ADOPTING FOR GOD

Adopting for God

The Mission to Change America through Transnational Adoption

Soojin Chung

NEW YORK UNIVERSITY PRESS

New York

NEW YORK UNIVERSITY PRESS
New York
www.nyupress.org

References to Internet websites (URLs) were accurate at the time of writing. Neither the author nor New York University Press is responsible for URLs that may have expired or changed since the manuscript was prepared.

Library of Congress Cataloging-in-Publication Data
Names: Chung, Soojin, author.
Title: Adopting for God : the mission to change America through transnational adoption / Soojin Chung.
Description: New York : New York University Press, [2021] |
Includes bibliographical references and index.
Identifiers: LCCN 2021011575 | ISBN 9781479808847 (hardback) |
ISBN 9781479808854 (paperback) | ISBN 9781479808885 (ebook) |
ISBN 9781479808861 (ebook other)
Subjects: LCSH: Intercountry adoption—United States—History. | Intercountry adoption—East Asia—History. | Interracial adoption—Religious aspects—Christianity. | Interracial adoption—United States—History.
Classification: LCC HV875.55 .C48 2021 | DDC 362.734088/2773—dc23
LC record available at https://lccn.loc.gov/2021011575

New York University Press books are printed on acid-free paper, and their binding materials are chosen for strength and durability. We strive to use environmentally responsible suppliers and materials to the greatest extent possible in publishing our books.

Manufactured in the United States of America

10 9 8 7 6 5 4 3 2 1

Also available as an ebook

To Daniel and Priscilla

CONTENTS

Introduction

I own a vintage photo of Harry and Bertha Holt, the founders of an adoption agency called Holt International, descending from a Pan American World Airways airplane with twelve Asian babies. Taken on October 14, 1955, the photo depicts the Holts alongside Robert Pierce, the founder of the Christian humanitarian organization World Vision, and several other men dressed in suits, all proudly carrying Asian children.[1] A photo taken from a different angle, displayed on the Holt International website, has become the iconic photo of transnational adoption and a symbol of altruism.[2] Even to those who are not familiar with the photo's history, the image is endearing—the adorable children wear traditional Korean *hanbok*, some smiling innocently while others look around curiously. But there is more to the heartwarming photo than this. If we look closely, we can surmise that the children are of mixed-race heritage. Some do not look East Asian. An uninformed person is left wondering why these mixed-race children flew across the Pacific without their parents, wearing traditional Korean dress.[3]

These children were a product of the Korean War, often referred to as "the forgotten war" due to the relative lack of public attention it received. Korea was under Japanese occupation until Japan surrendered to the Allied forces on August 15, 1945. Soon after Korean independence from Japanese colonization, Korea was split into two opposing governments. The Soviet Union accepted the ad-hoc American proposal for the division of Korea in 1945. The South was supported by the United States and the North by the Soviet Union. The Harvard- and Princeton-educated Syngman Rhee became the president of South Korea, and the guerrilla fighter Kim Il Sung became the premier of North Korea. With the two governments locked in hostility from the moment of the split, Korea became a major theater of the Cold War. In January 1950, U.S. Secretary of State Dean Acheson gave a speech at the National Press Club that left Korea and Taiwan out of the American defense perimeter. Less than half a year later, North Korea invaded South Korea and the Korean War broke out. By the end of 1950, American and Chinese troops had escalated the civil war into a global conflict.

The war devastated Korea. The casualties exceeded 2.5 million people—many of them civilians—and more than 10 million people were displaced, which created countless widows and orphans. By the time the war came to a halt with an armistice in 1953, Korea was one of the most destitute nations in the world. To compound the matter, American servicemen who were stationed in South Korea during the war impregnated numerous Korean women through military prostitution and fleeting love affairs. Many mixed-race children, along with orphaned "full-blooded" children, were abandoned during this time. The twelve babies captured in the photo were part of the abandoned mixed-race population. During the years following the war, America endeavored to rebuild the war-torn South Korea and sent $6 billion in humanitarian aid. Missionaries also stepped in to bring relief to the devastated country.

In this context, the photo of the Holts and the orphans represents much more than a heartwarming moment. Culturally, the Americans who staged the event wanted obvious imagery of the East and the West coming together, as seen in the sharp contrast between the attire of the Americans and that of the mixed-race children. One woman who appears to be East Asian is also wearing *hanbok*, while Bertha Holt is wearing a modest, Western-style dress. Politically, to the American public, the Holts represented U.S. democracy, where religious freedom flourished. South Korea was an innocent child in need of saving; North Korea was the vile, communist enemy; Christian America was the benevolent savior that would bring democracy and Christianity to South Korea.[4] Religiously, the child-parent paradigm represented the paternalism commonly found in American mission history. Harry and Bertha Holt—adoptive parents and evangelical Christians who identified themselves as missionaries— were both metaphorical and literal parent figures to the impoverished children in need of Western help. Indeed, when missionaries founded churches in Asia, the hierarchy between the missionaries and indigenous Christians was often framed with a child-father paradigm.

The intersection of Harry and Bertha Holt's identities, as American Christians and as white adoptive parents who promoted and facilitated transnational adoption from East Asia, represents the crux of this book.

Harry and Bertha Holt were what I call "adoption evangelists." The term is intended to have a dual meaning—it refers to those who accomplished traditional evangelism through adoption and those who "converted" Americans to the cause of adopting Asian children. Transnational adoption was popularized by Christians who emerged from, were influenced by, and in some cases worked within the tradition of Christian mission, evangelizing for the cause of adoption itself. As adoption evangelists, the protagonists in this book pioneered a new kind of missionary work, broadening the traditional definition of Christian mission.

In an era of global anti-communism and domestic racial strife, how did adoption evangelists' religious convictions inform and motivate transnational adoption from East Asia? How did they challenge and change America's perception of race and family? What methodologies did they use, and why were they effective?

This volume argues that missionaries were crucial players in the rise of the transracial adoption movement and, somewhat surprisingly, pushed Americans to redefine traditional family values and to rethink racist stances. Much of the common narrative about missionary work portrays it as propagating unmitigated cultural imperialism. This book challenges that understanding to show that the reality is more nuanced. While that cultural imperialism was certainly part of the story, Christian missionaries were also instrumental in shifting negative stereotypes about East Asians in the U.S., and ideas about race in general. Missionaries spent significant time immersed in cultures outside of the U.S., and they brought changed perspectives back home with them. They influenced foreign policy as well as ordinary citizens' views towards foreign countries, and they pioneered the transnational adoption movement in America. Gender is a key part of this story, as women played important roles in the mission field, doing much of the work of actually caring for the children.

Though the role of Christian missionaries in the rise of transracial adoption is known, there has not yet been a full historical look at their theological motivations—which varied depending on whether they were evangelically or ecumenically focused—what they did, and what the effects were for American society, relations with Asia, and thinking about race more broadly. This book offers a nuanced picture of the rise of an important twentieth-century movement, adding to the growing body of literature about how missionary cosmopolitanism changed America by underlining the ways the adoption evangelists' campaign for the adoption of mixed-race children challenged American perceptions of race and family. I distinguish between evangelical and ecumenical Christians and investigate how their purposes, audiences, and methodologies differed or aligned, with the result that together these Christians contributed significantly to the inauguration and popularization of transnational adoption from East Asia.

American Family History

After World War II, the so-called baby boom ensued. While most scholars understand the baby boom as the direct result of a transition from difficult times to more stable times, the era's family-centered rhetoric was also deeply influenced by the quest for national security and the geopolitical factors of the Cold War era.[5] There were other additional explanations for the significant increase in the birth rate and the cultural emphasis on families, including a general surge in prosperity, a strong desire for emotional stability, and patriotism. An intense obsession with family values runs through each explanation.

Postwar Prosperity

World War II left many parts of the world debilitated, poverty-stricken, and unstable, both economically and morally. Postwar America focused on rebuilding the economy and the sense of stability that had been lost during the fifteen years of suffering. Economic historians are in general agreement that 1950 was the starting point of the golden age of capitalism, during which the middle class, the Gross Domestic Product (GDP), and a well-educated workforce grew simultaneously.[6] The Eisenhower administration established a bipartisan economic policy for America, aiding public works programs and reducing taxes. Dwight Eisenhower, in his annual State of the Union Address in 1960, declared that since 1946, the real income of every citizen in the United States had risen nearly 20 percent.[7]

The visible emblem of the postwar economic boom was suburbanization. After World War II, returning soldiers escalated the demand for housing, which contributed significantly to the development of suburbs. Buying suburban single-family homes became relatively affordable. Around 1940, 50 percent of young adults (between 20–24 years of age) had lived with their parents. After the war, many young couples married and purchased suburban homes of their own.[8] During this time of rapid suburbanization, development was segregated on the basis of race, as sanctioned by federal government loan requirements. The Federal Housing Administration subsidized the mass production of subdivisions for whites while refusing to insure mortgages in black neighborhoods. This state-sponsored system of segregation was designed to provide suburban housing to white middle-class families, while people of color were excluded from the new suburban communities, involuntarily pushed into urban housing.[9] The government believed that single-race communities would solidify housing values and marketability by affirming the boundaries of racial segregation that were already deeply entrenched in American society.[10] The white middle-class suburban family thus became the hallmark of postwar American prosperity and identity.

The movement to the suburbs reinforced the family-centered values of the postwar society. This surge in postwar prosperity, coupled with suburbanization, drove many women who had previously joined the workforce to return to being housewives. To a generation that had delayed marriage and childbearing during the Depression and the war, raising a happy family in the suburbs became a goal that promised to bring emotional stability and contentment.[11] With the economic boom came an acceleration of consumption, with the spending focused on families, not individuals. In the five years following the war, the general consumption of goods increased by 60 percent. The most significant increase was in spending on household furnishings and appliances, which rose 240 percent.[12] The advent of television was one of the most important cultural changes of the time. The television—along with its values focused on consumption and pleasure—became the center of American homes. In 1950, only one-third of families owned a television set; in 1956, three-quarters of households owned a set.[13]

The Quest for Emotional Stability

World War II had brought family separation, frequent moves, and a constant sense of instability and anxiety that the new postwar families were eager to replace with the promise of security and familial love. *McCall's* magazine, one of the most popular women's magazines of the time, published an article in the Easter 1954 issue about the life of the ideal postwar family. The picture essay featured a typical white middle-class couple, Ed and Carol Richtscheidt, who lived in a suburban New Jersey house. The article showcased the defining characteristics of postwar family values, such as "togetherness" and a "new and warmer way of life."[14] The emphasis was not on individuals, but on a happy life as a family unit.

During the postwar era, marriage and childbearing were seen as the prerequisites for happiness. Anyone who did not share this vision was treated as having gone astray. Psychologists, journalists, and educators echoed the family-centered sentiment. Various women's magazines portrayed career women without families as unhappy and discontented. The psychologist Carl Rogers, the founder of the humanistic approach to psychology and psychotherapy research, disseminated an optimistic view of human nature that came to pervade religious and secular counseling. Popular culture promoted ideas such as "peace of mind" and "self-actualization."[15]

Popular culture was dominated by television shows and movies. Popular films and shows romanticized familial love, reducing family woes to the result of a lack of parental love—love was the solution to all family-related problems, from juvenile delinquency to domestic violence. This quest for emotional stability and the Romantic ideal of being unrepressed manifested themselves in family values as well. Happiness and fulfillment, rather than parental duties and familial responsibilities, were emphasized. The tensions and struggles of family life were downplayed, and American families became more self-absorbed, inward-turning, and isolated.[16]

Moreover, gender roles became stricter during this time. The historians Steven Mintz and Susan Kellogg argue that families of the 1950s were child-centered and female-dominated due to the acceptance of traditional gender roles and the demands imposed by fathers' commutes.

This created what they call a *filiarchy* in place of the traditional patriarchy. The private, domestic sphere was women's domain; men functioned as breadwinners and authority figures in the home.[17]

Patriotism and Domesticity

The cultural emphasis on family and the increase in the birth rate were partly due to a change in the national geopolitical culture. The glorification of domestic values embodied the hope that the future of America would be filled with the happiness and satisfaction denied by the war.[18] American soldiers in World War II were driven not only by universal moral values such as freedom and democracy but also by a private interest in protecting their own kin. Wartime advertisements appealed to this sentiment, for instance by displaying gruesome warzone images that read, "That this shall not be *Your* sister!"[19] When the war was over, the family-centered rhetoric proliferated even more. Radio stations, television shows, popular books and magazines, and newspapers celebrated the family values that had survived and triumphed over the catastrophic war. The insecurities of the Cold War also drove this emphasis on family values.

American patriotism and triumphalism were closely related to American family values because enjoying a joyous, carefree family life meant overcoming the war that had been dragging on for years. True American happiness was equated with a happy family. Looking back on the postwar period, the psychologist Joseph Adelson recalled that the zeitgeist of the time emphasized living in suburban homes and raising perfect children. He argued that men would be "secure in stable careers" and women "in comfortable homes," although the emphasis was on the "togetherness" of the family, not on individuals.[20] Motherhood was glorified, and fatherhood represented respectability for men. The patriotic meaning of parenthood was evident in a popular magazine of the time in which a writer argued that parenthood had taken on a new responsibility of profound significance, becoming an "absorbing, creative profession—a career second to none."[21] The notion that parenting was the most sacred "profession" and "career" was closely related to the inception of transnational adoption. For the Christians at the heart of this movement, adoption ministry, along with their parenting, became their career.

The Golden Age of the American Family

The sociologists Ronald R. Rindfuss and James A. Sweet conducted multiple layers of surveys and found that for virtually every ethnic, education-related, and age group surveyed, fertility rates increased significantly during the 1950s.[22] Unprecedented numbers of young adults married earlier than in previous decades, and a million more children were born each year than in the 1930s.[23] In this so-called golden age, infertile couples were marginalized. Many childless couples turned to domestic adoption as a solution. Domestic adoption agencies, whose initial goal was to meet the needs of the children, increasingly turned their attention to the needs of infertile couples.

Moreover, suburbanization and relative prosperity during the 1950s made nuclear families the ideal prototype. This development influenced adoption philosophy. In earlier adoption philosophy, the preservation of biological kinship was emphasized and supporting biological mother was the priority as adoption was seen as the last resort. The heightened emphasis on a nuclear family during the 1950s, however, encouraged the creation of a new nuclear family through adoption. The ideal adoption policy was redefined as creating a happy middle-class, suburban nuclear family.[24] Moreover, the percentage of adopted children who had been born to married women plummeted, as most newborn babies available for adoption were born to unwed mothers. The healthy, happy, nuclear family was the road to a fulfilling life, and many Americans endeavored to achieve this dream.

History of Anti-Asian Racism in America

Before the 1950s, the U.S. government and American society deemed Asians unassimilable aliens unfit for membership in America. The so-called Orientals were subjected to the government policy of Asiatic Exclusion in 1882. Under the provisions of the Exclusion, Asians experienced barriers to naturalization, occupational discrimination, and residential segregation.[25] In the 1920s and 30s, Filipino Americans in California were violently attacked due to widespread hatred. During World War II, President Franklin Delano Roosevelt signed an executive order to forcibly remove 112,000 Japanese Americans to an internment camp in Manzanar. Many died there and in the nine other camps where Japanese Americans were unjustly imprisoned during the war. Even after the war's end, Asians were systematically excluded from civic participation and demonized as uncivilized enemies. The American media painted dehumanizing portraits of Asians, doing everything from calling them names to perpetuating racist stereotypes.

A few Americans, however, voiced opposition to anti-Asian racism throughout U.S. history, albeit in varying degrees and with differing motives. After the Civil War, Radical Republicans spoke in inclusive language about Asian immigrants with the aim of reconstructing race relations in the South. Senator George Frisbee Hoar opposed Asiatic Exclusion, arguing that nothing was more in conflict with the "genius of American institutions" than racial discrimination.[26] Maryknoll missionaries, driven by their religious conviction, chose to relocate themselves to Manzanar, the Japanese internment camp, or to the nearby town of Lone Pine to show solidarity and meet the physical and spiritual needs of the Japanese.[27] During World War II, white liberals began to recast Asian Americans as assimilable and law-abiding "model minorities" in the hope of rehabilitating America's international image.[28] Liberal civil rights activists expanded their egalitarian rhetoric to include Asian Americans. These two forces—racism against Asians and the opposing anti-racist voices—have both been at play throughout immigration history, although the United States remained largely hostile toward its Asian American population until the mid-twentieth century.

The historian Lon Kurashige suggests that Asian immigration history be divided according to the implementation of significant policies: before exclusion, peak exclusion, late exclusion, transwar egalitarianism, and civil rights egalitarianism. He demonstrates that each era had differing dominant and subordinate policy communities. For example, the immigration-labor policy community was a dominant force during the exclusion era, while race relations and foreign relations policy communities were dominant during the egalitarian period.[29] U.S. immigration laws formed during international wars, the most notable being the 1952 McCarran-Walter Act that ended Asian exclusion by extending U.S. citizenship eligibility to all Asians. After the Immigration and Nationality Act of 1965, which removed discrimination against ethnic groups from immigration policy, the race relations policy group dominated the scene. A broad range of Cold War internationalist and domestic civil rights movements demanded equality for minorities, including Asian Americans.[30]

While Cold War politics expedited the implementation of anti-racist policies and major civil rights legislation, it was the culminative impact of the anti-racist grassroots movements that ultimately made the most progress in changing the public's view of Asians and Asian Americans. The government stimulated macro-level changes, while missionaries, social workers, and individual actors drove micro-level changes in areas where the government could not reach. Christians' transnational adoption efforts were one such micro-level movement, and they directly challenged Americans' narrow perception of race and familial matters. The Holts, for example, received tremendous media attention and opened the door for thousands of American families to adopt Asian children.[31] Oregon Senator Richard Neuberger declared that these families were modern incarnations of the "Biblical Good Samaritan," helping society's most vulnerable members.[32] Through such portrayals, a dramatic shift occurred: whereas once Asians had been viewed and depicted as strange, despicable pig-tailed coolies, they came to be seen as appealing and adoptable children in need of American help.

History of U.S. Adoption from East Asia

The reconceptualization of Asians (particularly East Asians) as easily assimilated members of the "model minority" and adoptable children proved effective on both the macro and micro levels. On the policy level, the U.S. Congress passed a special bill named the "Holt Bill," a piece of legislation that permitted the Holts to adopt Asian children beyond the quota specified by the Refugee Relief Act of 1953.[33] As a result, on October 1955, Harry and Bertha were able to bring twelve children (eight for their family and four for other families), an event *World Vision* magazine famously called "Operation Babylift."[34] On the grassroots level, the Holts' Operation Babylift enabled them to establish the Holt Adoption Program, which has placed half of all Korean children adopted since 1956.[35] Although adoption from Japan and China had occurred sporadically throughout modern history, the Korean War played a crucial role in the emergence of large-scale transnational adoption from

East Asia. South Korea became the number one "sending nation" and a birthplace of the transnational adoption movement. Between 1953 and 2018, approximately 170,000 Korean children were adopted by families in more than 29 countries. Americans adopted more than two-thirds (114,117) of these children. Adoption rates increased steadily after the Korean War erupted in 1950 and peaked during the turbulent decade of the 1970s.

Although the large-scale transnational adoption movement began in South Korea, occasional adoptions of Asian babies had taken place in Japan during the post-World War II U.S. occupation of Japan (1945–1952). American servicemen and Japanese women produced Japanese-white and Japanese-black "occupation babies," and while there were American efforts to adopt Japanese mixed-race babies, the adoption rate was significantly lower than that of Korea. Between the end of World War II and the 1980s, around 1,500 Japanese mixed-race children were adopted by Americans.[36] Unlike the Korean government, the Japanese government was relatively inclusive of the mixed-race babies, even issuing an antidiscrimination policy for the "new type of children." While mixed-race children and their mothers were socially ostracized in both Korea and Japan, legally and financially, Japanese mixed-race children enjoyed more equality in the country of their birth than Korean mixed-race children did in theirs. Transnational adoption from Japan decreased even further in the twenty-first century—from 1999 to 2018, only 601 children were sent to the United States.[37]

In the late 1950s, some Americans adopted Chinese babies through International Social Service-America Branch (ISS-USA). The ISS-USA initiated the "Hong Kong Project," which facilitated the adoption of Chinese refugee children living in Hong Kong. Due to the poor living conditions in Communist China, many Chinese fled to Hong Kong as refugees. In the process, some abandoned their children or died, leaving their children orphans. ISS-USA collaborated with Hong Kong agencies to bring the children to the United States, and by the 1960s, more than five hundred babies had been adopted through the Hong Kong Project.[38] In the 1980s and 1990s, due to China's "one child policy," transnational adoption became more standardized in China. The adoption rate continued to increase in the mid-1990s, making China one of the major sending countries.

As this brief overview has suggested, transnational adoption from East Asia began as a series of rescue missions by various missionary organizations, social workers, and governmental and non-governmental organizations. Many of the children adopted from East Asia were mixed-race children born to local women and American military personnel, and some were refugees. The family was the most cherished institution in 1950s America, and a flood of compelling family-centered rhetoric helped white Americans warm up to the idea of welcoming mixed-race orphans into their homes.[39] In the mid-1950s, many East Asian children who came to the United States for adoption were labeled orphans even though they had one surviving parent. These legally designated orphans were victims of poverty, social dislocation, and gender inequality.[40] The dominant cultural understanding of orphanhood and vulnerability often described the children as "waifs of war," the objects of American rescue.[41] The letters, newspaper articles, and books quoted from this period thus used the term "orphan" liberally.[42] In the 1960s, transnational adoption entered a new phase as many East Asian countries slowly rose from the ashes of war. The adoption of "full-blooded" Asian children born out of wedlock replaced the adoption of mostly mixed-race war orphans. By the 1970s, the adoption operation initiated by missionaries as an emergency intervention had slowly matured into a multi-billion dollar industry.

In recent years, many East Asian countries have started to place children in domestic adoptions, thanks to East Asians' increased openness to adoption. Consequently, the rate of American adoption from East Asia has decreased significantly. In 2018, for example, U.S. families adopted only 206 Korean children, in marked contrast to the 1,064 children adopted in 2008.[43] Another explanation of this decrease is related to the recent wave of adoption literature written by East Asian adoptees adopted from the 1950s onward. These adoptees, who have often been the subject of discussion by psychologists, sociologists, and anthropologists, use creative forms such as films, documentaries, poems, and novels to share their stories with the world.[44] Experiences of abandonment, identity crisis, and longing for their cultural roots layer the adoptees' stories. One adoptee expressed in an interview that she never related to her adoptive mother. The interviewee was "always wondering what my biological mother was like, and what she looked like, and how I was like her."[45] When the adoptee sought therapy in college, she realized how deeply she had been wounded by her biological mother's abandonment. The negative experiences voiced by adoptees are not unrelated to East Asian governments' reluctance to turn to international adoption as the first-choice strategy as they saw the negative consequences of international adoption, such as ethnic identity crisis and multiple reported cases of child abuse and neglect.

Historical Studies of Adoption

As has been noted, transnational adoption functioned in the larger context of Cold War politics and domestic anti-racist rhetoric. It was also part of the movements of missionary cosmopolitanism and Christian internationalism, although it is often overlooked in studies of Christian history. Transnational adoption extended beyond the private realm of family-making—it was entangled with issues such as war politics, race, foreign relations, and Christian mission. Examining the history of transnational adoption allows us to see how these issues came together to create a unique twentieth-century movement. Conversely, adoption history offers insight into Cold War politics, the domestic racial landscape, the role of religion in U.S. public life, and family history. The majority of the academic adoption literature, however, focuses on the negative psychological effects of transnational adoption. Scholars have extensively researched the psychological damage inflicted by adoption, the identity formation of adoptees, and adoptees' adjustment or failure to adjust in white American homes.[46] Because psychopathology studies have equated difference with damage, many psychologists have encouraged racially matched adoptions (child and adoptive parents of the same race or nationality).[47]

In historical studies of adoption, researchers often highlight the political agenda of postwar America.[48] Many locate East Asian adoption at the intersection of American militarization, empire-building, and Cold War ideology. Christina Klein, for example, does an exceptional job of unfolding the relations between transnational adoption and Cold War Orientalism, an ideology of racial tolerance that the U.S. created to justify its global influence. Recent historical studies have shown that transnational adoption was not an isolated event but operated within the larger context of the Cold War. One aspect that has been largely overlooked, however, is the role of Protestant activists in the movement. Although most historians recognize the indispensable part missionaries played in the early formation of the movement, no work has focused exclusively on the role of missionaries with attention to the diversity of their perspectives.

A close examination of missionary and lay Christian writings reveals the complex nature of the theology of adoption, which is worth investigating given the extent to which evangelical and ecumenical adoption evangelists' narratives differed, even as their concerted efforts drove the movement forward. Moreover, few of the historical studies on adoption look closely at the gendered aspect of the movement. Transnational adoption was pioneered primarily by female Christians who took on the identity of mothers.[49] This book makes a unique contribution to adoption history by highlighting adoption evangelists' religious convictions and the influence of the women actors of the movement.

Evangelical and Ecumenical Cosmopolitanism

Through transnational adoption, adoption evangelists challenged Americans to redefine traditional familial values and rethink race matters. David Hollinger, in his important book *Protestants Abroad*, argues that missionaries had a "boomerang effect" on American society— they traveled to distant lands only to bring changed perspectives back to America.[50] Missionaries' firsthand experience in the mission field influenced foreign policy and the American outlook on foreign countries. This book adds to the conversation about how "missionary cosmopolitanism" changed America by demonstrating the ways missionaries' campaign for transnational adoption challenged and changed Americans' views of East Asians and race in general. Unlike Hollinger, I argue that evangelical and ecumenical missionaries criticized America concertedly, albeit in different ways.

The terms "evangelical" and "ecumenical" are fluid concepts that gradually took shape throughout American religious history to indicate conservative and liberal Christians. After World War II, the binary division between the two types of Christianity became more apparent after decades of strain. Progressive Christians shifted their missional focus to humanitarian efforts and steered away from evangelism, which caused fundamentalists—an ultra-conservative Christian sect that shunned social engagement—to push back by becoming more sectarian and more disengaged from society. In an effort to separate themselves from the fundamentalists, the evangelicals actively engaged society while maintaining their conservative theological beliefs.[51] They were the self-declared third force between liberalism and fundamentalism. American evangelicals were far from monolithic in their cultural expressions, political views, and denominational affiliations. However, they shared some defining theological features: they regarded the Bible as the ultimate spiritual authority, emphasized spiritual salvation through faith in Jesus Christ (expressed by being spiritually "born again"), and shared a belief in the urgency of evangelism. They also practiced an "engaged orthodoxy" by maintaining their conservative faith while engaging the larger culture and society.[52]

I use the terms "ecumenical" and "mainline" Christians interchangeably. Ecumenism refers to ecclesial endeavors to achieve church unity and denominational collaboration. Ecumenical Christians, in general, emphasized social action, interreligious dialogue, Christian presence, and global friendship. They responded sensitively to the changing social and political atmosphere, and after World War I, they quickly embraced the Christian internationalist rhetoric of world peace following Woodrow Wilson's Fourteen Points and the League of Nations.[53] Progressive Christian thinkers such as William E. Hocking produced important works criticizing the imperialistic methodology and attitudes held by traditional missionaries. Unlike evangelicals, who gave priority to evangelism, they underlined Christian social responsibility.

I distinguish between these two groups of Christians in this book because their purposes, audiences, and methodologies concerning transnational adoption practices differed significantly. Noting the distinctive theologies of the individuals involved is the key to answering the question that has baffled so many adoption historians: Why did Christian missionaries have such a caustic relationship with secular social workers? Among those who had particular difficulty with ISS-USA were the Holts, who belonged to the evangelical niche. Understanding their conservative theology and religious convictions helps us understand the sharp chasm they created between themselves and ISS-USA. Moreover, understanding ecumenical Christians' theology helps us to situate them within the larger context of ecumenical cosmopolitanism and anti-racist movements of their time. In other words, investigating the religious history intertwined with adoption history provides a clearer picture of the role of religion in humanitarian efforts.

Regardless of theological differences, evangelical and ecumenical adoption evangelists worked together to elevate the social condition of abandoned children by taking an active role as adoptive parents. Transnational adoption was not an isolated phenomenon—the evangelical social conscience, ecumenists' active anti-racism propaganda, and the latter's increasing interest in global friendship all contributed to the inauguration and spread of transnational adoptions from East Asia. Consequently, this book's central argument is that both evangelical and ecumenical adoption evangelists collectively advanced the anti-racist narrative and popularized transracial and transnational families through the practice of overseas adoption.

Organization of the Book

This book analyzes archival materials produced by Christians who began the transnational adoption movement. By putting missionary writings (materials written by missionaries, mission agencies, denominational boards, and interdenominational organizations) in conversation with published scholarship, the book offers a nuanced account of the inception of the adoption movement.[54] The book identifies adoption evangelists who played a part in the emergence of the movement, analyzing their backgrounds and social contexts, theological rationales for and public rhetoric about transnational adoptions, methodologies of adoption, and contributions as expressed in their writings, both published and unpublished. Each chapter looks at a different aspect of the topic.

Chapters one and two focus on evangelicals. They illustrate how evangelical missionaries used the transnational adoption movement to awaken what I call the "evangelical social conscience" and solidify the "evangelical social commitment." Chapter one examines one of the key precursors of the transnational adoption movement: the child sponsorship programs established by Robert Pierce and Everett Swanson. Unsettled by the calamity of the war, Robert Pierce and Everett Swanson founded World Vision and the Everett Swanson Evangelistic Association (now Compassion International) in 1950 and 1952, respectively, to meet the needs of orphans during the Korean War.[55] These two pillars of orphan care ministry introduced the new concept of virtually adopting underprivileged children by sending financial support each month. This practice became an important foundation of the adoption movement and played a crucial role in awakening the evangelical social conscience.

Chapter two focuses on the Holt family, who solidified the "evangelical social commitment." The official inception of the Korean adoption movement is often attributed to Harry and Bertha Holt. Their use of a religious founding myth, insider language, and the persecution trope was extremely effective in popularizing transnational adoption among conservative Christians. In addition, the Holts portrayed themselves as a "heroic family," a notion many evangelicals found attractive. The Holt family's role as the founders of Korean adoption was confirmed in 1956 when they established their transnational adoption agency, which has placed half of all the Korean children adopted since the mid-1950s.[56] The Holts consistently prioritized their religious convictions above any other social conditions, a perspective that many social workers at the time found objectionable.

Chapters three and four investigate how ecumenical Christians saw transnational adoption as part of their broader agenda of anti-racism and anti-imperialism. They championed global friendship through global kinship. Chapter three explores Pearl Buck's anti-racist propaganda and her sharp criticisms of American hypocrisy. Pearl Buck fiercely opposed racial and religious matching, a philosophy that governed non-relative adoption during the early twentieth century.[57] Matching required adoptive parents to match the potential adoptees in terms of race, physical resemblance, religious background, and intellectual capacity. Pearl Buck was a Presbyterian missionary and a prolific writer who wrote countless articles and essays on the topic of anti-racial matching.[58] Moreover, she was an avid supporter of global friendship and unity who argued that adoption could foster world friendship. Chapter three examines Buck's prose and explores how she dismantled the resistance to transracial adoption that was prevalent at the time. The chapter also expounds on her primary motivations for promoting transnational and transracial adoption: her advocacy of American political and moral responsibility, her personal connections and motherhood, and her mission of global friendship and unity. If the Holts spoke to an evangelical audience, Buck popularized transnational adoption beyond the Christian niche and across America.

Chapter four covers Helen Doss, who, in 1954, published *The Family Nobody Wanted*, the first book to offer a first-person transnational adoption narrative. With this book, Doss essentially translated the ideas of Pearl Buck into narrative form.[59] The book was the most popular first-hand account to emphasize how God's love triumphed over cultural and racial differences. Helen and Carl Doss, a Methodist minister, adopted twelve children from various countries, acquiring the title "United Nations Family." This chapter expounds on Doss's narratives and traces a distinct theology of adoption and theology of belonging—a theology based on the divine love and image of God. It also examines how the Doss family became the archetype of an ideal multicultural family that maintained its American identity. Although Pearl Buck and Helen Doss had the same goals of dismantling racial prejudice and demonstrating how God's love triumphed over racial injustice, their methodologies differed. While Pearl Buck actively criticized the American public through her prose, Helen Doss illustrated racism's ungodliness and irrationality through stories.

The Conclusion summarizes adoption evanglists' pivotal roles in the rise of transracial adoption movement and answers the question of whether they had an abiding effect on the American racial and familial landscape in contemporary America. Although the adoption evangelists used different methods, they were united in the purpose of improving the condition of orphaned East Asian children during the 1950s. World Vision and the Everett Swanson Evangelistic Association used the child sponsorship program; the Holts promoted evangelical values by working closely with theologically conservative Christian families; Pearl Buck fought against racism and implemented non-matching transnational adoption; and Helen Doss emphasized diversity and Christian love. Distinct though their methodologies and theologies were, this group of Christians spearheaded the transnational adoption movement.

I have limited the scope of the research to the period between 1949 and 1960. In 1949 Pearl Buck established Welcome House, the first interracial and transnational adoption agency in the United States. This event marks the beginning of the transnational adoption movement because she broke the social norm of racially matching children to adoptive parents. However, the notion of adopting interracially and transnationally did not receive widespread support at this time. Another five years would pass before Helen Doss published *The Family Nobody Wanted* in 1954. With the Holts' adoption of eight children in 1955, transnational adoption became socially acceptable and even encouraged. In 1960, transnational adoption started to change: whereas Americans had once adopted mixed-race war orphans, now they were adopting "full-blooded" Asian children who had been born out of wedlock.[60] It was also during this time that transnational adoption slowly became a multi-billion-dollar industry, creating what Kimberly D. McKee calls the "transnational adoption industrial complex."[61] The entanglement of adoption, missionary work, and Christian theology after 1960 is a topic that merits further research.

Finally, this book is limited to one region and one group of people: I focus on transnational adoption as practiced between the United States and East Asia (focusing particularly on Korea). Moreover, although Catholics, Seventh-Day Adventists, and Orthodox Christians were involved in transnational adoption, this book examines the activities of selected Protestants.[62] Due to the paucity of sources written by Asian social workers, missionaries, and birth parents, I have relied mostly on American missionaries' writings and on some Korean newspapers from the 1950s. While I have included perspectives from adoptees when possible, a full consideration of this movement from the perspective of those who were adopted is a topic for another book.

1

The Foundation of the Transnational Adoption Movement

Robert Pierce and Everett Swanson founded two of the world's most influential Christian international non-governmental organizations (NGOs). Together, they reached millions of children. World Vision, a leading child sponsorship organization, today serves more than four million children in approximately one hundred countries. Compassion International has formed alliances with churches and denominations in Asia, Africa, Central America, the Caribbean, and South America to carry out worldwide relief and advocacy work.[1] All of this started when two ministers decided to do something about the catastrophic circumstances of Korean war orphans. Unsettled by the calamity of the Korean War, Robert Pierce and Everett Swanson founded World Vision and the Everett Swanson Evangelistic Association (ESEA; now Compassion International) in 1950 and 1952, respectively.[2] The two pastors' charismatic leadership, coupled with the political and religious atmosphere of the time, resulted in a rapid expansion of the child sponsorship movement in the evangelical niche.

Together, Pierce and Swanson laid the groundwork for adopting children financially and gave currency to the idea of adopting internationally. These two pillars of orphan care ministry inaugurated the concept of "virtually adopting" impoverished children. Thanks to the organizations' family-centered rhetoric, integration of evangelism and social action, and vivid images of wretched Korean waifs, virtual adoption programs expanded rapidly. By blurring the line between sponsoring and adopting, these programs inverted the dominant social structure of the racially homogeneous family and introduced a creative avenue through which sponsors could legally adopt Asian children. In addition, this innovation led to a foundational event in the transnational adoption movement: Harry and Bertha Holt, having been influenced by Robert Pierce's child sponsorship program, adopted eight mixed-race Korean children.

Consequently, Pierce and Swanson made an important contribution to the conservative Christian community by awakening what I call the "evangelical social conscience." Liberal Christians' active involvement with the social gospel movement tended to drive conservative Christians away from social justice issues, and by the 1940s, most evangelicals were advocating an exclusive focus on evangelism, often to the exclusion of humanitarian activities. Christian service was viewed as evidence of belief in a watered-down, unbiblical social activism. Pierce and Swanson, however, along with several of their evangelical peers, emphasized both evangelism and Christian social responsibility. They advocated a renewed dedication to both world mission and Christian social engagement, thus arousing an evangelical social conscience that had been dormant for centuries. In this way, evangelical relief organizations such as World Vision and ESEA created a neo-evangelical subculture within conventional evangelicalism.

Pierce and Swanson did not set out to eradicate systematic racism or increase cross-cultural engagement in America. Rather, they were faced with an immediate tragedy and decided to act as they saw fit, calling other Christians to do the same. Their actions had momentous results. In addition to pioneering neo-evangelicalism, they helped reshape evangelicals' perception of "the other." Their ministries' portrayal of the war orphans as adopted children paved the way for the American acceptance of Korean children as family members and legitimate citizens, who, because of their innocence and perceived malleability, came to represent exemplary immigrants. The potent image of an innocent child made it possible to bypass divisive theological debates and social stigmas. Whereas once Asians had been portrayed in the U.S. cultural sphere as hypermasculine exemplars of the "yellow peril," World Vision and the ESEA reconceptualized Asians as helpless children.[3] This chapter will analyze how the two orphan care ministries were conceived, what they accomplished, and most importantly, how these ministries inaugurated the transnational adoption movement and appealed to the evangelical social conscience.

The Changing Dynamics of World Mission

To better grasp how and why World Vision and the Everett Swanson Evangelistic Association (ESEA) emerged, one must situate the two leaders within the changing religious climate of the nineteenth and twentieth century. In brief, they belonged to the evangelical subculture of the twentieth century, which emerged as a response to shifts in the missiological paradigm of the previous centuries.

Most historians agree that the nineteenth century was the heyday of Christian mission. The so-called "Great Century" (a term famously coined by church historian Kenneth Scott Latourette) witnessed a surge of concerted and systematic Protestant mission activities.[4] Both conservative Christians and mainline denominations focused their energy outward and sent countless missionaries around the world. The global Christian population increased from approximately twenty-three percent in 1800 to thirty-four percent in 1900.[5] When prominent Christian leaders gathered in Edinburgh in 1910 for the World Missionary Conference, confidence in Christendom and mission zeal was at its zenith. The Conference demonstrated Protestant mission's triumphant optimism through the slogan "The Evangelization of the World in This Generation," a phrase adopted from the previous century's Student Volunteer Movement.[6] The Conference embodied the optimism at the height of imperialism, urging that non-Christian countries be converted and "civilized."[7] Robert E. Speer, one of the key leaders of the Edinburgh Conference, estimated that there were 1.5 million converts in the missionized areas around 1910.[8]

Most Christians in the West during this time viewed world mission mainly in terms of extension and expansion: missionaries were heroes and heroines subduing a hostile environment.[9] The climate that encouraged the imposition of Christian virtues on other cultures began to change after the Great War. The Christian West was morally challenged to reexamine its triumphalist rhetoric, as militaristic language such as "missionary conquest" and "world evangelization" started to falter after World War I. Mainline denominations embraced the Christian internationalist language of world peace and unity following Woodrow Wilson's Fourteen Points and the League of Nations.[10] As more progressive Christians started to critically self-reflect and change their mission policies to focus on humanitarian endeavors and calls for wider social engagement, fundamentalists resisted, enforcing traditional understandings of Scripture and becoming more sectarian.

The schism between extreme conservatives and liberals widened in the 1920s, and by 1925, several North American denominations were in sharp conflict with one another—with fundamentalists on one side and modernists on the other. The conflict within the northern Presbyterian Church (PCUSA) was the most intense, and the fundamentalist-modernist controversy erupted over issues such as the authority of Scripture, evolution, the nature of God's kingdom, and the death, resurrection, and the atoning sacrifice of Christ.[11] Although the controversy focused on theology and ecclesiology, it was closely related to the place and role of Christianity in culture and society.[12] While liberals began to see themselves as the bearers of a prophetic voice that had the potential to transform society and bring about social justice, fundamentalists became more exclusive and isolated, refusing to engage in Christian social endeavors.

The fundamentalists had to accept defeat when the large body of moderates swung to the liberal side. While the moderates maintained their conservative doctrinal commitment, they did not find the liberals' stance menacing or completely misguided. Indeed, when J. Gresham Machen, one of the most notable fundamentalists, founded the Independent Board of Presbyterian Foreign Missions as a reaction against the official denominational board, he was regarded as an extreme isolationist by the moderates. After the fundamentalists were publicly defeated in the 1920s, a coalition of "neo-evangelicals" emerged, distinguishing themselves from fundamentalists by engaging with mainstream culture and seeking to restore the social standing of Christian America.[13] As a self-declared third force between fundamentalism and liberalism in American Protestantism, they affirmed religious orthodoxy but abandoned sectarianism, aspiring to become more inclusive by collaborating with other denominations in a spirit of ecumenism. Christian unity—which was at the heart of ecumenism—was taken seriously by neo-evangelicals.[14] At the same time, they distinguished themselves from the liberal movement for fear of deviating from what they perceived as orthodoxy.[15]

Toward the end of World War II, youth revivalism played a significant role in solidifying the neo-evangelical identity. What started as sporadic youth revivals gained momentum and coalesced into a loose organization called Youth for Christ (YFC). On April 1944, Torrey Johnson, pastor of the Midwest Bible Church, led the opening rally for Chicago YFC, with Billy Graham speaking to over 2,000 people. Billy Graham, often regarded as the face of neo-evangelicalism, soon became the first full-time YFC staffer.[16] In 1944, Pierce became the director for the Seattle YFC chapter. Pierce was heavily influenced by Billy Graham, and their relationship lasted until Pierce's death.[17]

Having grown out of fundamentalist separatism, YFC attracted young American evangelicals filled with zeal for world mission and optimism about Christianity's place in the society. YFC was dedicated to spreading the gospel while reengaging mainstream society.[18] Unlike fundamentalists, who shunned secular cultural or political engagement, YFC neo-evangelicals combined effusive patriotism, evangelism, and popular culture (such as pop music and celebrities) to bolster civic faith and global outreach.[19] This experience later led Pierce to launch World Vision. Although less conspicuously, Swanson was also part of the movement of young Christians committed to evangelism with new attitudes toward mainstream culture. He became an evangelist for the Christian Business Men's Committee and later embarked on worldwide evangelistic tours similar to Billy Graham's.[20]

In the 1940s and 50s, major organizations such as InterVarsity Christian Fellowship (1941), the National Association of Evangelicals (1942), Youth for Christ (1944), and Campus Crusade for Christ (1951) established a subculture centered on active evangelism and circumspect yet creative cultural engagement. Campus Crusade for Christ, for instance, established itself on college campuses and appealed to students through shows, events, and music that drew on the youth culture of the time. Yet the organization's ultimate goal remained reaching students for Christ; it maintained a fundamentally evangelical commitment. Doctrinal conservatism and cultural assimilability similarly marked the myriad other neo-evangelical organizations that sprang up in this era.

Robert Pierce and Everett Swanson, along with other conservative Christians, pioneered and created this neo-evangelical subculture. Their populist, grassroots organizations appropriated the youth culture of the time, putting on events that included "radio-style intensity, pepped-up music, and fast-paced shows."[21] When World Vision and ESEA used films to appeal to potential sponsors, they demonstrated their cultural assimilability by appropriating consumer culture and the latest communications technology. Through such efforts, neo-evangelicals shed their association with an antiquated and backward-looking fundamentalism.

They embraced modernity and popular culture, and neo-evangelicalism came to be perceived as a "hip religion" by young Christians craving more social engagement and a civic faith.

A number of organizations emerged from within the neo-evangelical movement. World Vision and ESEA stood out among these organizations because of the weight they gave to humanitarian works. Although other neo-evangelical organizations creatively engaged in popular culture, their purpose often remained thoroughly evangelistic, often overlooking humanity's physical needs. Issues such as poverty, racism, and sexism were regarded at best as secondary concerns. The leaders of World Vision and ESEA believed otherwise. They believed that Christianity should play a positive and decisive role in transforming the world both spiritually and physically. They promoted Christlike love and service coupled with a passion for evangelism, campaigning for a renewed dedication to world mission and heightened evangelical social responsibility.

World Vision International
The Early Years of Robert Pierce

In Robert Willard Pierce's early ministry years, he was a poster child for evangelicalism, filled with evangelistic zeal. His efforts as an evangelist, a brief abandonment of his faith, his involvement with Youth for Christ, and a trip to Asia concertedly laid the ground for his child sponsorship ministry. Through his journey from an obsession with soul-saving to a new perspective on social issues, we can discover how a vigorous evangelist became a pioneer of neo-evangelicalism.

Pierce was born in Fort Dodge, Iowa, on October 8, 1914, to Fred and Flora Belle Pierce. In 1924, the family moved to Redondo Beach, outside Los Angeles. They were actively involved in the Methodist and Nazarene Churches, and young Robert Pierce made a personal commitment to Christ at the local Grace Church of the Nazarene when he was twelve. When his father died during the Great Depression, Pierce worked to support the family. He was a disciple of Earle Mack, and as a fervent evangelist, Pierce often rode the Gospel Car, bringing church members into town to preach the gospel. From a young age, he preached whenever he had a chance.[22]

While attending Pasadena Nazarene College, Pierce was elected student body president in his junior year. That same year, in 1936, he became involved in the Los Angeles Evangelistic Center. There he met his future wife, Lorraine Johnson, the daughter of the traveling evangelist Floyd Johnson. The two young students fell in love instantly and married on November 24, 1936, when Pierce was twenty-two and Johnson nineteen.

After getting married, Pierce's manual labor job ended abruptly, and he discontentedly drifted from job to job, yearning to preach full-time. He rededicated himself to preaching at a Nazarene annual convention, where he made such an impact that several pastors afterward invited him to hold revival meetings in their churches. Pierce traveled the West Coast preaching in various churches and building a regional reputation. Churches all over southern California filled with people eager to hear his message. During this time, he tasted the exciting lifestyle of a traveling evangelist and enjoyed his independence. His evangelistic ministry thrived, but his finances languished since he had to rely on the hospitality of the host churches and love offerings for lodging and income.

When Lorraine Pierce became ill with diphtheria, the couple halted their traveling ministry and returned to Los Angeles. In 1938, Pierce became an associate pastor for his father-in-law at the Los Angeles Evangelistic Center. Pierce came to resent his father-in-law for restricting Pierce's ministerial activity and not giving him a position of greater authority. In 1941, Pierce announced that he was leaving the congregation to speak at a series of conferences. During this time, Pierce had a psychological breakdown and abruptly abandoned his faith and his family. He filed for a divorce, but Lorraine convinced him to withdraw the divorce papers at the lawyer's office. He returned home but avoided the church and his old friends.

On December 1942, the prodigal son returned.[23] When Paul Rood, president of the World Christian Fundamentals Association, spoke at the Los Angeles Evangelistic Center, Pierce slipped into the back row and listened to Rood's sermon. During an altar call, Pierce fell prostrate on the ground in repentance. The next Sunday, when Pierce asked to be received back as "a doorkeeper in the house of the Lord," his father-in-law embraced him and welcomed him "home," giving him a position as a youth pastor.[24]

Pierce labored diligently at the Los Angeles Evangelistic Center but still found local church ministry monotonous. To him, as it did to many others at the time, evangelism evidently represented sacrifice, adventure, heroism, and "muscular faith."[25] The concept of muscular faith, which encouraged men to seek an exciting, adventurous, and adverse lifestyle, affirmed evangelical white manhood. Evangelists combatted non-Christian men not with their fists but with charismatic words. Through evangelistic journeys, many conservative Christian men asserted themselves as "manly" Christians even as they advanced the gospel. Evangelistic associations such as Youth for Christ and Christian Businessmen's Committee allowed conservative white men to forge close bonds as they ministered and competed together. The result was not just a tight-knit support system, but also a kind of spiritual white boys' club.[26] The direct preaching of God's Word also boosted their sense of manliness: in this subculture, saving souls was deemed superior to Christian service, which was often regarded as a feminine duty.

This view of Christian service had deep roots. Although evangelical revivalism involved female participation and gave a certain spiritual authority to women, by the twentieth century, the Victorian view of the family dominated conservative Christian circles. This view assumed that women were innately more moral and docile than men and thus more fit for domestic duties. Women were discouraged from entering the workforce for fear that they would become morally degraded.[27] Furthermore, evangelicals' affirmation of a patriarchal gender ideology limited women's involvement in ecclesial leadership and social involvement. The stereotypical gendered division of labor—men as the breadwinners, and women as homemakers—was the accepted norm.[28] In this environment, most conservative Christian women found their purpose and meaning in the domestic sphere.

Pierce, like many of his peers, accepted this ideology. He was also attracted to the exciting and unpredictable lifestyle of an evangelist. When the Eureka Jubilee Singers, an African American gospel group, invited him to join their evangelistic circuit in 1944, he accepted the opportunity without hesitation. Pierce, Lorraine, and their three-year-old daughter Sharon embarked on an evangelistic journey that would change their lives for good.[29]

The Establishment of World Vision

The family traveled for months, and Pierce's public ministry gained momentum. While traveling on the East Coast, Pierce heard about Youth for Christ (YFC), a zealous group of young people focused on global missions. This new youth revivalism spread throughout the country, attracting thousands of young people to a single rally.[30] Pierce was immediately captivated by YFC president Torrey Johnson's impassionate speech and charismatic leadership and longed to be part of the movement. In the fall of 1944, the Christian Businessmen's Committee of Seattle asked Pierce if he would hold a YFC rally in California. Pierce became the regional director for the Pacific Northwest, and along with Billy Graham and Merv Rosell, he became one of the most indispensable leaders of the movement. By 1945, he was serving as one of the regional vice-presidents of the Youth for Christ International convention.[31]

In 1947, Pierce went to China as an overseas evangelist. His daughter, Marilee Pierce-Dunker's statement, captures his experience in China aptly: "Bob Pierce was never the same after his trips to China. He went to China a young man in search of adventure, but came home a man with a mission."[32] In China, he spent months holding two services daily for massive crowds in large auditoriums. He was enthralled by the dramatic scenes of mass conversion, but something was different this time compared to his prior evangelistic gatherings. Pierce was deeply troubled by the poverty he witnessed. His exposure to the poorest of the poor changed him. He decided to become an advocate for the poor. When he returned to America in October 1947, people filled churches and auditoriums to hear Pierce's stories about Asia. Pierce told them that he had gone there to change Asia, but instead, he was the one who returned changed. Pierce considered himself an ambassador for God: he wanted to depict the conditions of the people for an American audience.[33]

Pierce planned to go back to China in 1949, but the Communist takeover by Mao Zedong made his return impossible. In June 1949, he received an invitation from Oriental Mission Society (OMS) missionaries to come to Korea. In March 1950, he headed to Korea under the auspices of Youth for Christ.[34] He preached from early morning to midnight for days, and thousands of people gathered at his rallies to hear his message.

By that time, the tension between North and South Korea was escalating, and war seemed inevitable. Only weeks after Pierce's return to the U.S., the Communist army crossed the 38th parallel. On June 25, 1950, the Red troops—led by Commander-in-Chief Kim Il Sung—invaded Seoul, the capital of South Korea.

Pierce was heartbroken. He passionately preached about the urgent state of Korea at the Billy Graham Portland Gospel Crusade, where his eyewitness accounts of his visit only weeks before the Communist invasion and the beginning of the Korean War stunned the eight thousand attendees. Frank C. Phillips, a veterinarian and Baptist layman, was one of them.[35] Moved by the message, Phillips loaned Pierce a desk, a phone, and the use of a secretary in the Youth for Christ headquarters. He orchestrated Pierce's funding and coordinated his speaking engagements.

Soon afterward, Pierce founded an organization "to meet emergency needs in crisis areas of the world by working through established missionary agencies."[36] Pierce named the organization World Vision, remembering the Youth for Christ world vision rallies and his Sunday School teacher at Grace Church of Nazarene, who had encouraged him to "keep a world vision."[37] This was only the beginning of the impact of female leaders on his life. World Vision officially incorporated on September 22, 1950, with Robert Pierce as the president. The organization adopted the statement of faith prepared by the National Association of Evangelicals two years previously, strengthening Pierce's role in the development of neo-evangelicalism.[38] One month after the incorporation of World Vision, Pierce quickly applied for and obtained status as a U.N. war correspondent, because no civilians were allowed into the country during the heat of the war.[39]

When Pierce finally reached Korea, he recorded the terror he found: "One afternoon, 3,000 Christians were murdered on the banks of the Han River, their hands bound by barbed wire."[40] His associates testified that they noticed a change in his preaching and demeanor after this exposure to the world of terror, disease, and human suffering. Russ Reid, an advertiser who worked with Pierce to produce World Vision's movies for many years, recounted, "Something's happened to Bob Pierce . . . He doesn't tell those lighthearted jokes . . . there's a sob in his voice, a heaviness in his heart."[41] After seeing the tragic aftermath of the war,

Pierce wrote on the flyleaf of his Bible, "Let my heart be broken with the things that break the heart of God."[42] This prayer became World Vision's watchword.

The Hidden Actors of World Vision

Dana Robert contends that women constituted the majority of the mission force by the late nineteenth century and that their commitment to social concerns transformed the face of American missions. Women, although less conspicuous than male missionaries, were guided in their mission practice by principles and strategies in various contexts. Women developed their mission theory according to their gender-based experience. This mission theory reflected their practice of holistic ministry, with an emphasis on both evangelism and meeting basic human needs. Because women were rarely ordained, their voices tended to be acceptable in the educational and medical fields.[43] Moreover, with the rise of the faith mission movement, direct evangelism became an important tool and mission strategy for women. They were the worker bees of missions, and they outnumbered men in mission fields.[44]

This model held true for World Vision. While Robert Pierce functioned as the face of the organization, the hands and feet of the ministry were the women working behind the scenes. Women, both missionaries and local Korean workers, took care of orphans and facilitated child sponsorship programs in various parts of Korea. They knew the children by name; they fed, bathed, and nurtured each child daily. These women assumed the identity of spiritual mothers. Pierce acknowledged the powerful influence of women on his ministry and life. While he still subscribed to a dualistic view of gender roles and enjoyed his position of male leadership, he wrote extensively about some of these women, both named and unnamed. The three most prominent women in Pierce's writings were Beth Albert, Tena Hoelkeboer, and Gladys Aylward. Beth Albert and Tena Hoelkeboer served as catalysts for the founding of World Vision. Gladys Aylward served as an inspiration for Pierce, and he actively supported and publicized her work.

Robert Pierce called Beth Albert "my beloved partner and fellow warrior, the one who was the most powerful trigger of the vision God gave me for world missions."[45] She was a registered nurse who specialized in leprosy medicine and techniques. After receiving her calling to be "a hundred percent for God," she worked in the Philippines, where leprosy was rampant after World War II.[46] After meeting some of the islands' most immediate needs, she proceeded to China. Robert Pierce first met Albert in Kunming, China, where she was running a ministry for lepers through the China Inland Mission. The governor of Kunming Province had given orders to eliminate anyone showing the marks of leprosy, so most of the lepers lived eight miles outside the city. Albert scrounged among the debris left by the G.I.s and taught the lepers how to bake bricks to build shelters. With no outside help, she supported the lepers through manual labor and her ingenuity.

When the lepers asked her why she was doing this for them, she replied, "Because I love Jesus and he loves you. He loves you so much he sent me to help you. You are precious to God, and God knows you are beautiful."[47] Retelling this story, Pierce emphasized that people came to accept Christ not because of her theology, but simply because of her Christian love. She found joy in working among lepers, and it was evident to Pierce that the community loved her.[48] His statement also demonstrated that women often forged deep, personal relationships with the people they were serving. Pierce recounted that his personal world vision started when he met Albert:

> The official records show that World Vision was incorporated in 1950. But in reality my own world vision from God was sparked on that first trip . . . In the real, practical sense, World Vision was born that day with Beth Albert when I saw people, who without any support, had proved they loved Jesus and the suffering needy around them.[49]

These stories retold in the hagiographic accounts have been intentionally edited to create a dramatic founding myth. Such myth-making was prevalent in popular evangelical literature at the time. The myths served as a testimony of divine intervention. Many evangelical pastors and evangelists included miraculous anecdotes that accentuated the supernatural aspect of their faith in their verbal and written communications. The oral history concerning various myths served as a strong impetus for Christians to participate in the mission. Myths functioned as a unifying force that inspired Christians with a sense of purpose and "calling" due to their supernatural and spiritual nature. For World Vision, the myth served as a foundation that rationalized the organization's cause and granted spiritual authority. Because God himself had commanded Pierce to do something about the situation, surely the organization had to continue what it was doing. The spiritual myths, therefore, pointed the readers directly to the divine.

Another episode that serves as a founding myth for World Vision occurred near the end of Pierce's China trip in 1947. This story, too, involved an important female missionary. In Amoy, Pierce was invited by the Dutch Reformed missionary Tena Hoelkeboer to preach to her school of four hundred girls. The next morning, Hoelkeboer handed Pierce a little girl whose back was bleeding from her father's caning. The student, White Jade, had upset her father by informing him that she had become a Christian. Her father threw her out of the house after beating her. Hoelkeboer demanded of Pierce, "Don't you dare think you can walk off this island without doing something for her . . . now, tell me, what are you going to do about her?"[50] Pierce gave Hoelkeboer five dollars, all the money he had left in his wallet, and vowed he would send the same amount every month.

Pierce's experience in Kunming left a strong impression on his heart. Hoelkeboer's question resounded in his mind. He wanted to take immediate action, and he made a commitment to God that he would help people like Beth Albert and Tena Hoelkeboer for the rest of his life. He wrote:

> As I left Kunming, I told God I'm not going to try and start anything . . .
> I'm going to spend my life backing up people I find . . . And that basically
> was what and why World Vision was created: To meet emergency needs
> in crisis areas through existing evangelical agencies and individuals.

This story became firmly embedded in World Vision's oral tradition, and Pierce recounted the story to his audience at evangelistic rallies and church meetings. By inviting others to join him in "backing up people," he created a new avenue that allowed evangelicals to participate easily without making a lifelong commitment to overseas missions. By financially supporting individuals and established agencies, evangelicals could satisfy the demands of their social conscience. Pierce made sure this conscience remained awake. Each time he invited people to join him, he repeated Hoelkeboer's deafening question: "What are you going to do about it?"[51]

Another missionary who made a deep impact on Pierce was Gladys Aylward, a British faith missionary to China who lived from 1902 to 1970, during the time when the independent missionary movement flourished. Many evangelical mission organizations were born, and by the time she was ready to go to China, the China Inland Mission was actively sending out missionaries.[52] Aylward followed the faith mission model because she shared the belief that soliciting funds was not biblical.[53] She raised funds by taking on various jobs, then traveled to China, where she founded an orphanage and adopted more than a hundred Chinese children who had been orphaned, abused, or abandoned. Her dedication moved many local people's hearts, and Mandarin, one of the prominent social figures of the area, called her the "mother of all."[54] The Chinese gave her the name Ai-weh-deh, the virtuous one.

Robert Pierce used his radio program as a platform for Aylward to tell her stories. His stories on the radio program and in World Vision publications led Hollywood to turn her biography *The Small Woman* into a 1958 Oscar-nominated film, *The Inn of the Sixth Happiness*.[55] World Vision sponsored Aylward in several international speaking tours. During his interview with Aylward, Pierce joked that World Vision had never intended to adopt thirteen thousand children. He thanked her for being his inspiration and said, "I'm nominating you, not the 'small woman,' but God's Great Woman!"[56]

Notably, most of the female missionaries Pierce praised were single, unmarried women in the field. At the time, celibate women had more liberty to exercise religious authority than married women did. Particularly within the Holiness movement (a movement among Protestant churches characterized by its emphasis on holiness and post-conversion experience), celibate women could attain spiritual authority and, unlike married women, assume leadership positions. With the rise of independent mission agencies, celibate women's role grew in importance. Gladys Aylward was the epitome of this phenomenon. It is also worth mentioning that Pierce's repeated inclusion of women in his myth-making reflected a common theme in the Holiness tradition. Because women were considered to be more emotional, they were thought to be more in touch with the divine. The anthropologist Dorothy Hodgson, for example, has challenged the Western accounts that present a patriarchal Maasai world by analyzing the ways women controlled the supernatural realm and brought about mass conversion to Christianity in East Africa.[57] Women's mysterious, literal life-giving power was often associated with the divine ability to bring life, thereby giving them a sense of spiritual authority.

One of the common themes found in the careers of Gladys Aylward and the other women missionaries was their personal involvement with the locals and the sense of motherhood they forged while taking care of children. As they nurtured street children, lepers, and abandoned babies, they used the language of personal commitment and motherhood. This approach and this language were also used by the women missionaries discussed in this book: Bertha Holt, Pearl Buck, and Helen Doss. Pierce and Swanson, in contrast, did not use the rhetoric of fatherhood or dwell on their personal responsibility to the children. Rather, in their public writings and speeches, they treated the orphan crisis as a project to be finished, a tragedy to be alleviated, and a territory to be subdued.

The Everett Swanson Evangelistic Association

The Early Years of Everett Swanson

Everett Swanson bore striking similarities to Robert Pierce. Both were involved in evangelistic ministries at a young age, actively participating in fellowships dominated by white male evangelicals; both served as local pastors for periods of time but longed for more adventure; and both made trips to Asia that altered their lives. After experiencing similar events that became founding myths, both men founded evangelical relief organizations specifically for Korean war orphans, and both used films and visual aids to normalize transnational child sponsorship programs, advancing the genre of the evangelical humanitarian activist film. The parallels between the men are not surprising: they both belonged to a specific evangelical subculture of the twentieth century, and they walked similar paths as together they decisively influenced neo-evangelical culture.

Swanson was born on December 13, 1913, in Sycamore, Illinois. His parents came from immigrant families who had settled in Sycamore. His father, Abel Swanson, ran one of the largest farms in the United States. Abel made sure his children were well disciplined and grew up far from any of the mischief a city could offer. The Swanson family was actively involved in Calvary Baptist Church—Everett Swanson's father was a Sunday school teacher, a deacon, and church chairman; his mother was the organist; the children participated in every church event. Lawrence Swanson, Everett's younger brother, recounted, "Our home was a disciplined home. We respected our parents and all other adults. No back-talk was allowed or tolerated."[58] In this strict home environment, Everett Swanson had an uneventful and quiet childhood.

As a child, Swanson was bashful. However, he was powerfully expressive about his faith. Ever since he converted to Christianity at the age of nine in 1923, Swanson was unafraid to stand up for his beliefs and shared his beliefs whenever he had an opportunity. At age fifteen, he entered full-time evangelistic work.[59] Soon after high school, Swanson traveled across America in his car and visited communities in need of revival. Preaching from a tent, he held evangelistic meetings that lasted days or weeks. On December 16, 1934, he married Miriam Edwards, and the couple traveled throughout the United States and continued the evangelism ministry.

After years of traveling, the Swanson family settled down to serve at Swedish Baptist Church (now Emmanuel Baptist Church) for seven years and at Central Avenue Baptist Church (now Christ Tabernacle Missionary Baptist Church) for six years. The family enjoyed the security and joy of serving a local church, but full-time evangelistic work still beckoned to Swanson. Immediately after his resignation from Central Avenue Baptist Church, Swanson received numerous invitations to preach all over the country. In January 1951, he set off for a six-month evangelistic tour of Japan, the Philippines, India, and parts of Asia and Africa. This tour was a turning point for Swanson: it was during this tour that he received a calling to overseas missions.[60]

The Establishment of the Everett Swanson Evangelistic Association

Swanson longed to visit South Korea, but the door was not open to him during the 1950s. He prayed for an open door, and the answer to his prayer occurred in the most unusual place—the men's bathroom at the YMCA Tokyo. While visiting the YMCA Tokyo office as part of his evangelistic tour, he heard a familiar hymn coming from the men's bathroom. The whistler was a Presbyterian missionary, Peter Van Lierop. The Van Lierops were missionaries in Korea, involved with humanitarian projects to aid the people after the war's devastation. Peter Van Lierop was visiting Tokyo for the day to attend a field council meeting. He recounted that Swanson was thrilled to learn that he was a missionary in Korea: "Swanson entertained the burning desire and vision of ministering to the Korean troops in the front lines. His face lit up when I told him I could write him a letter of logistical support. This became the door that opened his ministry of Compassion."[61]

The American military presence in South Korea played a crucial role in facilitating Swanson's access to South Korea. After a short trip to Korea in October 1951, Swanson was formally invited to work alongside the South Korean Army (ROKA) chaplains in 1952. His evangelistic ministry flourished, and many soldiers made decisions to convert to Christianity.[62] As much as he was inspired by the spiritual victories in Korea, he was devastated by the abject poverty, particularly the sufferings of children.[63] Swanson could not escape the images of the war orphans and abandoned children. Some of the mixed-race orphans, fathered by American soldiers temporarily residing in Korea, were not only caught in the crossfire of local skirmishes but also bore the cultural disgrace of being impure and orphaned.

The incident that motivated him to establish ESEA occurred one morning in the streets of Seoul. During a normal day of evangelistic work, he noticed sanitation workers gathering what appeared to be a few piles of rags from doorways and alleys down the street. As Swanson drew closer to the truck, he realized that one of the piles had more than rags in it—he made out the shape of a child sleeping in a fetal position under the rags.[64] Some of the children, huddled together to keep warm, were asleep; others had died in the night. The workers were putting away the bodies of abandoned children who died on the streets.

Swanson was shocked and horrified by the plight of the war orphans and returned to America a changed man. His missionary friend had challenged him: "You have seen the tremendous needs and unparalleled opportunities of this land. What do you intend to do about it?"[65] With this question ringing in his ears throughout the flight home, Swanson, like Robert Pierce, made a vow to do something about the Korean war orphans. Upon returning to America, he received $50 designated "for Korea," and a few days later, a $1,000 check earmarked "for the needy in Korea." Everett later wrote, "This was conclusive proof to me that God was in it."[66]

Swanson first used his evangelistic platform to relate the destitution of the children to the Baptist General Convention congregations. He also produced documentaries titled *Wrath Praising Him: Civilian Life in War Times* and *God's Parallel in Korea: The Story of War and Evangelistic Opportunity*. These documentaries were used to raise funds for the Korean war orphans.[67] Miriam Swanson and their family friends Gus and Helen Hemwall supported Swanson's early works. Gus Hemwall, a medical doctor and an active member of the Christian Medical Society, provided medical supplies and significant financial resources. By 1954, one-to-one sponsorship programs had been developed to allow individuals, families, and churches to support children by sending a few dollars a month. Sponsorship funds provided daily food, clothes, housing, medical aid, and Bible study materials to the children of Korea. After several years of helping Korean children on an ad hoc basis, Swanson founded the Everett Swanson Evangelistic Association in 1956 in the basement of his home in Chicago. The organization was incorporated as a nonprofit corporation with Everett Swanson as president, Miriam Swanson as vice president, and Gus Hemwall as secretary and treasurer.

The Child Sponsorship Program

For both World Vision and ESEA, the backbone of the ministry was the child sponsorship program. Although both organizations engaged in leprosy ministry, medical care for adults, and evangelistic rallies, their main focus was alleviating the devastating circumstances of Korean war orphans through monthly child sponsorship. War orphans had become a major problem in postwar Korea, and by 1954, of the more than 170,000 orphans, only 50,000 lived in orphanages.[68] Moreover, the so-called G.I. babies—born to American soldiers and local women— were in imminent danger, since they experienced a severe stigma. The G.I. babies were fatherless, and their mothers became outcasts who had borne racially impure babies.[69]

Robert Pierce started the child sponsorship program in 1953 as a form of direct support for children in Korean institutions. World Vision connected individual supporters to individual children, and supporters were asked to sponsor an orphan by giving ten dollars each month for at least one year. Sponsors received an opportunity to adopt either a boy or a girl orphan, and the sponsor would receive a picture of their child, a brief biographical note, and the child's footprint. World Vision produced numerous posters and pamphlets with the slogan "World Vision has a Korean orphan for *You!*"[70] Sponsors were encouraged to write to their child, and the children wrote back. A pamphlet promoting the sponsorship program read, "You too can become the 'dear my sponsor' to whom they can write their touching little letters of gratitude and whose name they will remember as they say their goodnight prayers."[71] Sponsors were encouraged to send gifts, as the children "enjoy Western-world style clothes—shirts, trousers, and dresses."[72]

By January 1954, World Vision was supporting 751 orphans in 20 orphanages, and by November 1955, the organization was ministering to 4,200 orphans in 57 orphanages. Christian workers managed each orphanage—World Vision worked primarily with the Presbyterian Church in the beginning, but eventually widened its partnership to other denominations. The orphanages used financial support from the sponsorship program for food, uniforms, schooling, medical care, and religious training for the children.[73]

Everett Swanson used a methodology and structure almost identical to that of World Vision's child sponsorship program. After two years of ministry experience in Korea, Swanson realized that the best way to minister to children in Korea was through resident Korean missionaries and Christians within the country. In September 1954, Swanson wrote a thank-you letter to all of the sponsors, emphasizing that without their help, "children would still be wandering aimlessly on the streets and roads of this war-torn land."[74] Similar to World Vision's program, enclosed in the letter was a picture of the child with some biographical information. ESEA included one thing that World Vision did not have: an academic report card for older children who received education through their sponsors' support.

Both Pierce and Swanson used adoption language liberally to describe the sponsorship programs. Swanson exclaimed in his letter, "This is your 'adopted' child! He is depending upon your support and prayers. Only eternity will reveal what your kindness and generosity has meant."[75] When Roy Rogers and Dale Evans, popular Hollywood celebrities, decided to sponsor twenty-five Korean War orphans, World Vision magazine showcased the incident, advertising that the Rogers had adopted twenty-five Korean orphans through World Vision. Both organizations stressed that the children, who were otherwise hopeless and helpless, had been saved and given a new life through adoption by their sponsors.

When adopting a mixed-race or Asian child was a foreign concept, World Vision and the ESEA normalized the idea by promoting the virtual adoption program. The link between the child sponsorship program and transnational adoption is further attested to by the adoption of Asian babies by two couples: Bertha and Harry Holt, wealthy farmers and devout evangelicals residing in Oregon, and Roy Rogers and Dale Evans, cultural icons of America at the time. Both couples sponsored children through the child sponsorship program, and eventually legally adopted mixed-race Korean children through World Vision orphanages.

The Holt Family's Adoption

The child sponsorship programs were a great success, and many Christians asked World Vision and ESEA about legally adopting a child. While neither organization was a legal adoption agency, Pierce and Swanson assisted the process. It was through World Vision that Bertha and Harry Holt executed their famous "Operation Baby Lift." In December 1954, the Holt family attended a meeting about the emergency needs of the children in Korea. The Holts were horrified by the images and stories of the mixed-blood children. After several months, they contacted Robert Pierce and told him that they would like to adopt eight G.I. babies.[76]

Because immigration law permitted only two refugee children per any one family, Harry Holt wrote to his senator Richard L. Neuberger about compiling a case for a special bill. Neuberger introduced a bill in the Senate, and in the closing moments of the Eighty-Fourth Congress, President Eisenhower authorized the bill. Bertha and Harry Holt traveled to Korea and observed the calamitous condition of the children caused by the tragic aftermath of ideological conflict. World Vision provided the Holts with a tour guide and an interpreter who took them to forty-seven World Vision orphanages throughout Korea.[77]

On October 5, 1955, a Pan American Airlines airplane arrived at the Portland airport. A crowd of reporters and photographers surrounded the plane. In the plane were Robert Pierce, Miss Cowan (a nurse employed by World Vision), and the Holts, smiling happily with their twelve orphans—eight for their family and four for families. All twelve babies were of half-American and half-Korean ancestry. World Vision made its Reception Center available to the Holts and provided medical care for the children.[78] Soon after this incident, Frank Phillips, Executive Secretary of World Vision, expressed the hope that many others would follow the Holts' example.[79]

One year later, during June 1956, Robert Pierce personally brought nineteen orphans to America. This influx of children was by far the "largest group of Korean war orphans ever to fly the Pacific."[80] Sixteen of the babies, ranging from ages one to four years, were quarantined in Japan for three weeks because of measles. Among these children was a little girl who was adopted by Roy Rogers and Dale Evans, the Christian Hollywood actors who had already "adopted" (sponsored) twenty-five orphans through World Vision. World Vision's magazine reported this event with a picture of Robert Pierce personally handing Roy Rogers his newly adopted daughter Debbie.

Everett Swanson also supported the adoption process and did the initial screening of the parents himself. His major criterion was that the parents must be born-again Christians. After the initial screening, he referred the parents to Harry Holt for immigration processing. Swanson stated that his "only interest in adoption [was] in getting children into Christian homes and that unless this [was] possible, he would prefer that they remain in Korea."[81] He further said that he fully trusted Harry Holt in Oregon, and he always referred the sponsors' requests to him. Despite Pierce and Swanson's convictions about humanitarianism and their goal of awakening the evangelical social conscience, their ultimate goal was evangelism—as we will see, they used the child sponsorship program to promote the conversion of children. Holt and Pierce eventually drifted apart in their personal relationship, as Pierce and Swanson became more focused on institutional efforts in child welfare than on transnational adoption in their later years. Without World Vision's and ESEA's inauguration of virtual adoption, however, transnational adoption would not have gained such currency in the mid-1950s.

"Dearest Debbie"

Roy Rogers and Dale Evans adopted Deborah ("Debbie") Lee Rogers, a Korean-Puerto Rican girl, who instantaneously became a poster child for transnational adoption. Rogers and Evans were a Christian actor and actress who were outspoken about their faith and engaged in various charitable activities.[82] They were also beloved celebrities and cultural icons known throughout America. They actively participated in the Hollywood Christian Group and Chapel in the Canyon in Canoga Park, California. Dale Evans was named Churchwoman of the Year for 1964 by Religious Heritage of America, Inc.

Rogers and Evans had been inspired to adopt when they watched a film from the World Vision orphanages in Korea about the plight of the war orphans. They asked Pierce to help them find a Korean girl to adopt.[83] Debbie was one of the Rogers' nine children, five of whom were adopted.[84] Debbie was almost three when she arrived at her new home. She lived a short life, dying on August 18, 1964, in a car accident en route home from visiting a Tijuana mission post.[85]

After Debbie's death, Dale Evans wrote a book titled *Dearest Debbie* commemorating the little girl who had brought such abundant joy. Using the device of a letter of remembrance to her daughter, Evans sought to comfort readers who had experienced the sudden death of loved ones. She was unafraid to express her profound grief and denial.[86] Dale Evans also wrote *Angel Unaware*, an account of the life of her daughter Robin, who was born with Down's Syndrome and who died after two and a half years. The book demonstrated how raising a child with special needs broadened Rogers' and Evans' hearts and encouraged them to pursue charity work for children around the world.[87]

In *Dearest Debbie*, Evans made clear the joy of adopting an Asian child and raising an interracial family. Debbie's Korean name was In Ai Lee. Rogers and Evans decided to keep the "Lee" part of her Korean name and gave their new daughter the biblical name "Deborah." Recalling the first time she met Debbie and saw her "pretty, solemn, frightened" face, Evans wrote that Debbie brought something that would always remain in her family—her spirit of joy and love.[88] Evans pleaded with her readers to consider adopting or sponsoring the suffering children:

> My heart aches for all orphans . . . The majority of these children are of mixed racial backgrounds, like our Debbie; most of them are sentenced to life in a hostile and unsympathetic society, without our help . . . We all have a responsibility of these orphaned ones.[89]

Evans recommended that any childless family or would-be adoptive parents welcome a child of another race or a child of mixed racial background. She encouraged her readers to become involved in World Vision's Child Sponsorship Program and help the orphans any way they could, either from a distance or by giving them a home. Her stories and use of sentimentalism had a powerful effect. With her compelling rhetoric, she reconceptualized Asians as innocuous and adoptable children. By the end of the book, her readers likely felt personally attached to Debbie—a child who was innocent, lovable, and capable of assimilating seamlessly into American society. "Asians," in this portrayal, were no longer masculine, threatening, and foreign; they were feminized, infantilized, and relatable. Furthermore, the element of grief in the story called forth powerful sympathy. The readers, along with Evans, were invited to grieve the loss of an Asian child and a beloved adoptee.

Evans also criticized American society's apathy about the suffering of orphans around the world, attributing racial conflicts and conflagrations to a lack of love in the world. She sharply rebuked Americans who considered themselves superior to people of color and emphasized that all humans were equally created in the image of God. She also recorded the hardships she experienced raising Debbie. For example, Debbie often fell ill during her first six months in the Rogers household because floors in America were not heated like those in Korea. Furthermore, Evans was frustrated with her ignorance of Debbie's culture and language. She learned some Korean words and short sentences through a World Vision pamphlet but had a difficult time trying to communicate with Debbie during the first year. In one anecdote, she recollected:

You held on to your Korean speech and to your Korean customs for what seemed to be a long, long time . . . One morning you took my hand and led me out into the driveway, waving your arms wildly and pouring out an excited stream of Korean words. Helplessly, I said, "Honey, Mommy can't understand you"—whereupon you stopped in your tracks, put your hands on your hips, and looked up and down in desperation (and, I think, disgust) at my ignorance, shrugged, and turned away from me back into the house. That was the last time you ever spoke a word of Korean.[90]

It is unclear whether Evans intended this story to be an endearing, silly episode or a devastatingly sad story about an adoptee's struggle with ethnic identity. A recent flood of narratives written by mixed-race adoptees of the 1950s suggests that Debbie, had she survived to adulthood, might have taken the latter view.[91] Because transracially adopted children could not find a "biological mirror" in their parents, they often suffered pain and difficulty as they sought to understand their ethnic identity and cultural roots.[92] Growing as people of color in white homes, Asian adoptees rarely matched the established racial identity models.[93] Moreover, as in Debbie's case, many adoptive parents were unfamiliar with adoptees' cultural heritage and failed to put in the effort to learn their native language and culture. We observe in the passage above that Evans assumed that eventually Debbie's "Korean speech" and "Korean customs" would fade. By stating that Debbie held on to her cultural heritage for "a long, long time," Evans may have suggested that Debbie's cultural heritage was inconsequential—something that never should have been permanent, and something she should have shed more quickly.

Evans wrote that despite the cultural differences, she came to adore Debbie incredibly quickly and intensely. She realized that divine love triumphed over racial and cultural differences. Debbie was baptized during the Billy Graham Crusade in Los Angeles in the summer of 1963. This event aligned with World Vision's ultimate aim of bringing children to Christ through child sponsorship and adoption. Evans concluded the book by stating that Debbie's adoption was a divine intervention to bring people's attention to orphans around the world. She wrote, "Since you have been beckoned home, God has led me to tell others, in this letter, about the blessings of housing an orphan—and there are so many blessings!"[94]

The book indeed received tremendous attention, and the Rogers family received thousands of letters of consolation. The Hollywood couple had gained knowledge and awareness from World Vision about the tragic plight of Korean War orphans. Their involvement with the child sponsorship program eventually led them to adopt five children. Because of their social status as beloved actors and active participants in the local church, their actions were met with admiration and respect, popularizing and normalizing the practice of transnational adoption. By choosing to work with World Vision, a rising neo-evangelical relief organization, the couple demonstrated that faith was an important motivation in their decision to pursue transnational adoption. Through the powerful language of motherhood and grief, Evans moved many readers—particularly women readers who related to the everyday joys and struggles of raising a child.

The Success of the Child Sponsorship Program

While Robert Pierce and Everett Swanson disseminated the concept of virtually adopting a child through the child sponsorship programs, the notion of sending monthly financial support to underprivileged children was not their original idea. The precise origins of child sponsorship are controversial, but the Save the Children Fund had used child sponsorship since 1920, as a direct response to prevalent famine in war-torn Europe.[95] Moreover, the China Children's Fund (CCF) had already established a child sponsorship program, and Robert Pierce recruited Ervin and Florence Raetz from CCF to replicate its sponsorship programs in Korea.[96]

What, then, was unique about World Vision and ESEA's child sponsorship programs? What made them so popular and well known, and how did they awaken the evangelical social conscience? There were three prominent reasons for these programs' success: their founders' insider evangelical privilege, their family-centered rhetoric, and their effective portrayal of Korea through multi-media and vivid imagery.

Insider Evangelical Privilege

In the period following World War II, the animosities between theologically conservative and liberal parties widened and created a division between ecumenical mainline Christians (symbolized by councils of churches) and the new evangelicals. The conservative churches united in strong opposition against the ecumenical movement, including organizations such as the World Council of Churches (WCC). The liberal response to this distrust was just as bitter: Eugene Smith, the New York secretary for the WCC, remarked that evangelicals' "bigotry had produced nausea, wide-spread and justified."[97] By 1947, most evangelicals believed that missionary activities should be directed at saving souls and were suspicious of humanitarian activities.

However, with the rise of neo-evangelical institutions such as National Association of Evangelicals, the climate of opinion that prevailed in the late 1940s began to change. Using the slogan "Cooperation Without Compromise," the National Association of Evangelicals, along with other neo-evangelical organizations, declared itself an alternative to both fundamentalists and mainline denominations.[98] Although some neo-evangelicals made a conscious decision to separate themselves from the fundamentalists, until the early 1950s, fundamentalists and evangelicals often functioned loosely together. Some of World Vision's early endorsements came from fundamentalist supporters.

In an attempt to both maintain fundamentalist patronage and challenge the evangelical social conscience, Robert Pierce and Everett Swanson helped evangelicals see their place in society by integrating the call for evangelism with a plea for social action. These two pillars of child sponsorship organizations helped create postwar neo-evangelicalism by gently provoking the roots of Christians' personalized compassion and a sense of obligation. They underscored individual needs over systematic issues, often by invoking a sense of duty and guilt via vivid imagery. They successfully distanced themselves from the liberal social gospel movement by avoiding discussions of systematic, structural issues. Their contribution to the development of the evangelical social conscience also worked in their favor, as neo-evangelicals found the notion of accomplishing evangelism while engaging in humanitarian works appealing.

While Pierce and Swanson saw the importance of humanitarian works, they considered Christian service less significant than meeting the "spiritual needs" of non-believers. The two missionaries preached the absolute necessity of evangelism and believed that Christianity was the only way to achieve salvation. Pierce implied that meeting the physical needs of the people was necessary to meet their "real" (spiritual) needs.[99] He argued that Christians must not allow relativism to water down the foundational doctrinal truth of the uniqueness of Christ. He even believed that individual conversion could lead to material benefits and societal change.

Pierce and Swanson linked evangelism and social action by using insider evangelical language, without having to resort to the language of the liberal social activists. For example, one of the most common methods they used was to convince the sponsors that they could teach the Bible and evangelize the children through the child sponsorship program. One crucial method of communication was the use of Bible verses. Pierce and Swanson used verses such as "Train up a child in the way he should go; and when he is old, he will not depart from it" (Proverbs 22:6) and "Even so it is not the will of your Father which is in heaven, that one of these little ones should perish" (Matthew 18:14) to inspire their sponsors to acknowledge the eternal impact of their actions. They emphasized that through sponsorship, the children received biblical training that would prepare them to become evangelistic leaders of the next generation: "With your help, you, as a part of World Vision, can bring not only physical life, but to thousands eternal life through Jesus Christ."[100]

By framing spiritual needs as more urgent than physical needs, Pierce and Swanson won over many recalcitrant evangelicals who were otherwise indifferent to social issues such as racism and poverty. Moreover, the people who received their messages trusted them because Pierce and Swanson appeared similar to themselves, true evangelicals who were committed to the gospel—after all, they actively preached the Bible throughout Asia—while simultaneously meeting the most basic human needs. Indeed, Pierce and Swanson repeatedly identified themselves as evangelicals.

On the conceptual level, their mission theory was more closely aligned with evangelical missiology than with mainline missiology. As will become apparent in my discussion of Pearl Buck, mainline Protestants centered their missiology on Christian ecumenism and indigenization. Contextual theology was stressed, and imposing a Western view of Christianity was discouraged. In contrast, Pierce and Swanson emphasized Bible learning and evangelism through adoption. The militaristic trope of "conquering" heathen lands reveals the deep-seated superiority and American exceptionalism commonly found in white evangelicalism.[101] In this sense, Pierce and Swanson did not fall far from the tree— they thoroughly basked in their insider privilege.

At the same time, it must be acknowledged that even broaching the topic of social justice was a risky move, especially when addressing fundamentalists, who were still licking their wounds after their public defeat in the fundamentalist-modernist controversy of the 1920s. Robert Pierce, rebuking the separation between social action and evangelism, contended, "Our Lord preached the gospel of the kingdom, and that's social. The same word in both Hebrew and Greek for righteousness can be translated 'justice.'" He quoted biblical texts such as "Seek ye first the kingdom of God and his justice" and "blessed are they that hunger and thirst after justice."[102] When challenged, he explained that he fully believed in the Bible, which was the reason he carried out both evangelism and humanitarian works.[103]

Both organizations stressed that the chief objective in all of their efforts was to bring young people to a personal knowledge of Christ. Pierce and Swanson designed all of the programs in the orphanages with evangelism in mind. Prayer and a specific Christian emphasis permeated educational activities. The children attended regular worship services and received systematic discipleship training. For example, Robert Pierce established the "Little Shepherd Movement," a program aiming for evangelization and spiritual growth. It included Bible study and Scripture memorization to promote spiritual growth. The orphanages collaborated with local Korean churches to bring spiritual guidance to 9,500 orphans aged nine years and older.[104] Pierce convinced his sponsors that what they were doing was not merely sending financial support, but "feeding the sheep."[105] He emphasized that the pictures of the children represented not just individuals' need, but humanity's need for the hope of Christ.

Family-Centered Rhetoric

World Vision and ESEA played a crucial role in transforming the image of Korean orphans from wretched waifs to beloved American sons and daughters during the early 1950s. In both organizations, the transformation of the "hungry, dirty, helpless" orphans into "well-fed, well-dressed, well-educated" adoptees occurred through the child sponsorship programs.[106]

One of the most common methods used by World Vision and ESEA was "before" and "after" photos of children. On the left was a photo of a sickly, famished child; the right-hand photo depicted his transformed condition after sponsorship.[107] A typical text read, "Prompt medical care by World Vision transformed this orphan from a starved, sickly boy (left) into a robust smiling youngster (right)."[108] The narrative emphasized that while the child was dying, helpless, and fatherless, the sponsors became his life, help, and father:

> "I was dying . . . and you restored me to life."
> "I was naked . . . and you took me in and clothed me."
> "I was hungry . . . and you fed me and gave me something to drink."
> "I was handicapped . . . and you gave me hope."
> "I was helpless . . . and you helped me to pray."
> "I had no father . . . and you became my father."
> "I was drifting . . . and you gave me direction."
> "I was unlearned . . . and you taught me."
> "I was confused . . . and you pointed me to Jesus Christ." As a World Vision child sponsor *you* influence one impressionable child who needs your love and prayers.[109]

One reason Americans who encountered the family-centered rhetoric of World Vision and ESEA were eager to welcome the children was that the Korean child reaffirmed the power of the family as a "normalizing institution."[110] This reaffirmation of family as a normalizing institution through the practice of adopting transnational children appeared to nullify the racial strife and segregation found in the public sphere and replaced the strife and segregation with an inclusive, intimate, and racially diverse private sphere. Moreover, due to evangelicals' pro-life penchant, conservative Christians deemed childcare and adoption ministry a potential solution to the problem of abortion.[111] The evangelical culture of family-centeredness, the pro-life ideology, and the perceived innocence of children worked in synergy to promote the new evangelical humanitarianism.

By blurring the line between *sponsoring* and *adopting*, the two organizations inverted the dominant social structure of the racially monotonous family and created an idealized notion of kinship and racial inclusion. Instead of minimizing the effects of the "racial other," Pierce and Swanson portrayed Korean children with vivid imagery, thus countering the violent imagery of the "yellow peril" that had influenced American attitudes toward Asians in the previous century. Pierce and Swanson portrayed the children as helpless, innocuous victims of the war. Their work in opening the hearts of evangelicals to Korean orphans was essential to the success of the adoption movement. In the rhetoric of Pierce, Swanson, and the organizations they founded, Asians were no longer threatening, but deserving of compassion and rescue, and sometimes of pity.

Ironically, in their struggle against racism, Pierce and Swanson repeated the mistakes of Orientalists by making Asians objects of tragedy in need of Western rescue. Edward Said, in his seminal work *Orientalism*, famously defined Orientalism as a dominant Western discourse that portrays the East as enigmatic, static, irrational, and exotic. Historically, Orientalism distorted and exaggerated the civilizational differences between Arab peoples and cultures and Westerners. The heart of Orientalism was the ideology of difference, which defined "the Orient" as "other than" the Occident and made the two entities mutually exclusive. Further, the differentiation was a product of the West's position of power, domination, and imperialism.[112] Pierce and Swanson unwittingly adopted the discourse of Orientalism by stressing the exotic, mysterious "otherness" of the children in the "far East." The children were often portrayed as needy, backward-looking, and uneducated. Consequently, many American families who read Pierce and Swanson's newsletters or viewed their films understood the Asian children from an unchallenged Western perspective and, as a result, failed to understand the children's racial and cultural heritage.

Many pamphlets displayed words handwritten by children, such as 감사합니다 ("thank you" in broken Korean) accompanied by the words "this is your child in the Orient" in large font.[113] The exciting, exotic otherness of an Asian child was accepted in an intimate, private bond created between the sponsor and the adopted child. Unfortunately, many evangelicals' deep-rooted cross-cultural incompetence continued to linger even after they adopted Asian children. Some conservative families could not acclimate to living with a culturally and racially different child, and sent the child back. Moreover, as will become clear in subsequent chapters, even within transracial adoption, there was a hierarchy: half-Caucasian children were favored; then "fully" Asian, followed by half-African American children.

Depicting Asians as docile and innocuous individuals came with an additional cost: these portrayals contributed to the later prevalence of the model minority myth. Because of the compelling imagery of the child as an emblem of innocence, helplessness, and malleability, it became relatively easy for American families to overlook the fact that the children came from a foreign land—the orphans, to them, were children first and Asian second. Pierce stated that despite physical differences between the races, children have one thing in common: an immediate, pressing need for love. The cultural perception of a menace from the East—the yellow peril—was replaced with softer imagery of orphans in need of Western care and love. The rhetoric of love and compassion helped foster the later American acceptance of Asian children as family members and legitimate citizens worthy of a new status. The children were the best kind of immigrants.

World Vision and ESEA stressed repeatedly that children were in need of American help:

> Because they long for love and in many cases seek help for physical existence, they look to us—World Vision and its friends like you—to provide the love and care that they long to know and so desperately need. Wouldn't you like to bring joy to a little heart?[114]

Pierce wrote to the sponsors that "Dear my sponsor" was a very real person to the children, and that they were probably the only family the little ones would ever know in this world.[115] Pierce further emphasized the grave responsibilities the sponsors owed the children:

> Children don't choose their way of life . . . adults choose for them, by caring for them, loving and guiding them, or by defaulting to chance through neglect and abandonment. *You* can help a child receive Christ as Savior. *You* could give one of these children an opportunity to live a

happy, useful life of Christian fulfillment. Without your help he might not have a chance to live at all.

The short essay concluded with a direct question from the child: "Would *You* like to adopt an orphan just like me? And you can write to me and have my own personal picture and story. I'd like to be *your* child. Could I?"[116]

World Vision and ESEA's appeal to the public was effective and strategic, since the images of innocent children allowed the organizations to circumvent divisive theological and social stigma. The potent family-centered rhetoric was one of the primary explanations for Americans' readiness to welcome and accept the Korean war orphans. The family was the most fundamental and cherished institution in American culture, and thus family values facilitated the spread of the child sponsorship programs of World Vision and ESEA. Family-centric rhetoric coupled with compassion-evoking photos and language propelled the growth of the movement, contributing to the later acceptance of Asian adoptees as legal citizens and beloved sons and daughters in both the public and private spheres.

Although many were blind to their own racism and Orientalist mentality, some well-intentioned conservative Christians sought to fight systematic racism in their own way. Because the family was the microcosm of the nation, the adoptive parents hoped that racial unity within the family could lead to the eradication of racism on the national and societal levels. The family was not only a remedy for anti-racism but also the antithesis of communist collectivism in the 1950s. Adopting the children and converting them to be good, Christian, democratic children became their goal.

The Portrayal of Asia

Probably the most compelling method used by World Vision and ESEA was their vivid portrayal of Asia. They made their appeals to ordinary people at the grassroots level. Their strategy relied on active publicity, graphic images of the orphans, and guilt-provoking language. This approach set the two organizations apart from smaller charities that promoted child sponsorship. Pierce and Swanson were particularly successful with their filmmaking and storytelling about individual orphans. Films and vivid imagery were the primary vehicles they used to popularize the child sponsorship movement and reach broad audiences within evangelical circles. Through shocking and graphic images, they enlivened the evangelical social conscience and provoked compassion. Pierce's association with Rogers and Evans helped him to expand his influence in Hollywood as well.

The two founders wanted Americans to experience Asia vicariously through up-to-date reports and films. They described the sights, sounds, and smells of Seoul streets and Buddhist temples, underlining the exotic elements and the otherness of Asia. Their depiction of Asia resembled European paintings of the nineteenth and early twentieth centuries in which the Arab world is painted as an exotic, fascinating, and mysterious place that evoked Orientalist fantasies. At the same time, they depicted a continuity of American and Asian culture and faith—Pierce found the evangelical faith of Chiang Kai-Shek particularly inspiring and praised his strong Christian commitment.[117] Christians had come to embrace new technology and media, and Pierce and Swanson's films were well-received among moviegoers.

Robert Pierce considered himself a man in the gap and sought to function as a cultural bridge between the East and the West. In his first short film, *China Challenge* (1948), Pierce explained the rationale behind his filmmaking—because one picture is worth a thousand words, he wanted the audience to witness the tangible physical and spiritual needs of Asia directly.[118] He inaugurated the genre of the evangelical social action film, also known as the humanitarian activist film, with an underlying emphasis on evangelism. He wrote the script of *China Challenge* himself and, as the narrator, infused it with his unique emotional sensitivity and keen insight into human needs.

In both *China Challenge* and *38th Parallel: The Story of God's Deadline in Korea* (1950), he opened with exotic images of the mysterious Orient to attract a curious Western audience who had limited access to television at the time. Having once captured his audience's attention, Pierce gradually moved to depict the sordid social conditions: a blind beggar with vermin-ridden clothes, a bloated boy dying of starvation in the street, and innumerable women and children suffering from tuberculosis and pneumonia moved the viewers to empathy. As he depicted the children, he frequently narrated passages such as "When my father and mother forsake me, then the Lord will take me up," quoting Psalm 27:10.[119] He also emphasized the spiritual dimension of the social problem—he attributed the sufferings of Asia to Satan's terrible reign and suggested that Asians were spiritually enslaved to false gods.[120] Pierce always concluded his films with an upbraiding of evangelicals for their apathy and an exhortation to involvement.

Everett Swanson, likewise, produced documentaries such as *Wrath Praising Him: Civilian Life in War Times* and *God's Parallel in Korea: The Story of War and Evangelistic Opportunity* to depict the sights and sounds of Asia. Somber and realistic, and less entertaining than Pierce's films, his documentaries captivated Christians with their appearance of truth. The documentaries challenged Americans to take part in the high calling to bring the gospel and social change to Asia. Pierce and Swanson's films and documentaries were a great success and facilitated the spread of the child sponsorship programs by raising awareness of the situation and bringing financial support. The money raised through the media laid an essential foundation for later sponsorship programs.

In addition to films, Pierce and Swanson used vivid imagery and individual stories of orphans to spread the sponsorship programs. With charismatic rhetoric, the two leaders invented the idea that sponsoring an orphan would bring excitement and meaning to the sponsors' lives. World Vision printed pamphlets that read, "For the thrill of your life 'adopt' a Korean Orphan!"[121] By evoking a range of emotions, from compassion to guilt, they motivated many devout evangelicals to adopt helpless orphans. Neither Pierce nor Swanson was concerned about the convoluted, systematic character of poverty. For them, alleviating poverty meant meeting the immediate needs of the individual before their eyes. They showed images and told stories about individual victims. Pierce published vignettes about individual children in his books *Orphans of the Orient* and *The Untold Korea Story. Let My Heart Be Broken*, a biography with various testimonies, became a bestseller that exposed World Vision to non-evangelical audiences. Politicians and the mainstream press came to see Pierce as an expert on Asian affairs.

Evangelical Social Conscience

One of the reasons for the effectiveness of Pierce and Swanson's strategies was that they appealed to the general public, not the government. The pleas for funds were not directed to social elites but to ordinary people—most of the money for the global program trickled in a dollar or two at a time. Pierce famously stated that he would "rather have eight thousand people praying for us and giving us a dollar apiece, than one man giving us eight thousand dollars."[122] They also specifically catered to the sponsors' needs by providing a personal connection with the children. On July 31, 1956, Swanson shared in a letter to supporters that they had arranged for translators at each home so that letters could be read to the children, per the sponsors' request.[123] Their focus on micro-level aspects of the ministry had macro-level social and religious outcomes.

The two organizations' active publicity, involving celebrities, graphic images of the orphans, an evangelistic focus, and guilt-provoking language, was not above reproach. The International Social Services' (ISS) American Branch criticized Pierce and Swanson for mixing proselytizing with child welfare. Wells C. Klein, General Director of ISS's American branch, expressed the opinion that the evangelical voluntary agencies were publicity-minded and were far more interested in "obtaining dramatic or public relations results rather than providing real care for children."[124] Arthur Herzog, ISS Public Relations Director, complained that Pierce raised the hopes of adoptive parents only for them to find no children available. Pierce had advertised that approximately eight hundred children were awaiting American homes, when in fact there were none.[125] However, ISS acknowledged that World Vision and ESEA were still the major supporters of institutional programs in Korea and tried to find common ground for collaboration. Harry Holt also despised Pierce's publicity-seeking, but Pierce asserted that such publicity would aid the child sponsorship program.

Despite their shortcomings, Pierce and Swanson adroitly contextualized their message of social justice for evangelicals who viewed evangelism and social justice as mutually exclusive by exploiting insider evangelical privilege, family-centered rhetoric, and vivid imagery. While their contribution may seem minimal, considering their continued emphasis on evangelism, their method of incorporating humanitarianism was significant for their time. As they rebuked apathetic conservatives and provided a concrete way to engage in social issues, Pierce and Swanson stimulated the evangelical social conscience and helped create the new subculture of neo-evangelicalism. Because of the close association of child sponsorship programs with the practice of adoption, the time grew ripe for the transnational adoption movement to begin.

2

Hero or Villain?

The Holts and the Korean Adoption Boom

If Robert Pierce and Everett Swanson laid the foundation for transnational adoption and awakened the evangelical social conscience, the Holt family solidified the evangelical social commitment and popularized the transnational adoption movement. The Holts, like Pierce and Swanson, belonged to the neo-evangelical subculture, but held to a theology that was closer to fundamentalist doctrines. There are two established perspectives regarding the humanitarian activities of Harry Holt. On the one hand, he has been lionized as the founder of the transnational adoption movement in Korea—during his lifetime, hagiographic accounts and media articles painted him as the single most influential figure in the emergence of the movement. On the other hand, in recent literature on international adoption, he is commonly portrayed as a religious activist who failed to cooperate with secular social workers.[1]

As this chapter will show, both of these perspectives contain a good deal of truth. Nevertheless, the story is more complicated and nuanced than either portrait suggests. Furthermore, to understand this story, we must treat the Holts as a family unit, rather than focusing exclusively on Harry Holt, as many have done. To fully grasp what the Holts' activities imply about Christian missions and American identity in the postwar era, we must situate them within their religious and social contexts. Politically and socially, the Holts acted within the context of Cold War internationalism and were affected by the increased cross-cultural engagement of that era. Religiously, they were extremely conservative Christians who were attempting to pioneer the new field of transnational adoption among evangelicals.

This chapter examines the Holts' unconventional method of placing adoptees exclusively in Christian homes. I explore the significance of their evangelical theology and the reason for the sharp contrast between their philosophy of adoption and the policies developed around adoptions by social workers of the time. I delve into the significance and perils of the practice of "proxy adoption" that the Holts advocated. I also shift the focus away from Harry Holt as an individual hero and demonstrate how the Holt family's image as a "heroic family" moved the hearts of countless evangelicals. Because the Holt family's adoption endeavors in South Korea played a crucial role in the emergence of large-scale transnational adoption from East Asia, it is imperative to examine the forces that drove their success.

Harry and Bertha Holt

Harry and Bertha Holt were not the first to adopt transnationally from East Asia. In addition to Protestant missionaries who organized adoption agencies and fostered the movement, another group that significantly contributed to the adoption movement was American servicemen stationed in East Asia. The informal adoptions of children by servicemen started with fictive adoptions of *mascots*. The mascots came to military units from various places, but mostly from the streets. Servicemen often placed the displaced children in orphanages, but sometimes they brought them to their units and made the little boys into military mascots. Mascots had both practical and symbolic roles—practically, they helped with domestic labor, but more importantly, they served as the emblem of the paternalistic U.S.-Korean relationship, in which the U.S. at once rescued and colonized.[2]

While the symbolic adoption of military mascots sometimes led to legal adoption of Asian children, the cases of legal adoption was more sporadic than organized. For spontaneous, sporadic actions to become a *movement*, there must be a strong impetus and a clear agenda at the right time. That is precisely what the Holts had—what they perceived to be a strong divine impetus, support from the media, and the opportune time of the golden age in American family history. In addition to the factors mentioned above, most importantly, the Holts instilled American Christians with a sense of divine mission and obligation. Sacred biblical principles coupled with American heroism motivated would-be adoptive parents to eagerly seek out transnational adoptions in Korea. The aforementioned factors made Harry and Bertha the father and mother of the transnational adoption movement in Korea, which in turn ushered in a wave of transnational adoptions from countries throughout East Asia.

The Divine Calling

Harry and Bertha Holt were farmers who lived in a rural area of Creswell, Oregon. Around the time they began their adoption ministry, the Holts had six biological children between the ages of nine and twenty-one. Similar to the founding myths of World Vision and ESEA, the Holt story began with a moment of epiphany, bearing a resemblance to the typical revivalist language of "conversion." Just like people recounting the moment of conversion, these religious leaders—Robert Pierce, Everett Swanson, and the Holts—used the language of epiphany and God's providence. Bertha Holt, in her book *The Seed from the East*, described the moment as something that "forever changed our lives."[3]

Their story began when they watched several films sponsored by World Vision in 1954. Robert Pierce was recruiting sponsors to support World Vision's child sponsorship program, and as part of his efforts, he played documentaries focusing on war widows and orphans in Korea. Pierce was calling evangelicals to follow their consciences in this social matter, and the Holts were among the conservative Christians who responded to the challenge. Harry and Bertha Holt were dumbfounded to see the martyred Korean pastor, the war widows and orphans, the amputees and lepers, and the tragedies that surrounded the Korean War. What touched them the most was the account of the mixed-race "G.I. babies."[4] Bertha recounted that witnessing the plight of hundreds of illegitimate children "shattered" their hearts.[5]

At that time, mixed-race G.I. babies—babies born to Korean women and American servicemen—experienced a triple stigma: they were mixed-race, they were fatherless, and their mothers were treated as prostitutes who had borne racially "impure" babies.[6] Fearful mothers often hid their mixed-race children until it was no longer possible to keep the secret. Mixed-race children were often beaten by other children who had never known Asians with blond hair or blue eyes.

The Holts wanted to do more than provide financial support for mixed-race children. How the Holts came to this conclusion is an important part of understanding the impetus and rationale behind what they perceived as a divine calling. As days went by, after watching the documentary, Bertha Holt's desire to bring back the Korean war orphans grew. She wrote, "More and more I found myself wishing we could bring some of the Korean orphans into our home where we could love and care for them . . . I kept reminding myself that to continue this sort of planning was like living in a fantastic dream; but the dream continued to grow."[7]

She went on to write that her dream was confirmed as divinely inspired when Harry Holt also expressed the same urge. He said that he could not erase the pictures of the orphans from his mind, and his burden would not go away: "I look out here at this beautiful playground God has so generously given us and something inside of me cries out at the thought of those poor little babies starving to death, or being thrown into dumps to be gnawed on by rats."[8] Harry further declared that he would have no peace until he went to Korea to adopt mixed-race orphans. Bertha concluded, as she heard Harry repeat almost the identical things she had been meditating on throughout the week, that God was "working in their hearts," and that "only God could bring about such a miracle."[9]

As Pierce and Swanson had done, Bertha Holt laid out a dramatic founding myth that set the direction of their narrative. Her use of words such as "miracle" and "dream" served to legitimize the Holt's adoption ministry. Other evangelicals who had been intrigued by World Vision and ESEA's films committed themselves to adopting as they became convinced that the Holts' work was indeed divinely inspired. Miraculous signs have a long history in both the biblical world and church history, and they have traditionally functioned as a form of direct communication between the divine and humanity. Bertha Holt's rhetoric is important because her use of a founding myth helped to create zealous Holt followers who religiously subscribed to the Holts' adoption policies. Interestingly, as in the case of World Vision's founding myth, HAP's founding myth was also initiated by a female actor. Bertha was the one who received the "dream" from God; she was the one who recognized that God's words to both Bertha and Harry were a "sign" from God. As discussed in Chapter 1, in fundamentalist and evangelical circles, women were generally considered more spiritual and emotional than men, and hence more in tune with the divine. It was no coincidence, then, that women played a significant role in the oral and written traditions that made up the evangelical founding myths.

In Bertha's description of the founding myth, we also discover the notion of a "call" or "calling." Since the early church, the term has been applied to the vocations of candidates for religious leadership positions and to those holding spiritual authority. During the Protestant Reformation, Martin Luther crystallized the doctrine of the call in his commentary on the Book of Galatians. Luther differentiated two types of call: those made "by means" and those "without means." The first was a mediated call by which God spoke to individuals through the intervention of other people. The second was an unmediated call by which God himself asked individuals to carry out a divine mission, as with the Old Testament prophets.[10] The doctrine of calling was thoroughly engraved in evangelical tradition and was regarded as sacred. Bertha Holt, by depicting their mission as an unmediated call from God, placed herself and Harry Holt in the prophetic role of accomplishing a divine mission—the mission of finding permanent Christian homes in America for Asian children. Through a mystic, miraculous founding myth emphasizing an unmediated call from God, the Holts won many evangelicals' undivided loyalty. To evangelicals, a divine appointment was the highest form of legitimacy, one that no human government or institution could bestow.

Because the Holts viewed their work as a sacred duty bestowed by God, anything that stood in the way of this calling was viewed as an obstacle to overcome, a "spiritual attack from Satan."[11] Harry Holt recalled that whenever there was any doubt about his mission and calling, he reminded himself that God was with him. He wrote, "The enemy was giving me a good working over. He seemed to say, 'what are you doing out here away from home? You are nothing but a farmer and not a very good one at that.'"[12] His doubt was quenched when he shook his Bible open and pointed at certain verses. Holts wrote confidently that the verse was Isaiah 43:5, 6, and 7: "Fear not for I am with thee . . . I will bring thy seed from the east, and gather thee from the west . . . bring my sons from far, and my daughters from the ends of the earth; Even every one that is called by my name: for I have created him for my glory, I have formed him; yea, I have made him."[13]

Isaiah 43 became the foundation for Harry and Bertha Holt's theology of adoption, and Bertha used the phrase "seed from the east" as the title of her book.[14] In another book, *Bring My Sons from Afar*, Bertha explained their interpretation of the passage. She wrote that while previously they had considered "I will bring thy seed from the east" and "bring my sons from afar" the same command, they both discovered that the two sentences were not the same—according to her, "I will bring" was a promise from God; "bring my sons from afar," in contrast, was a command, not a promise.[15] Harry and Bertha Holt were convinced that they had been given a direct command from God to establish an adoption agency to "bring God's sons from afar."

The Holts' primary motivation for adoption, then, appears to have been not political but religious. They viewed themselves as ambassadors of God's work. Bertha Holt stressed that adoption was the entire family's duty, given by God. Harry and Bertha's five girls and one boy unanimously supported the adoption. Deciding that they had "room in their hearts and home for eight," the Holts welcomed eight children into their family.[16] Moreover, although the Holts did not hold the formal title of missionaries, in Korea they were widely referred to as missionaries from America. Their religiously driven relief work helps us understand their later feud with secular social workers. The Holts' rigid ways drove them to be somewhat isolationist and hostile in their dealings with these workers. The tension escalated when Harry started to promote proxy adoption, which will be examined later.

Because of the country quota restrictions on immigration laws, public demand led Congress to include in the Refugee Relief Act (1953) a provision for visas to be issued to 4,000 orphans to be adopted before the end of 1956.[17] The Holts wanted to bring back as many children as possible from Korea, but the Refugee Relief Act of 1953 restricted the adoption of foreign orphans to two per family. Convinced that it was the "Lord's doing," the Holts decided to petition for a special bill to allow the adoption of eight children. Harry Holt wrote a letter to Senator Richard L. Neuberger concerning the special bill.[18] Neuberger, along with Wayne Morse, the other senator from Oregon, enthusiastically endorsed and sponsored the bill. The bill was introduced in the Senate, and Edith Green introduced the bill in the House. In the Eighty-Fourth Congress, the bill was passed. Senator Neuberger predicted that the bill would not pass until early 1956, but Congress passed it in summer 1955, and the famous Holt Bill was officially authorized by President Eisenhower.[19] Bertha Holt exclaimed that "the rapid enactment of this bill was no accident for the Lord sponsored it."[20]

At his personal expense, Harry Holt flew to Korea for the first time in 1955. During his stay in Korea from May to October 1955, Harry Holt worked with World Vision and visited various orphanages. They traveled by bus into remote rural areas in search of children who would meet the health standards of the U.S. immigration service. While documenting the process, a *World Vision News* article featured a story about Christine, a blonde mixed-race girl who had almost died after being beaten by Korean children. Her mother begged an army chaplain to take her away so Christine could have a chance to live. The chaplain brought Christine, just over two years of age, to Raetz. When Harry saw her, he "knew she was the one that the Lord had picked out for his new family."[21] Harry Holt described the miserable condition of the children, stating that the Korean children frequently mobbed mixed-race children. According to him, mixed-race children were simply not safe in Korea.[22] On October 5, 1955, Harry and Bertha Holt brought back twelve children—eight for their family and four for three other families.[23] In 1956, they founded the Holt Adoption Program (HAP), which today is known as Holt International Children's Services. HAP/Holt International has placed half of all Korean children adopted since 1956.[24]

Although Bertha Holt was indispensable in the inception of the adoption movement, her role is often overlooked. After the death of Harry Holt in 1964, Bertha Holt worked ceaselessly for the advancement of the agency and founded additional adoption centers in other countries. In 1972, she established a counseling and support center for single mothers in Il-San, South Korea and a school for disabled children that later became Holt School. She was given the "Mother of America" award by President Johnson in 1966. In 1995, she received the *Mugunghwa* (Rose of Sharon) Award from the Korean Ministry of Health and Welfare for her years of social welfare ministry.[25] Until her death on July 24, 2000, Bertha Holt advocated for homeless children and helped them find permanent families.[26]

The Construction of a Heroic Family

An important change from Pierce and Swanson to the Holts was the shift of emphasis from individual heroism to *family* heroism. As previously discussed, Pierce and Swanson, who lived out a "muscular faith" marked by an exciting, adventurous, and challenging lifestyle, were often portrayed as individual heroes who inaugurated the child sponsorship programs. Their families and wives were seldom mentioned in their biographies. Harry and Bertha Holt, however, worked together as a unit and a family, and this partnership was often highlighted in popular portrayals of the family. The Holt children, likewise, were featured in magazines and newspapers. The imagery of the heroic Holt family aptly encapsulated the gender norms and mission theory of evangelicalism of the time—male headship, female domesticity, and "Christian home" missiology.

Despite the family-centered media coverage, Harry Holt remained the face of HAP as the male head of the family. He was described with phrases such as "heroic," "bold," "determinate," and "taking up [the] challenge," typical terms used to imply evangelical masculinity. Myriad newspapers and magazines portrayed him as a hero who had sacrificed his life for helpless orphans. The media attention was so overwhelming that Harry was met by press contingents wherever he went.[27] When Harry Holt returned to the United States on October 14, 1955, Portland International Airport was packed with a crowd of reporters, photographers, and other media-related personnel. The commotion was so great that some people wondered whether President Eisenhower was visiting the town.[28]

Specifically, Harry Holt was praised in both the American and Korean media as a religious hero who had saved hundreds of Korean waifs living in misery. For example, in an article entitled "Mr. Holt 'Moves the World'" published in *The Oregonian* on April 9, 1956, he was depicted as a hero who had singlehandedly "worked his will against the massive inertia of human society" by taking up the challenge of saving Korean orphans.[29] According to the article, Harry Holt struggled through "an insurmountable mountain of red tape" and never gave up because of his conscience and faith.[30] The article went on to describe Harry Holt's grandiose dream of finding homes for *all* of the Korean-American waifs.

Harry's "spark of initiative and the flame of determination," according to the author, enabled the movement. Claiming that Harry Holt has "given life" to hundreds of children, he rhetorically asked: "Given his example, can anyone doubt the power of the individual?"[31] The phrase "power of the individual" was clearly intended to portray Harry as a lone hero.

Ron Moxness, a reporter for the *American Mercury*, wrote an article characterizing Harry Holt as a typical American hero who had actualized the American dream of making a fortune out of nothing and then contributing his wealth back to society. According to Moxness, Harry—a native of Nebraska with little formal education—was able to buy some land and developed a profitable lumber business after moving to Oregon in 1937. The article portrayed a hardworking hero who sacrificially gave up not only his time but also his money for the Korean orphans.[32] Moxness concluded that while good agencies were working to alleviate the plight of Korean orphans, *only* Holt, "the farmer with the big heart and generous purse," had dedicated his entire life to the Korean war orphans.[33] Using Christian language, the writer wrote that Harry "shepherded" numerous children, which made him an "international Good Samaritan."[34]

The language of male heroism was both the product and a catalyst of the evangelical perception of masculinity. Harry Holt, a white evangelical male, was portrayed as someone who embodied a stereotypical determination, strength, and tenacity that inspired his evangelical male readers and wooed a female audience. In contrast, in line with the notion of female domesticity, Bertha Holt was portrayed as a loving, supportive wife and a mother who raised perfect children. The religious climate of the time helps us understand the neo-evangelical culture to which the Holts belonged. One of the topics neo-evangelicals were unwilling to dialogue with mainline Protestants was the issue of masculinity and femininity: mainline Protestants held a more egalitarian view of gender norms, while neo-evangelicals believed in male headship and female submission. The chasm widened after World War II, when progressive Christians began their debates concerning the ordination of female pastors. In the face of the ecumenists' gender reforms, fundamentalists and evangelicals alike resisted challenges to traditional Victorian gender norms.[35] The exacting church hierarchy gave men alone access to leadership roles, and most evangelical men supported hierarchical gender roles.

In the late eighteenth and nineteenth centuries, missionary wives played modest supporting roles in the mission fields—as "assistant missionaries," they rarely had a vote in discussions of mission theory or strategy.[36] However, they played a significant role within domestic culture and developed a mission theory based on the "Christian home." The goal of the Christian home movement was to model what a "Christian home" should look like—a place of nurturing, evangelism, and discipleship—for the indigenous population. Even as the Christian home functioned as an extension of the colonial project, it had the effect of giving white Western Christian women a greater sphere of influence than they would otherwise have had.[37] Through the movement, missionary wives were "evangelists" both for the gospel and the ideal home. The mission historian Dana Robert, for instance, argues that the movement was a cornerstone of nineteenth- and twentieth-century Anglo-American mission, because it validated women's participation in all aspects of mission work, including "homemaking, evangelism, fund-raising, teaching, and even social reform."[38] Bertha Holt, through adoption, accomplished all of these tasks. She raised funds through writing books, taught and "evangelized" her adopted children while tending to her domestic duties, and ultimately ushered in social reform by starting a new movement.

The incorporation of Harry Holt's rugged, male heroism and Bertha Holt's nurturing female domesticity, coupled with Christian home ideology, constructed a narrative of a "heroic family." The Holts not only modeled an ideal Christian home, but also demonstrated American heroism through their home. When Harry Holt appeared in the media, he was portrayed as an audacious, solitary hero. When the Holt family appeared in the media, however, family-centered rhetoric was used: Holt was no longer portrayed as a rugged pioneer, but as a family man. According to one news article, Harry Holt, who "just loves children," willingly gave up plowing his 350-acre farm to save the children.[39] An article titled "The Power of Faith" reported that Harry prayed with his family every night.[40] Harry and Bertha were seen as the perfect team who had clearly "heard the Lord calling them."[41] Harry ended the interview by referring to the work as "our" work, instead of "his": "Ours is a work of faith in the Lord Jesus Christ."[42]

Politicians and lawmakers also acclaimed the Holt family as a whole. Senator Neuberger, who played a pivotal role in making the Holt Bill a reality, commented in his address to the U.S. Senate that "if brotherhood of man still has meaning in this troubled world, then that sentiment is exemplified by Harry Holt and his family."[43] Senator Neuberger famously compared Harry Holt and his family to the "Biblical Good Samaritan." Korean newspapers also portrayed Harry and Bertha Holt in an extremely positive light. Around 1956, Korean media outlets started to use the phrase "father of Korean adoption" to describe Harry Holt. *Dong-Ah Newspaper*, one of Korea's largest newspapers, called Harry the "father of mixed-race orphans," and *Kyunghyang Newspaper* similarly called him the "father of mixed-race children." Similar titles he obtained were the "father of Korean War orphans" and "father of the lost children." Bertha Holt was affectionately called "Grandma Holt" by Koreans later in her life and earned the title of the "Apostle of Korean orphans."[44] Similarly, Korean Americans commended the Holts. The Honolulu-based Korean American newspaper *Kookminbo* compared the Holt family to the Good Samaritan. The newspaper rhapsodized that while the Good Samaritan had only helped one man, the Holts were helping countless children in dire need.

Various Christian newspapers and magazines reproduced the founding myth of HAP. The Holts, as a family, were portrayed as a heroic family in these stories. David Wisner, a reporter for *The Wesleyan Missionary*, wrote that the Holts were the "bright spot" in the Korean orphan situation.[45] He emphasized their extraordinary faith in boarding a plane to Korea even before the outcome of the special legislation was known.[46] Bertha, expressing how happy her family was to bring the children into their home, said that adopting them was an excellent opportunity to "teach them of our Savior's love and share with them the Christian inheritance," once again evoking the ideology of the Christian home.[47]

The most exuberant praise of the Holt family came from Robert Pierce. In one *World Vision News* article, Harry was portrayed as a family man who was deeply moved by his fatherly duty to the orphans, someone who could "never forget their tiny outstretched arms."[48] Pierce also praised Bertha Holt for being a model American woman who had "worked hard to make America a sanctuary for family life," affirming the Christian home ideology.[49] The Holts embodied the ideal postwar American domestic life—a father who provided for the family and a mother who raised perfect children. Among the "perfect" children that the media highlighted, Molly Holt was the most prominent. Molly, the second-eldest daughter, played an important supporting role as her parents launched HAP. When she visited Korea for the first time after graduating from nursing school, she felt a clear calling from God to stay in Korea. Molly spent most of her adult life caring for the orphans at the Ilsan Center in Korea and gained the title "Mother Teresa of Korea."[50]

The discourse that glorified Harry Holt's individual contribution, Bertha and the children's supporting role, and the heroism of the family as a whole was presented as one coherent story in Bertha Holt's book *The Seed from the East*, published in 1956. Bertha stated that the motivation behind the book stemmed from the numerous letters the Holts had received concerning the adoption process. In response, she wrote the first of several books about the history of the Korean adoption project to raise money for the effort.[51] As a byproduct, her books strengthened the public perception of the Holt family as a "heroic family." The narrative of this heroic family resonated among evangelical readers for several reasons. First, during the baby boomer era (often referred to as the "golden age" of family history), raising a family was seen as the most sacred vocation. Second, within evangelical circles, foreign mission was still glorified and carried an implication of spiritual superiority. Third, the Holts' "Christian home" model was a continuous affirmation of evangelical gender norms, and as a result, it fit comfortably within evangelical theology. Fourth, after the evangelical social conscience had been awakened by the child sponsorship programs, the time was ripe for evangelicals to commit to overseas mission by adopting foreign children and forming heroic families of their own. Instead of devoting their entire lives to discovering foreign lands, they welcomed Asia into their homes.

The evangelical social commitment that the Holt family called up can be traced through numbers. After Harry Holt's return from Korea, the Holt family received a flood of letters from across the country, with an average of twenty-five letters from prospective parents every week. Harry Holt, in his newsletter *Dear Friends* on December 27, 1956, wrote that he had received several thousand new applications for children. Overwhelmed, he said he hardly knew how to proceed. He continued confidently, "However, *we* feel that this is the Lord's work and if He has sent these applications to us for a purpose, *we* hope to receive wisdom from Him."[52] Bertha closed *The Seed from the East* with a prayer: "Father, please open the hearts and home and pocketbooks of the American people to help the mixed-race children in Korea."[53] This was an apt closing, considering her vital role as a supporter who constantly prayed while Harry was in the "field." To her, the home was the mission field.

Global Response

As detailed above, in the 1950s, the public largely viewed transnational adoption from East Asia as a benevolent humanitarian project spearheaded by the heroic Holt family. The concerns voiced by social workers of the time were rarely known to the public, except for occasional publicity about the tragic deaths of adopted children. However, from the beginning, North Korea vehemently castigated the United States for adopting children from Korea. Pyongyang radio initiated a new campaign denouncing America as a "nation of slave traders." It accused the Americans of stealing "the flow of South Korean war orphans to foster parents in the United States as well as South Korea's proposal to export surplus population."[54]

South Koreans were also blamed for selling their own kin to American slave traders. One Pyongyang radio station announced that South Korea proposed emigration to alleviate unemployment and that this was a "vicious attempt of the U.S. imperialists and the Syngman Rhee gang to sell Koreans by force."[55] The broadcast commented the "traitors sold 1228 South Korea orphans under the age of 14 to the United States between 1954 and 1957," handing them over to "American slave traders." They claimed that the children were being sold like animals in the foreign land.[56] Despite the North Korean media's vehement protests, the notion that the transnational adoption movement was infused with American imperialism and paternalism did not significantly influence popular American sentiment of the time.

The South Korean government's response to the Holts' activities, in contrast, was extremely positive and helped advance the movement from the "sending" side. President Syngman Rhee, who enthusiastically supported the transnational adoption movement, called Harry Holt an "apostle of international understanding and good will."[57] In 1958, President Rhee awarded Harry Holt the highest public award given to those who contribute significantly to the common good of Korean society.

Harry Holt expressed gratitude for the award and remarked that the co-operation of the Korean government and the American embassy had been an enormous help in his compassion ministry.[58]

President Rhee's motivation was multifaceted. Ideologically, he campaigned for *ilmin juui* (one people ideology), an extreme form of nationalism that promoted racial homogeneity of shared bloodline and ancestry. He also advocated the reunification of North and South Korea and stated that a unitary Korean nation must be "occupied by one united people."[59] His emphasis on racial purity was a common belief shared by many South Koreans, and as a result, mixed-race children suffered ostracization and severe discrimination. The children were given the debasing label *twigi*, an offensive term meaning "half-blood." Moreover, since many mixed-race children were born as a result of prostitution in *kijichon* (a U.S. occupation camp town), the children and mothers were shamed by Korean society.[60] Although prostitution was illegal in other parts of South Korea, the U.S. military government permitted it. The Korean government also saw the opportunity to attract foreign currency through entertainment and the prostitution business. For the Korean government, the mixed-race children were, therefore, an unfortunate byproduct.

Politically, Rhee's motivation betrayed his pro-American tendencies. As the poster child of foreign missionary educational ministry, Rhee welcomed any foreign relief aid during the Korean War and relied heavily on transnational adoption as the ultimate solution to the orphan crisis. Economically, dependence on foreign humanitarian aid was beneficial because most of the government money went to the military, with little to no attention given to social welfare. The Christian Children's Fund's (CCF) William F. Asbury, the regional administrator for CCF Korea, commented on the lack of a child welfare system in Korea, stating that there was "no adequate legislation and an insufficient understanding of social responsibility."[61]

While President Rhee promoted racial homogeneity, some Korean Americans swung in the opposite direction. University of Wisconsin professor Chung Jin argued that there was no genuinely homogeneous ethnicity. He asserted that mixed-race people were superior to the so-called "pure" Koreans just as hybrid plants produce superior fruits.[62] The Nobel laureate novelist Pearl Buck, a missionary in China and campaigner for the adoption of mixed-race children, also espoused this idea of hybrid superiority.[63] Against the backdrop of eugenics prevalent at the time, Chung and Buck repudiated the idea that only racially homogenous children were suitable for adoption.

Conflict with Social Workers

As discussed above, various media outlets and Bertha Holt's writings shaped the American perception of the Holts as a heroic family that pioneered the transnational adoption movement in Korea. What was less known to the public was Harry Holt's caustic relationship with secular social workers, particularly the International Social Service American Branch (ISS-USA). Harry Holt, in his newsletters, portrayed himself as a heroic soldier fighting for God's kingdom. He regarded social workers' concerns as a form of "persecution." The media's positive depiction of the Holt family validated his narrative. By spiritualizing everything about his methodology, he was able to use the conflict with social workers to his advantage by framing the opposition as a force of spiritual opposition. Evangelicals, who were accustomed to the trope of "spiritual warfare," readily joined Holt's battle with the social workers. From the founding myth to the persecution rhetoric, Holt's method of spiritualizing and bringing religion into the adoption practice proved extremely effective among evangelicals—they believed that the only ingredients necessary to become adoptive parents were a definite call from God and sincere goodwill. The conflict between ISS-USA and HAP was multifaceted and complex, but there were two practices that ISS-USA found most fundamentally objectionable: the Holts' religiously driven adoption methodology and the proxy adoptions facilitated by HAP.

Adoption and Evangelism

The Holts' primary criterion for selecting adoptive parents was religion. The Holts hired a private company to investigate whether adoptive families were "saved" and "born again Christians," a criterion that challenged the expertise and autonomy of the secular social workers who conducted thorough investigations of prospective families' socio-economic background, emotional and financial stability, and family history, among many other factors. The language of being "born again" was the hallmark of evangelical theology; it can be traced to the Great Awakenings in Great Britain and the American colonies. Many revivalists, such as John Wesley and George Whitefield, preached the necessity of a transforming encounter with Jesus Christ and emphasized the conversion event in the life of a believer. The phrase "born again" continued to distinguish evangelicalism from ecumenism in the era when Billy Graham, along with other twentieth-century neo-evangelicals, was fervently preaching a "born-again experience."

In a similar fashion, Harry Holt stated on multiple occasions that his main goal was to place children in Christian homes and create born-again Christians. Reassuring his readers that the Holt Adoption Program did not have rigid financial requirements, he stressed that being born-again Christians was the most important criterion. To clarify this criterion, he used historical revivalist language: having the "assurance of salvation," "accepting Christ as the Lord," and "returning home." He argued that all children were God's children, and thus he was responsible for placing the children in homes where they could be raised as born-again Christians.[64] Holt made a firm distinction between people who merely claimed to be Christians and born-again Christians who truly believed that "there [was] only one way to heaven . . . the Lord Jesus Christ."[65] Moreover, he often used the newsletter as a tool for evangelism. He wrote lengthy interpretations of the gospel, quoting various biblical passages.

While Pierce and Swanson, in their child sponsorship advertisements, alluded to the connection between evangelism and social justice, Holt made the connection particularly apparent and strong. Pierce and Swanson used vivid imagery to gently arouse the evangelical social conscience; Holt blatantly demanded evangelical social commitment by preaching conservative doctrines and invoking a sense of guilt. To him, refusing to adopt children meant removing the opportunity for these children to receive salvation. Although his fundamentalist doctrine was stout and his exhortation demanding, his method was effective. Evangelicals who were otherwise indifferent to social issues began to respond. Because Harry Holt did not frame adoption as a "social justice" issue, it is likely that conservative Christians were more willing to participate than they would otherwise have been: adoption, in the Holts' portrayal, could be regarded as an extension of evangelism and part of the practice of building a Christian home. Ironically, the result was the development of an evangelical social commitment that went beyond a social conscience.

Because Harry Holt's objective was to produce born-again children, he rejected applications from non-Christian adoptive parents. In his newsletter, he wrote that he could not place a child contrary to his convictions because adoption was God's ministry and he felt responsible to God to see that "wherever possible they [children] are placed where they will receive fundamental teaching."[66] He also wrote that Mormonism, Christian Science, Unitarianism, and Jehovah's Witnesses directly contradicted the fundamental teaching of Scripture and represented false teachings that were dangerous and deceptive, "founded and established by Satan himself."[67] Holt concluded that if children were to be raised under these false teachings, they would grow up with a "terrific handicap."[68] Since the Holts were so fixated on selecting Christians only, they were much more lax in other areas that social workers deemed important, such as financial stability, mental health, and family history.

Moreover, since the Holt Adoption Program was not a licensed child-caring agency, the Holts worked independently of state social workers. This approach set the Holts in sharp contrast with Pearl Buck, who voluntarily registered her organization as a state-approved child-caring agency. William T. Kirk, the international director of ISS and general director of the organization's American branch, expressed concern that Harry Holt's unorthodox way of selecting Christian families was unnecessary. In his letter to Eugene Carson Blake, president of the National Council of Churches, Kirk wrote that social workers had already worked hard for many years to select a sufficient number of qualified adoptive parents to receive mixed-race children in Korea. When ISS reached out to Harry Holt to make available all the information they had accumulated, Holt simply stated that he only accepted "born-again Christians" and accused the agencies of conspiring against him because of his religious beliefs.[69]

Many social workers and government workers were disgruntled by the media's extremely positive portrayal of the Holts' activities because the media told only one side of the story. Raymond W. Riese, Child Welfare Director of North Dakota Public Welfare Board, wrote that Holt's actions were "well-intended but unprofessional" and did not provide adequate protection for children.[70] Similarly, Margaret A. Valk, a Senior Case Consultant for ISS, stated that a great deal of publicity regarding Harry Holt's adoption program in Korea had been harmful because it escalated public interest without adequate investigations by local social agencies. She lamented that because there was no requirement for social information or background checks, several unfortunate placements had occurred through HAP.[71]

Regarding these negative comments, Harry Holt remained obstinate in his belief and insisted that HAP followed the proper procedures and safeguards mandated by the Immigration and Naturalization Service and the laws of the country of the children.[72] He wrote rather defensively that he was the servant of the Lord Jesus Christ and what people said about him was unimportant. He equated his "persecution" to that of Jesus Christ, stating, "When my Lord was here they took him out and spit upon him and beat him and hung him on a cross to die . . . so I am not going to answer your unwarranted attack upon myself."[73] He went on to directly criticize what he perceived to be ISS's inefficiency: "Their [ISS's] inefficiency of operation has disgusted everyone who has had to deal with them. The reason fewer children are taken to International Social Service for placement is because it is well known that they are often kept in orphanages for years before they are adopted . . . if they are ever adopted."[74]

Harry Holt's acerbic relationships were not limited to secular social workers. Even former missionaries like Pearl Buck criticized Harry Holt's policies for being too fundamentalist and rigid. Moreover, Harry Holt published numerous newsletters containing sharp criticisms of other adoption agencies, which led to difficult relationships between HAP and both secular and Christian organizations. For example, Harry Holt accused Calvitt Clarke, the founder of China's Christian Fund (CCF), of holding "many children for ransom" because Clarke considered orphans "just a little bit better than a goldmine."[75] According to Holt, CCF made only "a half-baked attempt to find home[s]" for children.[76] Holt further accused Clarke of stealing donation funds for his selfish interests. In response to this abrasive attack, Clarke wrote:

> Frankly, Mr. Holt, I am greatly surprised at your writing these letters. You are only hurting innocent children so dependent upon CCF . . . Perhaps

we have been more conservative than you have but such conservatism has been for the protection of the children. I personally have never criticized your efforts . . . But your letter to our CCF people is sensational and interesting but cruel and untruthful.[77]

Joseph H. Reid, Executive Director of ISS, similarly commented that it was unfortunate that a matter of such high purpose as securing homes for orphans had degenerated to the "level of name calling."[78] He wrote, "I was shocked that you, a Christian, would deem Mr. William Kirk 'a propagandist . . . who was hired to conduct smear campaigns.' Mr. Kirk is a dedicated social worker devoted to the same aim that you are."[79] Reid insisted that though their views may have differed, Harry Hold should acknowledge that ISS's efforts stemmed from an honest conviction.[80]

A small number of media outlets took notice of Holt's rocky relationships with other agencies and published articles about his lax policies and hostile relationships with social workers. For example, *Coronet* magazine wrote that Holt's standards for adoption "were considered lax by most welfare agencies."[81] Arnold Lyslo wrote in his article "A Few Impressions on Meeting the Harry Holt Plane, the 'Flying Tiger'" that he was deeply disappointed and puzzled by the adoptive parents' reaction. The adoptive parents he encountered at the Portland International Airport seemed "colorless in emotions," according to him. He suspected that the families were of a "strict religious sect" judging from the way they dressed and behaved.[82] Lyslo further criticized HAP's method of bringing children in small cardboard boxes with round holes, "stacked one above the other."[83]

Lyslo felt the whole event was centered around publicity—there were cameras everywhere, and children froze or trembled in utter shock and confusion amid flickering flash-bulbs. Stating that he could not erase the terrified looks on the faces of the children, he expressed his anger that some parents did not remove themselves from the situation quickly enough: "It seemed that they were totally unconcerned as to when their child would need his next feeding, etc. They appeared to be in a complete daze—at the expense of the child."[84] He further wrote that to his horror, some adoptive couples were unhappy or disappointed in their children. He concluded his article by stating that the whole fiasco had been created because of Holt's "inadequate planning," and he predicted that the situation could have been avoided under the guidance of professional social agencies.[85]

Proxy Adoption

What ultimately created the deepest chasm between social workers and the Holts was HAP's practice of proxy adoption. Through proxy adoption, Americans were permitted to adopt abroad in overseas courts by appointing proxy agents to act on their behalf. The children obtained U.S. immigration visas faster and without investigation by social agencies when they were adopted abroad. The children came to their new families already adopted without having met the parents. Social workers saw this as a major problem because they believed that foreign children did not receive equal legal protection as domestic children. ISS-USA, in particular, believed that executing proper adoption procedure overseen by trained social workers was the best way to protect the children; those who supported proxy adoption—most notably Harry and Bertha Holt—believed that protection meant removing children from harmful situations in Korea as quickly as possible.[86]

Workers in the ISS-USA, the Child Welfare League of America, and the U.S. Children's Bureau accused Harry and Bertha Holt of executing an unscrupulous, unsound adoption practice that put children in danger. Minimum standards to ensure careful investigation and a probation period were mandated in domestic adoptions; however, proxy adoption excluded the minimum standards altogether.[87] Professionals also voiced concern regarding prospective parents' lack of cultural awareness and education, which should have included rudimentary Korean language skills and knowledge of Korean cultural habits, food, sleeping arrangements, and so forth. Protesting that proxy adoption lacked accountability and created opportunities to exploit children, these social workers collaboratively produced a statement warning against this unscrupulous practice.[88]

William Kirk directly criticized the Holts' programs, stating that the Holts' proxy adoption was harmful both to the children and the families: "Because these children are coming to families not able to deal with the problems of adjustment presented, they have the potential of prejudicing whole neighborhoods and communities against these children."[89] He went on to write that because Harry Holt was working so closely with the Korean government, ISS workers in Korea encountered great difficulty in dealing with Korean officials. President Syngman Rhee, who avidly praised Holt's efforts, had been quoted as saying, "Get these children out of Korea" and that he "doesn't care if they throw them in the sea."[90] Kirk expressed concern that both Holt and the Korean government were interested in removing the children from Korea by the quickest means possible and without concern for the long-term consequences. Similarly, Susan Pettiss, in her article "Adoption by Proxy" in *Child Welfare* published in October 1955, wrote that the risks involved in a transnational adoption was greater than in a domestic adoption, and thus a "living together period" before the legal adoption was imperative. She argued that proxy adoption was a practice that fell into the category of "unprotected placements."[91] She wrote tirelessly in various magazines about the perils of proxy adoption, directing her criticisms toward Harry Holt in particular.

In 1958, the Child Welfare League and ISS co-sponsored a project to study the effects of proxy adoptions, which, according to them, encouraged "a mail order baby business involving thousands of helpless youngsters."[92] The main argument of the study was that for homeless children who had spent their earliest years in deprivation or neglect (especially in war-torn countries), safeguards were doubly important. The project, prepared by Laurin P. Hyde and Virginia Hyde, comprised seventy-seven proxy adoption case studies providing evidence that proxy adoption "represented a long step backward in the development of sound adoption laws."[93]

The Hydes discovered that out of seventy-seven families, twenty-nine reported that their adoptions had not succeeded or were in question. They reported cases of "physical abuse of children, breakdown of adoptive homes, adoption of children by persons who were unstable or mentally ill, and placement of upset or emotionally disturbed children with persons unprepared or unable to help them."[94] Adoptive parents' financial instability compounded the problem. Hyde Report cited sixteen cases of physically abused or maltreated children. One child was abandoned soon after her plane landed because the adoptive parents "didn't like her looks."[95] The study concluded that proxy adoption was not only a hazard to children and adoptive families but also a danger that undermined state child protective legislation and adoption practices throughout America.

Another matter that bothered social workers was the lack of privacy in the Holts' proxy adoption procedure. In one of Harry Holt's pamphlets, Virginia and Laurin Hyde noticed that one could easily order a directory of all the children adopted by families for just two dollars. When Victoria Hyde ordered the directory as part of their research, she immediately received a directory listing over five hundred families and their children who had been adopted through HAP, with "no questions asked as to who she was and why she wanted it."[96]

Case studies that circulated among social workers detailed child neglect, child abuse, abandonment, and even death. For example, Van Dorm Sims, a child who was adopted by proxy through HAP, was admitted to a children's hospital and died soon afterward. The autopsy revealed that he had died of plasma cell pneumonia due to *pneumocystis carnii*. The adoptive parents reported that on the plane that brought Van Dorm were several children who later died of pneumonia. Helen E. Boardman, Director of Social Service, criticized HAP for not providing extensive medical exams before the trip.[97] One report estimated that out of one thousand babies on the plane, about ten babies died, and a hundred were ill and died soon after arrival.

Another case was that of Susie, a Korean girl adopted by the Henry Buller family through HAP. Because HAP did not conduct a proper background check or the thorough investigation that was required by the social welfare standard, Susie was given to unfit parents who were emotionally unstable. Wilmer H. Tolle, director of the Joseph County Department of Public Welfare, wrote that the "Bullers had no real affection for the child and their purpose in adoption was an extension of wishes to become missionaries and to salvage a deteriorating marriage."[98] On May 13, 1957, Mrs. Buller was committed to the Dr. Norman Beatty State Mental Hospital through the local court. She had acted violently and threatened her husband, the child, and her parents.

The Bullers did not possess the minimum financial stability that was required by social welfare standards. They lived in a small trailer that was described as "filthy, cluttered, and very cold most of the time."[99] The Bullers' relatives had to forcibly take Susie away because the trailer was so cold they feared for Susie's health. The Bullers' pastor testified that

Susie had to receive special medical care after suffering a bad case of polio. Individuals in the community who had firsthand contact with the Bullers also testified about the Bullers' abuse and neglect of the child. They described Mrs. Buller as emotionally unstable, and Mr. Buller as "withdrawn, sullen, and moody."[100] The social workers were upset that all this trauma for Susie could have been prevented had HAP done proper research before the adoption.

The social workers complained that Harry Holt had free rein over his projects in Korea. Holt had become a touted figure in Korea after receiving the highest award given by the South Korean government. President Rhee fully supported Holt's endeavors and bent laws to accommodate Holt's needs. For instance, when Harry Holt wanted to build the Holt orphanage next to a powder factory, the Korean government changed the law that forbade construction near such factories due to the risk of explosion. The social workers were concerned about the way the government freely accommodated Harry Holt without taking all the risk factors into consideration.[101]

The most notorious incident, known not just among social workers but also to the public, was the case of Edith Ott, a Roseburg housewife who was charged with the second-degree murder of her adopted Korean daughter. According to the indictment, the daughter, Wendy Kay Ott, age twenty-two months, died on June 14, 1957, less than a year after she was brought to the United States through HAP on October 9, 1956. The indictment charged Ott with "killing Wendy Kay Ott by striking her on the head."[102] The Otts had three other adopted children, all brought to America by Holt. District Attorney Avery Thompson filed a petition requesting that the children be removed from the couple due to "neglect" and "barbarous treatment."[103] Judge Woodrich stated, however, that he found the children "happy, unafraid and lonesome for their parents" in the foster home where they were waiting to hear the court's decision.[104]

Harry and Bertha Holt passionately defended Edith Ott. Harry Holt, in a letter to the *Oregonian*, stated that the Ott incident was only a means used by the state agency to "get at him."[105] He proclaimed that taking away the remaining children was an "unjust and malicious attack."[106] He explained that Wendy Kay Ott was a "very fragile little girl" who had almost died three times while she was under Holt's care. He wrote that social workers had "always bitterly opposed our work with the Korean orphans," and he predicted that they would attack them at the first opportunity. He closed the letter by stating that the Otts were good Christians who had opened their "hearts and home to two little Korean-American orphan children at considerable sacrifice and expense to themselves."[107]

Bertha Holt, in her statement at a meeting at Mocks Crest Evangelical United Brethren Church, stated that the welfare workers were "angry because they want[ed] jurisdiction" over the adoptions. She referred to the murder charge as "the devil at work" trying to discourage a "wonderful Christian family."[108] She concluded by affirming that what they were doing was "the Lord's work," and nothing could stop them from fulfilling their calling. District Attorney Thompson, after hearing these comments, stated that he was amazed at the Holts' statements "in view of the fact that he doesn't know what is going on down here."[109] The murder charge was eventually dismissed at trial for lack of evidence. In the trial, Bertha Holt testified for Ott.[110] In his newsletters, Harry Holt appealed to his readers to help him continue the proxy adoption process. He proudly stated that proxy adoption saved legal costs for the adoptive parents and was more efficient than other methods. The only precaution Holt required was that the parents make sure there was not even the slightest doubt in their heart about the decision to adopt. He urged his readers to write letters to their congressmen asking them to 1) quickly pass the bill to increase the orphan quota and 2) continue to allow adoption by proxy.

As should be evident by now, Harry Holt's adoption method was based largely on emotions rather than on scrupulous investigation or rationality. Even in his newsletters, he encouraged his readers to explain to congressmen how badly they wanted a child and how impossible it was to get one in America without proxy adoption. He predicted that if Congress received a flood of letters, it would eventually "do something about it."[111] He wrote that welfare groups were building up strong opposition to him because "social workers have no authority over and do not get any income from children adopted by proxy."[112] He wrote plainly that if the social workers' plan to influence Congress succeeded, his readers would not get children. Reminding them once again that their work was the Lord's doing, he urged them to write letters "today, and make it strong."[113] Harry Holt's method of invoking faith rather than going through proper regulation procedures presumed that raising children in America was better than raising them in Korea, even if that meant separating the child from their home country.

His zealous approach was a continuation of evangelicals' bold optimism concerning world evangelization. Not unlike the previous generation's watchword "the evangelization of the world in this generation," Holt envisioned the evangelization of Asian children under his watch. His spiritual elitism and American exceptionalism were evident in his writings; he saw himself as a bold, heroic solider fighting for God's kingdom by bringing helpless Asian children to the promised land of America. South Korea was often portrayed as uncivilized, backward, and unchristian, in sharp contrast with affluent, civilized, Christian America.

The sense of urgency found in his language was not merely a demonstration of his impatience. Rather, the imminent *parousia* (second coming of Christ) excited missionary fervor because it was a visible goal to be accomplished. Many evangelicals embraced a premillennial theology and believed that the second coming could be hastened through the completion of world evangelism. Holt's adoption ministry, for him, was eschatological in nature—by adopting and evangelizing Asian children who otherwise would not have learned about the gospel, he believed he was bringing *parousia* one step closer. This Anglo-Saxon eschatological triumphalism produced an evangelical social commitment, resulting in the mass adoption of Asian children among evangelicals.

Harry Holt apparently truly believed that good intentions justified the bypassing of all welfare regulations. Many social workers, however, voiced concerns that good intentions alone were not sufficient in dealing with such an important matter as a child's life. They criticized the one-sided picture of the Holt Adoption Program that was painted in the media. They claimed that these positive portrayals did not give the "opportunity [to] learn of the 'diseased Korean babies' or abused and neglected children."[114] Lawrence E. Laybourne, *Time* magazine's director of corporate affairs, became aware of this problem and endeavored to bring a corrective to the overly positive depiction of Harry Holt. He wrote that while he did not doubt Holt's good intentions, the amount of favorable publicity hid a growing number of unfortunate results of Holt's method.[115] Laybourne wrote a letter to his associates urging that

Time-Life research staff conduct an official investigation and "dig a little deeper into Mr. Holt's activities" for future articles on the subject.[116]

Adoption and Christian Mission

The interaction between the Holts (Harry Holt in particular) and the social workers clearly demonstrated the Holts' religiously driven motivation. In *Seed from the East*, Harry and Bertha Holt stated multiple times that what they were doing was "the Lord's undertaking."[117] The book was filled with prayers. Bertha, watching the giant tripod and the flood of cameras and sound machines that surrounded their home, prayed that they would "not [. . .] become so interested in the miracle" but remember "the One who had made it possible."[118] Their ministry centered on firm Christian dogma was at the heart of their conflict with the social workers because the Holts perceived any resistance to their methodology as opposition from the Devil. In her thoroughly hagiographic account, Bertha equated Harry Holt with Moses fighting against Pharaoh, who represented the social workers.[119]

The Holts' focus on adoption as part of their larger vision of Christian mission was apparent in their parenting method. The Holts made sure their children—both biological and adopted—were raised under Christian teachings and a Christian worldview. Every day, they gathered to pray together. Harry would say "*Kito*" (*Pray* in Korean), and the children would promptly fold their hands and bow their heads. When Harry read the Bible to them, they sat quietly around him and listened. As a family, they sang hymns, formed a choral group, and repeated Psalm 23 every day in their living room. When someone asked how they raised their children, Bertha proudly said that they taught by the Bible, "the best book on child training."[120]

Because Harry and Bertha Holt's definition of Christian mission was relatively narrow and fundamentalist, fighting racism was not their priority. Instead, discussion of race was a natural byproduct of their adoption of children of mixed-race or Asian heritage. While their main goal was evangelizing the children, they spread anti-racist rhetoric and an anti-racist worldview within the American evangelical and fundamentalist cultures. Through the family-centered rhetoric of *Seed from the*

East, Bertha Holt demonstrated that Christianity and racism were mutually exclusive.

Bertha's view of race issues closely resembled the ideology of "colorblindness" that became salient in the 1950s and 1960s in the context of the civil rights movement and global anti-racist internationalism. The term, in opposition to color consciousness, expressed the ideal of a nonracial society in which color of the skin was of no consequence for individuals or for governmental policy. Proponents of colorblindness emphasized what human beings had in common rather than directly challenging racial hierarchies.[121] Bertha, for example, stressed the commonality of all children—they were "bundles of extremely lovable humanity."[122] She further wrote that while the children's "features were a little different," they were the same as her biological children in their innocence, curiosity, and malleability. Just like Wanda and Molly (her biological daughters), she wrote, "they responded to love just like all other children."[123] Bertha Holt emphasized that all children desired and responded to love, and they were equally created in the image of God. In line with the Holts' religious approach, she approached race issues from a religious point of view. Criticizing the "heartless" social workers who enforced the racial matching system, she commented that no trained social worker could make a perfect match, and it was only God who could make the perfect match from "heart to heart."[124] In all this rhetoric, she avoiding engaging directly with racial injustice or racial hierarchies, perhaps for fear of being painted as a liberal activist.

The colorblind approach to racism, as recent literature points out, is problematic in several ways. Willful blindness to race has often been criticized as an attempt to paper over existing inequalities and systemic racial hierarchies. As it will become evident in subsequent chapters, even in adoption practices, there was a clear racial hierarchy—white adoptive parents preferred Asians to half-black children. Neglecting racial differences can lead to "colorblind racism," wherein race-neutral elements legitimize preexisting racial inequalities. Colorblindness has often led whites to claim they are beyond race even as they fail to address the enduring presence and significance of racial inequalities.[125]

Moreover, by focusing on commonalities and ignoring racial differences, Bertha Holt and Christian news outlets reinforced the idea that Asian children's ethnic identities and places of origin were inconsequential and effaceable. For example, in describing the Holts' activities, World Vision's newsletter proudly stated that the "fortunate" Korean children would soon "forget their life in Korea" and would have only "memories of kind parents whose hearts were big enough to take them in."[126] "Plenty of warm food and clothing and lots of good milk to drink" would apparently help the children leave their lives in Korea behind and live comfortably with their newfound Caucasian families.[127] Many Asian and half-Asian adult adoptees who were adopted into white homes during this time have reported that they struggled with their ethnic identity because they grew up as "honorary whites," and they felt that they needed to assimilate rather than celebrate their ethnicity.[128]

The most significant contribution of Harry and Bertha Holt's transnational adoption efforts was their reconstruction of evangelicals' perception of race and family. Evangelical missionaries such as Pierce, Swanson, and the Holts contributed to Christian foreign mission by making it feasible for evangelicals to engage in social issues and to modestly change their attitudes about racial issues. The evangelical missionaries did not engage in radical anti-racist activism; instead, in their family-centered rhetoric, they advocated a colorblind approach to race. While the Holts did not draw a direct connection between the transnational adoption movement and the civil rights movement, the Christian ethos—the belief in the human dignity of all people—was present in both movements. Considering the fact that race issues rarely received any attention at all from conservative Christians of this era, the missionaries' contribution was more significant at the time than it may appear now.

Granted, not all evangelicals who were exposed to the Holts' activities "saw the light." The Holts occasionally received violent letters accusing them of "bringing oriental blood into the United States" and "importing slave labor to work on our farm."[129] And although the overwhelming majority of their letters were filled with encouragement and prayers, it should be noted once again that the adoptive parents' zeal was at times misguided or tinged with paternalism. One woman wrote, "Send me an ugly baby, or a retarded one that nobody wants. I'll transform that little life with love and tender care."[130] While her good intentions are evident, her statement betrays her subconscious bias against the racial other and the disabled. Her will to "transform" the child also revealed her sense of American exceptionalism.

The inception of the transnational adoption movement from East Asia, in short, was spearheaded by the "heroic Holt family." The Holts had an unwavering religious conviction, which helped them stay focused and determined despite a flood of criticism. Their commitment was also met with a timely response from Korea—the government urgently wanted to remove Korea's mixed-race children, who represented national shame. The Holts held a distinctively conservative theology that fostered an evangelical social commitment. Even as this theology provoked myriad conflicts with social workers of the time, their faith-centered rhetoric and their presentation of themselves as a heroic family were extraordinarily effective in spreading their message to a conservative Christian audience. Next, we will turn to the activities of Pearl Buck, a liberal Christian who went beyond evangelical circles to popularize transnational adoption across America.

3

Mother of Transracial Adoption

In 1949, Pearl Sydenstricker Buck founded Welcome House, the first transracial and transnational adoption agency in the United States, marking the beginning of the transnational adoption of mixed-race "Amerasian" children (a term she coined).[1] She defied the conventional matching system and invented "special needs adoption." While it is difficult to reconcile her Christian upbringing with her overt dislike for traditional missionaries, Buck's Christian worldview was a crucial catalyst in her promotion of special needs adoption, as she was profoundly affected by the surge of Protestant liberalism, the emerging ecumenical Christianity, and Christian Internationalism from the 1920s to the 1960s. Her firm belief in racial equality and global friendship—values that characterized the ecumenical movement—prompted her to advance transracial and transnational adoption. She thereby invalidated the long-established social norm of "matching" adoption.

Buck and other Protestant thinkers such as William Hocking and John Mott defended racial minorities and the principle of human equality at a time when the situation of minority groups was precarious both in the U.S. and abroad. These ecumenical, internationalist Christians used anti-racist, anti-imperialist rhetoric that was distinct from liberal internationalism. They emphasized global friendship and human equality, unlike the liberal internationalism of the time, which focused on international law and institutions. Christian internationalism connected the local with the global, emphasizing a global community in which both diversity (locality) and unity (universality) were celebrated. Through transnational adoption, Buck sought to spread her holistic and oppositional focus on racism and her systematic and penetrating disgust with American imperialism. Her Christian values were closely in sync with the ecumenical mission thought that flourished from the 1920s to the 1960s.[2]

This chapter underscores Buck's identity as a humanitarian who distinguished herself from secular child welfare workers by basing her missiology (theological practice) and philosophy of adoption on Christian values. Contrary to the prevailing understanding that a secular, liberal ideology drove Buck's humanitarian advocacy, I argue that her belief in human equality was fundamentally rooted in her Christian values. This outlook led her to actively fight racism in America and to advocate the adoption of mixed-race Asian children and children with disabilities. Although her writings were permeated with Christian language and ethics, they appealed to the general public. Unlike the evangelical agencies, which catered to a conservative Christian audience, Pearl Buck normalized the notion of transracial adoption across America through her potent prose.

Following a brief biographical sketch of Pearl Buck, I examine her work in the context of the growth of Protestant liberalism. This perspective accentuates her role as the pioneer of the transracial and transnational adoption of Amerasian children. Later in the chapter, I will show how her ideology was congruent with the prevalent ecumenical theology of her time, refuting the currently dominant view that locates her approach to race and family in Cold War liberalism during the rise of postwar American global hegemony by situating her within a Christian framework.

To be sure, geopolitical factors cannot be entirely divorced from Buck's agenda. Buck often described war-torn Asian countries as perilous environments where communism could flourish, thereby creating a link between adoption as a private humanitarian effort and adoption as a public, political endeavor to eradicate communism and achieve democracy. From this perspective, the humanitarian act of helping children was a profoundly political act during the Cold War.[3] However, this perspective also tends to view transnational adoption as an opportunity to secure American global hegemony by creating an image of America as a benevolent savior. Buck's goal, however, was anything but American global hegemony. In fact, her vision for global friendship and anti-racism stemmed from her lifelong philosophy that all human beings were equally created in the divine likeness.

Pearl Sydenstricker Buck

Biography

Pearl Sydenstricker Buck was born on June 26, 1892, in Hillsboro, West Virginia. Since 1880, her parents had been Southern Presbyterian missionaries in Hangzhou, China. Buck was born during her parents' sabbatical after Buck's older siblings had died of a tropical disease. At five months old, Buck was separated from her country of birth and culture when the Sydenstrickers moved back to the Chinese village of Chinkiang.[4] During her childhood, she was homeschooled by her mother Caroline Sydenstricker in the morning, while a Chinese teacher tutored Buck during the afternoon. Buck became fluent in Chinese and English and accepted the Chinese culture as her own. She lived in close intimacy with the Chinese, since her parents preferred not to live in the missionary compound. This direct exposure to Chinese people taught her to treasure the indigenous culture and its moral values.[5] The deep bonds she developed with the Chinese became a crucial impetus for her later development of a mission theory based on global friendship.

Her father, Absalom Sydenstricker, was an itinerant evangelist who spent months at a time away from home, bringing the gospel message to the countryside. Driven by his rigid and conservative religious conviction, he unyieldingly preached Christian doctrine. To his dying day, he despised the "social gospel" movement that burgeoned during the second half of the nineteenth century.[6] He was indifferent and even antagonistic to Buck's scholarly aptitude, and his contempt for women shaped Buck's childhood and adolescence.[7] Absalom's missiology and stance on gender were close to the fundamentalist stances, and they doubtless contributed to Buck's deep-seated disgust at rigid Christian doctrines and her eventual departure from the Presbyterian mission board.

When the Boxer Rebellion broke out in 1900, Buck and her family evacuated to Shanghai, where she attended boarding school until 1909. She moved back to the United States the following year to study philosophy at Randolph-Macon Woman's College in Lynchburg, Virginia. Buck showed exceptional intellectual promise and found comfort in an environment where women's intellectual capacities were encouraged and appreciated. She applied to the Foreign Mission Board of the Presbyterian Church for a teaching position in the missionary school at Chinkiang and returned to China in 1914.[8] A few years later, Buck married a Presbyterian missionary who specialized in agricultural practices, John Lossing Buck. She gave birth in 1920 to Carol, who was mentally disabled. Carol's life and struggle influenced Buck's worldview and faith tremendously and became a major impetus for her later humanitarian work.[9]

John and Pearl Buck both enrolled in master's programs at Cornell, and Pearl Buck began her career as a writer while pursuing an M.A. in English.[10] The couple had temperamental differences and struggled to maintain their marriage. They divorced in 1935, and shortly afterward Buck married Richard Walsh, her publishing agent. She was a prolific writer and received the Pulitzer Prize in 1932 for her acclaimed book *The Good Earth*, a reflection of a lifetime spent among the Chinese peasants.[11] She was awarded the Nobel Prize in Literature in 1938. Even after suffering from the terror of the Nanking Massacre and the Communist Revolution, she remembered China fondly.

In her later life, Buck was an active humanitarian who supported women's rights, educated the American public on racism, and advocated for transnational and transracial adoption. In 1941 she founded the East and West Association to foster cross-cultural understanding and racial harmony. She also became an adoptive mother of six mixed-race children and in 1949 founded Welcome House. Since 1949, Welcome House has placed five thousand children in adoptive homes. Buck wrote prolifically on the issues of adoption, children with disabilities, racism, and overcoming cultural barriers.[12] In 1964 she established the Pearl S. Buck Foundation to help Amerasian children in poverty, and she donated Green Hills Farm, her personal estate in Bucks County, Pennsylvania, to be its headquarters.[13] On March 6, 1973, Pearl S. Buck died of lung cancer in Danby, Vermont. She is buried on the grounds of Green Hill Farm.[14]

Pearl Buck's Religious Context

Pearl Buck's public ministry and humanitarian work began in the context of the rise of Protestant liberalism in the 1930s. In the two decades following World War I, mission work was subjected to extreme scrutiny throughout the world. The Western countries, once an emblem of sacredness and justice, were destroying one another in bloody warfare. Their Christian morality came into question, and confidence in

Christendom abated. Isolationism and a quest for normalcy replaced idealism. Darwinian thought and modernism permeated American society and seeped into some parts of the church.[15] Emerging liberalism challenged the previously widespread confidence in Christendom. Voices advocating social change over evangelism abounded. It was during this period that the controversial volume *Re-thinking Missions: A Laymen's Inquiry after One Hundred Years* was published. This book was the fruit of two years of research by several major denominations, with William E. Hocking—a liberal Congregationalist and a Harvard professor—as the project's overseer. In the theological section of the report, Hocking sought to rectify the imperialistic methodology and attitude often held by missionaries by advocating more collaboration with other religious systems. He argued that the uniqueness of Christianity was found not in particular doctrines, but through its presentation of truths also available in other religious traditions.[16]

This Christian self-criticism was met with fierce opposition, and many denominations that had initially endorsed the project refused to acknowledge its validity. The report was far from what the denominations had expected to see, and only two of the seven sponsoring denominations approved it.[17] Even amid the changing religious climate, radical voices like Hocking's were an unwelcome blow to the sacred font of American imperialism.[18] The Presbyterian Board of Foreign Missions soon issued a statement criticizing Hocking's report and affirming the evangelistic basis of the missionary enterprise.[19] In contrast, Pearl Buck fully endorsed the text, even to the extent of calling it "the only book I have ever read that seems literally true in its every observation and right in its every conclusion."[20]

In January 1933, soon after her exuberant praise of the report in the *Christian Century*, she published an article titled "Is There a Case for Foreign Missions?" in *Harper's Magazine* in which she denounced the doctrine of original sin and the divinity of Jesus.[21] The two articles were fiercely attacked by the Westminster Seminary professor J. Gresham Machen, who had become despondent about what he considered the unorthodox theology of certain Presbyterian missionaries. He wrote a pamphlet, *Modernism and the Board of Foreign Missions of the Presbyterian Church in the U.S.A.*, that sharply appealed to the board to purify itself of all modernists in the field.[22]

His reaction was part of his prolonged feud with Robert E. Speer, the secretary of the Presbyterian Board of Foreign Missions from 1891 to 1937. Arguing that the board was unworthy of conservative support, Machen characterized the leadership of the Board of Foreign Missions as vague and theologically "indifferentist."[23] Furthermore, Machen demanded that Buck be removed as a missionary, claiming that she "did not consider a belief in the deity of Christ essential, that she did not believe in the miracles described in the New Testament, and she did not believe in original sin."[24]

In May 1933, Buck resigned from the Presbyterian Board of Foreign Missions, stating that she wanted to save the board from further embarrassment caused by differences of opinion between her and the board concerning the orthodoxy of her theological stance.[25] The board accepted the resignation "with deep regret" and expressed its "sincere appreciation" for her years of ministry in China.[26] Machen, who had hoped for a complete repudiation of Buck, was disgruntled by the board's polite words. To express their dissatisfaction, Machen and fourteen other elders founded the Independent Board in 1934 as an alternative to the Board of Foreign Missions.[27]

During an interview with the *Milwaukee Journal* on May 3, 1933, Pearl Buck said she was still a Christian, and her faith still motivated her to do good works. In place of evangelism, she emphasized social work, thereby situating herself neatly within the emerging ecumenical Christianity. While Buck no longer held the formal title of missionary, her years of mission work and her identity as a missionary played a pivotal role in urging her to what she saw as Christian social responsibility. She stated during the same interview, "I expect to go back to China, and to continue my life just where I left off, only without the formal title of missionary . . . I'm a Christian by conviction and shall continue being one."[28] She was not driven merely by secularism and liberal ideologies— her words reveal that religious conviction and her humanitarian efforts were not divorced from each other.[29]

Mother of Transracial Adoption

The History of Welcome House

The birth story of Welcome House shows Buck's personal connection to the adoption movement.[30] On an ordinary December day in 1948, she received an unexpected letter that changed her life. As she was sorting through piles of mail, she found a long white envelope from an adoption agency. The letter inquired, "Can you help us?" She described the experience as the receipt of a "sudden, unexpected, and unprecedented gift from heaven."[31] It was a Christmas card from an adoption agency about Robbie, a mixed-race fifteen-month-old who needed a home.[32] His mother was a young, white American missionary kid, and his father was an Indian man. The young woman's missionary parents forbade marriage. The young woman was brought to America in haste; the child was immediately given up for adoption.[33]

The agency wrote that they considered Robbie the finest child they had ever had in the agency, but he proved unadoptable because of his darker skin. It was also a social welfare policy at the time to place all children with matched parents—in this case, Indian American adoptive parents. Robbie had stayed in several foster homes and moved five times during his fifteen months. To find him a home, the agency inquired throughout the country and even in Hawaii, but no one wanted to adopt Robbie. Agency employees even reached out to the Indian embassy, only to receive the caustic reply that there were thousands of such children, and the embassy could not be responsible for them. The agency decided it could no longer keep the child—the only alternative place for him was an African American orphanage.[34]

Buck and her husband were infuriated at blatant injustice and took Robbie in themselves until they found a permanent home for him. Initially, it was indignation that moved her to get on the phone. However, as she held Robbie, who was anxiously sucking his thumb with his eyes "huge and tragic," she felt her anger replaced with intense love.[35] She lamented that she was too old to adopt Robbie since he needed younger parents to see him into manhood. However, she later acknowledged that had she been young enough to adopt him, the story of Welcome House would never have been written.[36]

Within a week after she met Robbie, Buck was given a newborn, only nine days old. His name was Peter, born to a Chinese father and a white American mother.[37] In the weeks that followed, Buck relentlessly approached adoption agencies to find homes for the babies. The attempt was fruitless. When she demanded what would become of the children, Buck received only a simple shrug or the explanation that agencies could not afford to accept unadoptable children.[38] The reality was clear: nobody wanted to adopt mixed-race children. Upon this premise, she proceeded toward the first stage of her organization.

Buck started to persuade friends and local people in her county to help her establish an adoption agency specializing in mixed-race children. She lived in a small, quiet community founded upon the precepts of the Quakers and Mennonites. The county council attentively listened as she poured her heart out, describing the appalling treatment of the mixed-race children. She then proposed founding an agency that would place special needs children in adoptive families, and specifically mixed-race children. Her worries that the community would not accept such a proposal was quenched when one of the members exclaimed, in his stout Pennsylvania-Dutch accent, "We not only want them, but we will be proud to have them."[39]

With the help of the community, Buck searched for families to adopt the two boys. The first family was a Pennsylvania-Dutch couple, a high school teacher and his wife. Other children began to come to her agency, and soon Buck had nine half-Asian children, varying in age from a few months old to fifteen years. As the multiracial family grew, Buck and some community volunteers formed a board of directors and made a formal application to the State of Pennsylvania to set up a private adoption agency. The cautious yet sympathetic officers had never heard of Amerasian children and decided to do an investigation to see if there was a real need for a special agency. The State Department of Welfare canvassed other states, and the answer was overwhelmingly in the affirmative. Many adoption agencies throughout the country replied that mixed-race children were the most significant problem faced by adoption agencies.

The State of Pennsylvania approved Welcome House, Inc., which became the first adoption agency to specialize in the adoption of mixed-race, especially mixed-Asian, children. Welcome House was permitted to receive and place for adoption children from any state in the Union, born in America but of Asian or part-Asian ancestry. Through a referral system, many agencies collaborated with Welcome House and referred mixed-race children to Buck.[40]

Letters sent from various adoption agencies and social workers to Welcome House proved the dire necessity of an agency specializing in interracial adoption. To illustrate just a few, Rochester Community Home for Girls, Inc. wrote: "We had contacted practically all the large child-care agencies on both the East and West Coasts and in Hawaii, and could obtain no solution to our particular problem. We are happy to know there is such a resource [Welcome House]."[41] Family and Child Services of Washington, D.C. was confident that its mixed-race children "would have remained in foster care for an indefinite time had it not been for the resource of Welcome House."[42] Hamilton County Welfare Department in Ohio wrote that the children adopted through Welcome House were making good adjustments in their newfound homes. They reported that at a meeting of the State Adoptive Service, Welcome House was discussed most favorably, and many adoption agencies were relieved that such an agency finally existed.

One incident Buck repeatedly shared in her articles and in her book *Children for Adoption* was the story of Lennie, a half-Japanese five-month-old. His mother, a young Japanese woman, died after giving birth to Lennie, and the heartbroken father placed his child for adoption because his family would not accept the child. It was Lennie who convinced Buck that mixed-race children could be adopted. In one of Buck's speaking engagements, she suddenly decided to appeal to the large crowd of well-dressed, intelligent people on behalf of Lennie. The next day, she received a letter from a young Presbyterian minister and his wife. Buck warned the minister that having a half-Japanese son could one day be a hazard to his career due to the narrow-mindedness of some Christians. The young couple did not care.

Buck ended the story by recounting that several years later, when the minister was applying for a church, he wrote a letter concerning his adopted son. The church replied: "We have reduced the applications to two, yours and another young man's. We see by your application, however, that you have adopted a little half-Japanese son. You are the man we want."[43] Buck remarked that while she was deeply disappointed in missionaries such as Robbie's biological grandparents, she still had hope in Christianity because Christians like Lennie's parents gave a glimpse of Christlike love in this world.

Welcome House expanded its program to include the adoption of other special needs children—not only mixed-race children, but also children with disabilities, older children, and African American children. Buck proudly wrote that not one child who had special needs was weak in mind or even in body, except for one child injured at birth. She worked with psychologists and held seminars to train prospective adoptive parents to ensure that the physical challenges were minor and prove that these challenges were unrelated to the mixed ethnicity of the children. Since its founding in 1949, with the stated purpose of "finding and placing in good adoptive homes mixed-race children and overcoming racial prejudice," Welcome House has placed five thousand children in adoptive homes.[44]

Pearl Buck's Christian Values

With Richard Walsh, Pearl Buck adopted five children from the United States and Europe in the 1920s and 1930s, a black German-American daughter in 1953, and a black Japanese-American daughter in 1958. As a leading opponent of racial and religious matching, she contended that religious and racial matching should not be a prerequisite for adoption.[45] *Matching*, a philosophy that governed adoption during most of the twentieth century, required adoptive parents to match the potential adoptees in terms of race, physical resemblance, religious background, and intellectual capacity. As a leader in transracial adoption, she advocated non-matching and special needs adoption.

While Pearl Buck's humanitarian work—particularly her founding of the transracial adoption movement—is widely known, few scholars connect her work with her Christian motivation and values. The prevalent view, as represented by Emily Cheng, attributes her anti-racist approach to Cold War liberalism and postwar internationalism. Cheng argues that Buck's fundamental belief in the individualism and universal equality of human beings reflected the core of U.S. Cold War imperial expansion.[46] According to this perspective, the charitable acts of humanitarianism were used to rehabilitate the image of imposing American imperialism, hence recasting Western powers as benevolent rescuers instead of colonizers.[47] This remaking of American imagery, according to historians such as David Foglesong and Emily Rosenberg, was part of the United States' drive "to remake the world in its own image."[48]

It is true that Buck's philosophy of transnational adoption was developed in the context of Cold War imperial expansion and the subsequent call for internationalism. Cold War politics and American culture were closely intertwined in the 1950s, as postwar reconstruction necessitated the rehabilitation of not only physical infrastructure but also cultural, emotional, and social infrastructure.[49] As the country's cultural groundwork was being re-laid, Cold War internationalism arose, emphasizing global peace, international cooperation, and international control of atomic science. This internationalism underscored the international responsibility of Americans as citizens of the "free world." President Truman exhorted Americans to develop the "human brotherhood that alone will enable us to achieve international cooperation and peaceful progress in the atomic age."[50] As a cosmopolitan and a forerunner of global friendship, Buck was keenly aware of the rhetoric of Cold War internationalism and affirmed the principles of world peace, international cooperation, and the flourishing of democracy. Furthermore, Buck's call for internationalism was interwoven with her anti-communist rhetoric—for example, she argued that adopting mixed-race children would prevent communism from overtaking Asia by forging a positive bridge between the West and the East. Moreover, she supported the United States' war efforts and worked to foster attitudes of unity with its allies.

Her philosophy, however, was deeper and broader than a mere secular internationalism based on Cold War imperialism. Her Christian worldview and philosophy of human solidarity had been established well before the emergence of Cold War internationalism. Buck's advocacy of special needs adoption stemmed from her lifetime opposition to discrimination and her personal philosophy of human solidarity.[51] Her ideology of human solidarity was cultivated during her childhood when she experienced alienation herself. As a missionary living in a foreign land, she was on a constant quest for human solidarity and a cosmopolitan outlook. Whenever she faced racism, she declared that such discrimination ought not to happen elsewhere in the world. Moreover, her anti-racist rhetoric strongly reflected the ecumenical movement of the 1920s and onward. Buck's language of global friendship was a reiteration of other missionaries' and mission organizations' ideology during the war relief time. Unlike most other internationalists, she was unafraid to critique her own American culture, policies, and people.[52]

Ultimately, Pearl Buck distinguished herself from secular child welfare workers by basing her missiology and philosophy of adoption on Christian values. One of her most prominent writings revealing her Christian underpinnings is her article "Is There a Case for Foreign Missions?," published in 1933. It is not a coincidence that her work bore a striking similarity to William E. Hocking's *Re-thinking Missions*. Buck and Hocking both held distinct mission theories that emerged during the rise of Protestant liberalism and the withering in many quarters of evangelical missionary work.[53] Hocking also made a notable contribution to the proceedings of the Jerusalem Conference of 1928, where the council produced a statement regarding racial relationships and the duty of Christians. The Council's statement, likewise, had numerous parallels with Buck's anti-racist rhetoric.[54]

To Buck, mission work meant demonstrating Christlike love rather than carrying out the traditional church-centered evangelism.[55] Lamenting that missionaries were apathetic to the highest good of their host nations due to their "narrow and superstitious religion," she contended that seeking the wholeness and betterment of the indigenous people should be the priority of foreign missions.[56] Her firm belief that the betterment of the people should be primary later fueled her child-centered approach to transnational adoption. She staunchly argued that adoption should not cater to adoptive parents or social workers. The sole purpose of transnational adoption, for her, was meeting the needs of the children.

Engaging in the adoption movement was Buck's direct response to her belief in divine love. She chastised the missionaries who drew a sharp distinction between body and soul: she argued that God did not distinguish between the two, and that social work itself, when done with Christlike love, was part of the Christian gospel. Buck's belief in human solidarity and spiritual collaboration with other religious traditions motivated her to pave the way for transracial adoption. She believed that when people of different religious faiths collaborated to help children, all of humanity could be united in one global community.[57] She particularly praised Asian cultures for taking care of their children: "In a peculiar, unprecedented, unparalleled way, the children of Asia are loved as ours are not."[58] She argued that Asians were able to see the divine likeness in the human being and that the individual's rights were, therefore, fully respected and honored.

Buck demonstrated an optimistic anthropological view and denied the doctrine of original sin. She believed that all human beings were equally created in the image of God and thus ultimately good, not evil. Furthermore, she held a high view of general revelation and believed that non-Christians could obtain a saving knowledge of Christ beyond the four walls of the church. Castigating closed-minded missionaries, she scoffed that she would rather kneel humbly before the shrine of Buddha than before the God of the missionary.[59]

However, she wrote, "Is There a Case for Foreign Missions?" precisely because she believed that the answer was *Yes*. Buck believed in Christ, and that was sufficient motivation for her Christian duties, including her adoption practice. While she respected and collaborated with all religious traditions, she saw something unique in Christ. Among people who had perceived Christ, however dimly, she found something she could find nowhere else.[60] She declared, "If I am not willing for Christ to die, what hypocrisy is mine if I will do nothing to keep him alive in the hearts and understandings of men, what selfishness if I keep him for myself alone, or for my race! I must be great enough to share Christ if I would keep Christ mine."[61] Pearl Buck's Christian values and anti-imperialist beliefs propelled her to develop a unique child welfare philosophy of special needs adoption.

Special Needs Adoption

Special needs adoption involved children who were hard to place due to their race, mixed heritage, physical disabilities, mental illness, or age. Systematic efforts to expand the bounds of adoption in the areas of ethnicity, religion, and physical and mental disability did not occur until after World War II. Even in 1948, the Child Welfare League of America, founded in 1921, reported that out of seventy-five American adoption agencies, half of them completely ruled out placing a child whose biological parent had a mental illness. Eighty percent of the agencies reported that they would place only the perfect child with perfectly matched adoptive parents.[62] It was not only African Americans and Native Americans who suffered discrimination; Asians were deemed unassimilable aliens and were subjected to the Asiatic Exclusion Act of 1924. Under the Exclusion Act, Asians experienced occupational discrimination, offensive racism in the media, and residential segregation.[63]

Amid such hostility and overt racism, many missionaries and Christian leaders voiced anti-racist rhetoric and promoted global friendship despite differences in race and ethnicity. The missionaries who regarded themselves as ambassadors of Christ and fought racism and injustice were those Buck was searching for in "Is There a Case for Missions?" Before the world wars, missionary conversations about world unity revolved around world evangelization, as evidenced by the Edinburgh 1910 watchword "the evangelization of the world in this generation."[64] This triumphalist language faltered, however, during World War I. On January 8, 1918, Woodrow Wilson gave the Fourteen Points speech on principles for world peace and internationalism. Internationalist language continued to gain ground in the 1920s when American Christian thinkers—including Pearl Buck, William Hocking, John R. Mott, and many others—began to use internationalist rhetoric that underlined world peace and world unity.

To meet the demands of the shifting religious climate, the International Missionary Council (IMC) emerged in 1921. IMC was an interdenominational association of Protestant churches founded with the aims of promoting ecumenical expression, facilitating significant missiological studies of the period, and engaging with issues from racism to religious freedom. Mott, the chairman of the IMC, declared, "Christian missions are indeed the great and the true internationalism. Our 29,000 missionaries are ambassadors, interpreters, and mediators in the most vital aspects of international and inter-racial relationships."[65] In 1928, just five years before the publication of Buck's article, the IMC held the Jerusalem Conference of 1928, where non-white churches were far better represented than at the Edinburgh 1910 meeting. Instead of a small group of minorities, more than 50 of the 231 participants were from Asia, Latin America, and Africa.[66] It was no coincidence that Hocking, who profoundly influenced Buck's missiology, made a notable contribution to the proceedings at the conference.

One of the key discussions was about the "Christian mission in light of race conflict." W. Wilson Cash, Secretary of the Church Missionary Society, who attended the meeting, recounted that his most ineffaceable memory of the council was the day they discussed the race problems occurring all over the world. The main speakers were an African American, a South African, an Indian, and a Filipino. Cash wrote that seeing men and women who had suffered from white domination talk passionately, yet without bitterness, challenged him immensely. The session ended, he wrote, with an impassioned speech from an Indian woman who cried out, "We must solve the problem in our own lives by a desire to know our neighbors!"[67]

It is true that Cash's emphasis on racial reconciliation rather than racial justice revealed a certain naïveté and idealism. The account reads as though he may have expected the racial minorities to do the work of forgiving and earning reconciliation. Nevertheless, the Council's Statement produced at the end of the meeting more fully addressed the issue of racism. The Statement reaffirmed that the absolute sacredness and inviolability of all humanity and the spiritual worth of every man and woman in his or her own right were the kernels of the Christian doctrine of man. The statement rightfully rebuked "any discrimination against human beings on the ground of race or color, any selfish exploitation, and any oppression."[68] Furthermore, the Statement warned that churches ought not to discriminate against immigrants on the grounds of color or race, particularly emphasizing a full and boundless welcome of refugees. The council reprimanded selfish, wealthy nations that tended to their own economic situations—it exhorted these nations to abandon the temptation of adopting such shortsighted measures and to think of the best interests of the world as a whole.

Another mainline missionary who represented the ecumenical mission principles of anti-racism and world friendship was Edmund Davidson Soper, of Garrett Seminary. Soper, in his book *Racism: A World Issue*, took a global approach to racism, and much like Pearl Buck, contended that all human beings were fundamentally the same.[69] Soper called the churches to repent of all forms of racism. He quoted from the Book of Revelation, where a great multitude of people from every nation, tribe, people, and language celebrated before the throne of God.[70] The ecumenical missionaries of the 1920s and onward believed that eliminating racism was the key to achieving peace and reconciliation among nations. Buck, Hocking, Mott, Soper, and countless mainline missionaries pleaded for world fellowship and cooperation with persons of color.[71]

This vision of anti-racism was conspicuous in Buck's advocacy of special needs adoption. Buck argued that adoption was appropriate and necessary for *any* child without family ties, regardless of age, race, and physical or mental capacity. Criticizing the matching system, Buck perceived that the "real barrier to the adoption of mixed-race children" was not that they were unwanted, but that the child welfare structure required that children and adoptive parents match.[72] Using her public platform as a writer, Buck sought to convince her readers to consider special needs adoption, children with disabilities, and the poor social conditions that failed to support single mothers.[73] In these articles and stories, Buck revealed an ideology of family formation that reflected her broader perspective on the world. She asserted that human beings had a common capability to love and to be loved: "Parenthood has nothing to do with color, race, or religion. It has to do with far deeper likeness of mind and heart and soul."[74]

Buck's goal was to eradicate the stigma of interracial adoption by breaking the conventional matching system. She appealed to Americans: "There is no escape for the colored child . . . I should like to see you take an active part in all groups of people who are working for the removal of race discrimination, because children cannot be saved from the evil effects of race discrimination."[75] Ironically, despite her campaign for the recognition of the equality of all human beings, she argued that mixed-race children were "superior children," better than either side of their ancestry.[76] She used the illustration of hybrid roses, corn, and fruit to demonstrate that the "hybrid" breeds superior beings.[77] The historian Kori Graves argues that Buck used this theory of hybrid superiority to encourage families—including black families—to adopt mixed-race children. To change people's opinions about mixed-race children, she constantly portrayed the children as more beautiful and intelligent than those of the so-called "pure" races.[78] By combining her argument about hybrid superiority with a plea for Christian social responsibility, she effectively communicated that the seemingly private act of adoption could lead to social change.

There were, however, several problems associated with her theory of hybrid superiority. One of the problems, as Graves mentions, was that her narrative solidified the model minority stereotype that started to emerge during World War II. White liberals, perceiving that domestic racism against Asians would damage America's ability to fight for democracy, began to recast Asian Americans as a law-abiding and courteous people that assimilated seamlessly into American society. The Chinese exclusion laws were finally repealed in 1943, and the myth of the "yellow peril" was replaced by the myth of Asians' collective success. The term "model minority" was officially coined by the sociologist William Petersen in his 1966 article "Success Story: Japanese American Style"; it denoted Asian Americans' purportedly strong work ethic and family values. A similar article depicting Chinese Americans as model immigrants was published the same year in *U.S. News and World Report*.[79] By portraying Asians as model minorities and contrasting them with "problem minorities," the media created a racial wedge and downplayed the deep-seated institutional racism endured by black Americans.

Buck's theory of hybrid superiority strengthened the model minority narrative by recasting Amerasian children as model adoptees and ideal immigrants who would assimilate perfectly into white homes. By doing so, she inadvertently treated the children's heritage as inconsequential, as many conservative Christians such as Robert Pierce or Harry Holt also tended to do. Furthermore, Asian American scholars rightly point out that the model minority myth obscures the differences between Asians and Asian Americans, thereby reproducing oppression.[80] Although Buck's theory of hybrid superiority had many problems, she did at least challenge the principle of eugenics, the pseudoscience that promoted the cultivation of a superior human population through controlled breeding. Indeed, Buck strongly and explicitly repudiated the idea that only Caucasian children free from disability were qualified for adoption.[81]

Buck also fought against religious matching, stating that religion was the strongest force in keeping children orphaned. During her time, many states demanded that children be placed for adoption with families of the same religion as their birth parents. She wrote, "It is reprehensible that adoption agencies that were supposed to consider above all the welfare of the child, have such religious limitations upon adoption instead of joining together to educate the public with a view to changing such prejudices."[82] She argued that children are born without consciousness of their religious background. Because often the religion of the birth parents differed from that of the waiting would-be parents, many children remained in institutions for a long time, unable to be adopted.

Her greatest grievance was against social workers and lawmakers. Resenting what she saw as their treatment of children like property, she remarked that there was "no magic in blood relationship," yet under the law, blood still took precedence over the reality of love. She wrote that the "human qualities of love, understanding, and acceptance alone" should dictate the destiny of a child, not race or religion.[83] Although a child is born without consciousness of race or religion, she argued, he is conscious of the need for unconditional love. She particularly criticized the Southern states, which strictly prohibited transracial adoption.

The two racial groups Buck defended the most fiercely were mixed-race Amerasian children and children of African American descent. As discussed in Chapter 2, the condition of the mixed-race G.I. babies, or Occupation babies, was precarious in Asia, due to the systemic problems of poverty, political instability, and social prejudice. Buck wrote extensively about the predicament of the Amerasian babies, often describing how her encounters with Korean mixed-race orphans and beggars had led her to believe that Koreans were genuinely puzzled about what to do with an entirely "new type of child."[84] Due to the endeavors of people like Buck, the American media started to describe the plight of these children as well. They depicted the fate of the children as appalling and bleak, warning that these children were destined for a life of degradation and misery if they remained in Asia.[85]

Koreans and American missionaries alike advocated the removal of mixed-race children from Korea, albeit with different motivations. Koreans argued for the removal of mixed-race babies to maintain a racially homogeneous society. Korean ethnic nationalism based on a belief in a commonly shared prehistoric origin and bloodline that existed before the Korean War, and this understanding was reflected in President Syngman Rhee's campaign for *ilmin juui* (the one, united people ideology). Rhee wanted to send G.I. babies abroad and expressed at a Cabinet Meeting that "he did not care what happened so long as the children were out of the country—and quickly." Buck even quoted Rhee as saying that he wanted them removed even if that meant dropping them in the Pacific Ocean.[86]

Buck's belief in human solidarity and the transcendent character of love was hopeful, but not naïve. She admitted that while love was color-blind, people were not. She acknowledged that it was more difficult to break the racial barriers facing African American children than those facing other mixed-race children. Caucasian adoptive parents preferred Asian or Native American children, and the recalcitrant racial hierarchy of the time branded blackness as "unassimilable."[87] In many states, crossing the black-white color line in adoption was illegal. To cite just two examples, in South Carolina, parents of color could not get custody of white children. In Amityville, New York, a white couple could not adopt a black child despite their uncommon desire to raise a black-white family.[88]

Several scholars, such as Susie Woo, have assessed the racial hierarchy that existed within transracial adoption practices. Woo concludes that half-black children were "socially, legally, and culturally" categorized as black, since in the eyes of most white Americans of the time, "Negro-Korean" children could not be redeemed by white blood. The "model" Korean half was not enough to counter deep-rooted racial prejudices.[89] This finding is particularly disturbing considering the fact that Harry Holt, like many other conservative Christians, held this view despite his efforts at placing mixed-race Asian children. There was a clear hierarchy of half-white, full Asian, and half-black children, in that order. Because Buck stressed Asian children's assimilability, they were welcomed into white homes, although less readily than half-white Amerasian children were.

Buck used her public platform to advertise and promote transracial adoption in both white and black homes. Writing for a largely black audience in *Ebony* magazine, Buck attempted to persuade her readers that they could help alleviate racism by adopting mixed-race children. Despite such efforts, there were simply not enough African American families interested in adoption.[90] Lamentably, Welcome House started to use a signpost that read that they had no "Negro homes" in 1956. The first successful placement of a child with African American parents did not occur until December 1958.[91] To further complicate the issue, several African American social workers opposed the placement of black children with white parents because transnational and transracial adoptions posed "a growing threat to the preservation of the black family."[92] Cenie J. Williams, Jr., president of the National Association of Black Social Workers, insisted that even if institutionalization were the only alternative, black children must not be placed in white homes.

In one of her last articles, "I Am the Better Woman for Having My Two Black Children," Buck addressed this very issue. Depicting the lives of her adopted daughters Henriette and Cheiko, both half-African, she affirmed that their chances were better with love than without and that she considered them her treasures. Referring to each of them, she wrote, "To all criticism I have but one reply. She is happy with us and we are happy with her. That is all that is required to make a good family."[93] In this article, Buck failed to provide a real answer to the troubling systematic racial hierarchy that persisted in transracial adoption. Her answer that a white mother could conquer racial prejudice is at worst imperialistic and at best idealistic. Although she rightly pointed out that any difficulty associated with adopting transracially was a result of social stigma and suspicion, not biology, she did not discuss how the social stigma surrounding black or half-black babies might be broken. However, by providing her own experience and expressing her personal commitment to half-black children, she demonstrated that on a personal level, it is possible to overcome racial prejudice. To her, the adoption of her black German daughter represented not only her personal commitment but also a public statement against racial injustice. Her hope of expanding her personal experience to address more systematic, institutional racism was in sync with her rhetoric of motherhood, which will be examined later.

Despite her shortcomings, Pearl Buck—a "multiculturalist" before the phrase was popularized—paved the way for special needs adoption. Through countless anecdotes and case studies, she proved that older children, children with mixed racial backgrounds, and children with deafness, heart conditions, palsy, or limited sight could become part of happy, loving families. Buck's writings and speeches steadily changed the public's perception of special needs adoption by providing continuous evidence that such children were adoptable.

Three primary motivations behind her campaign for special needs adoption emerge from Buck's writings: American political and moral responsibility, personal connection and motherhood, and her mission of global friendship and unity.

American Responsibility

Pearl Buck considered that orphaned children in Asia should be adopted by Americans for two reasons: political duty and moral responsibility. First, the United States was politically committed to anti-communism and world peace; thus, the national government was responsible as the leader of the free world to rescue these poverty-stricken children. Buck contended that from a political as well as a humanitarian viewpoint, Americans needed to be involved in the future of the mixed-race children who would otherwise become victims of the worst communist propaganda.[94] Moreover, Buck argued that American policy had failed in China because there were too few Americans who could mediate between China and the U.S. She proposed transnational adoption as part of a solution to foreign policy issues because mixed-race children could promote amicable relations between the U.S. and Asia, preventing further losses of Asian countries to communism. Pearl Buck envisioned forming a new category of citizens composed of Asian and mixed-race children to alleviate the tensions that had built up around Cold War politics. These new citizens, according to Buck, would create a sense of international kinship and friendship that would respond to the needs of postwar restoration.[95]

Political reasons, however, were only a small part of her argument. More importantly, Americans had a moral obligation to Amerasian children because many of them had been left fatherless as a result of fleeting love affairs between American soldiers and local women.[96] Buck pointed out that few American men, though they were morally responsible for their mixed-race children, stood by the Asian women whom they impregnated. She asked:

> How is it that these fathers will not be found? Do they never remember their children? In the night, when they sleep with their pretty American wives, do they never remember other nights, when Asia lay in their arms? Do they wonder where their Asian children are and how their Asian children look? Are they willing to let them wander the dusty Asian streets,

vagabonds without home and country? Is this not to destroy that which they have reproduced of themselves?[97]

Buck described herself as a hunter looking for the fathers of the mixed-race children left behind in Asia. She wrote that as long as these fathers cared for the children and helped alleviate the situation, the men could remain anonymous. Ironically, women responded to her writings more than men did. Buck received 151 letters, and only one was from a male. The rest were written by wives and mothers, some with small contributions for children for whom they felt responsible. The single letter written by a young man had five dollars enclosed, with the witty remark: "I have never been to Asia, but I expect to go next year and I would like to make a deposit."[98] Buck complained that no men were stepping up to take charge of the situation.

Buck was unafraid to criticize U.S. servicemen, who were generally treated by the media as American heroes and emblems of patriotism. This was a bold move, especially for a female writer of her time. Her literary reputation was often damaged by sexist prejudice, and a few critics dismissed her novels as saccharine and excessively feminine.[99] In the face of criticism and resistance, Buck endeavored to divulge U.S. servicemen's hypocrisy and sexual immorality. Such efforts were closely related to her feminist activism, including her campaign for birth control, sex education, and gender equality in the workplace. As an "evangelist for equality," Buck endorsed the Equal Rights Amendment as a feminist priority and spoke passionately to other women regarding gender equality.[100]

Refuting the notion that women belonged in the home, for instance, Buck castigated women whom she saw as reducing themselves to "social idiots," unaware of their intellectual and social potential. In her book *Of Men and Women*, she exhorted women to discard the "privilege" of remaining in ignorance and mental laziness, spending lavishly on self-adornment and amusement. She chastised women who sought to escape life's problems by retreating into the home.[101] In an interview with the television journalist Mike Wallace in 1958, she declared that some women were "making their homes their graves," burying themselves in ignorant bliss and refusing to assume their social duties as citizens of their nations and of the world. She also argued for the importance of equal education and wages.[102] Her view of women's rights was radical at the time, although she did not identify as a feminist.

In spite of Buck's pungent criticism of American servicemen, she was also one of the few public figures who wrote compassionately about the struggles of American soldiers in Asia. In her article "Children, American-Asian," she introduced an American soldier who had written a letter to Buck asking about what he should do regarding the Korean family he had left behind. He had been sent to Korea as a private in the American army when he was only nineteen—he had never been away from home before, and he found himself lonely and depressed. The only company he had was a Korean girl he met at a nightclub. She was a hostess there, and she spoke English well, unlike other girls. With reluctant permission from the girl's mother, they had a marriage ceremony performed by a Buddhist priest. They had two children, first a boy, then a girl. When his term of service was over, he applied for an extension but was refused—he was forced to leave his Korean family.[103]

The young soldier wrote about the devastating conditions the wife faced. Buck knew about it all too well—she knew that the mixed-race children could not go to school because of the persecution and ostracism they would encounter. She predicted that the mother would be compelled to find another American who would support her temporarily, and repeat the process. The fate of the children would be no better—in Korean culture, fatherless mixed-race children were treated as illegitimate, denied the chance for education or jobs. Buck wrote bitterly that a woman who had a child out of wedlock had no recourse but to become a prostitute after the departure of her American lover. Without a father, the Amerasian children were isolated and lost, because it was the child's father who had to register the children's births and take care of them. Amerasian children, then, were doomed to share the deplorable fate of their mothers.[104]

Buck asserted that the mixed-race children were not just the responsibility of the American servicemen but also a corporate responsibility. She was particularly frustrated with the military and legal systems that failed to address this issue. Military officials refused to recognize the existence of children fathered by Americans. When Buck brought the subject to the attention of a general, his reply was, "Our men are much too busy for this sort of thing to happen."[105] She also criticized immigration regulations that were hostile to interracial couples. Until the early 1950s,

Asian nationals were excluded from immigration and naturalization based on race. The McCarran Walter Immigration and Nationality Act of 1952 encompassed several reforms that allowed Asians to be eligible for naturalization. However, because only a hundred quota slots were granted annually, family reunions of interracial couples were extremely selective and difficult to obtain.[106]

Buck ultimately appealed to the public by contending that all of American society was responsible for the mixed-race children because the fathers were the "husbands and sons" of Americans and the "products of our schools, churches, and communities."[107] As a proud American, she feared that the legacy of the American remnant in Korea would be "a child in rags and filth" with blue American eyes and lice-ridden blond hair. Buck exclaimed dramatically that the people of Asia were crying out, "Look what the Americans left us!"[108] She asserted that "as the children's father's people," Americans owed the children everything. Denouncing racism, she declared that the true American believed in human equality regardless of class, creed, race, or sex.[109] Buck knew very well that one person could not undertake the enormous task of saving the children. She pleaded with Americans to take on this stupendous task because she had confidence in her people.

Personal Experience and Motherhood

Another impetus that led Buck to pioneer the transnational adoption movement came from the deeply personal experience of encountering Amerasian children. Her childhood experience of feeling that she was the "wrong color" was also part of the reason for her fight against racism and campaign for cross-cultural understanding. Despite her close integration into Chinese life, she always felt like a minority, which led her to ask, "What would I do if I belonged to a group in my own country against which race prejudice worked?"[110] Buck's initial reaction when she encountered mixed-race children was to avoid them. She repeatedly, yet unsuccessfully, attempted to convince herself that the children did not exist:

> The children do not exist, I told myself firmly as I stared into faces that were certainly not Asian. Beggar children pursued me on Asian streets and I gazed into dirty beautiful little faces, faces with blue eyes, grey eyes,

hazel eyes, faces surrounded by tangled brown hair, red hair, blonde hair. "You don't exist," I muttered while their filthy small hands clutched at my skirts. "No, no, you don't exist," I whispered when I saw them in orphanages. And "no," I cried, when I saw a ragged gang of them sheltering under a bridge in a snowstorm. "No, you are not there!"[111]

She finally gave in and spoke English to one child. He did not understand it. She put a coin in his hand and watched him run off.[112]

Buck wrote that she tried to harden her heart, for her responsibilities were already many. However, she could not erase the images of "their faces . . . the tiny wrinkled ones of the newborn."[113] The images lingered in her mind persistently. It did not take long for her to be "bewitched by the children" as they stole her heart "by their wit and beauty."[114] Buck described that all the orphans around the world had the same "orphan look" in their eyes, however well fed and well clothed. It was a sad look—or worse, an empty look.[115] The theme of motherhood in her adoption practice is deeply embedded in her writings. In her poem "To an Amerasian Child," she expressed the overpowering emotions of wanting to be "left alone," asking the child to make his own fate:

> Child! Cease haunting space!
> Your eyes are too blue
> In your Asian face.
> With your Asian grace,
> Cease haunting space!
> Child! Make your own fate!
> I never decreed,
> In love or in hate,
> Your birth place or date.
> Make your own fate!
> Too late, too late,
> My heart now sighs.
> I see that face,
> I see those eyes.[116]

She closed the poem by saying that it was too late to turn away because she had seen the face and eyes of the child. In this short poem, Pearl

Buck expressed her staggering sense of motherly love and compassion for the child.[117]

Rather than taking emotions out of the picture, she acknowledged that her activism was partly driven by her compassion and personal experience. This was a bold corrective to a toxic cultural perspective in the 1950s that viewed American women as susceptible to emotional responses to world tragedies and easy prey for communist ideas. In particular, the altruistic efforts of women's organizations were often seen as "bleeding heart liberalism," driven by the women's guilt about their wealth and their boredom. Women were also seen as victims of communism because of communists' stated ideology of gender equality.[118] Instead of avoiding such criticisms, Buck championed a distinctively feminine form of service and routinely promoted it with the language of motherhood. This approach put her in sync with feminist organizations such as the Women's International League for Peace and Freedom (WILPF) that incorporated maternal metaphors into their political activism. Anna Garlin Spencer, the national head of WILPF, argued "in the name of womanhood" for the sustenance of life, addressing social issues from welfare of women and children to reforms in education.[119]

Despite regarding motherly love as an important building block of a family, Buck contrasted true motherhood with sentimentalized mother instinct. She contended that the maternal instinct was a blessing only when combined with true love, wisdom, and the ability to care for the child both physically and financially. If the maternal instinct remained a superficial animal instinct, it created disastrous situations such as abandonment and institutionalization. In criticizing social workers who encouraged the maternal instinct in birth mothers after their children's birth, Buck wrote that maternal love should not be confused with maternal instinct—maternal instinct came naturally after birth, but true motherly love was sustainable, life-long, and accompanied by a deep sense of responsibility and duty. When a birth mother was unable to perform motherly duties, she wrote, despite her instinct, love might fail or develop into hatred for the child. Buck warned that such hatred might go unrecognized by the mother, but was obvious to the child.[120] She exhorted the social workers to refrain from evoking unnecessary guilt or maternal instinct from birth mothers and from pressuring them to keep their children. She asserted that the entire child welfare system must be child-centered, focusing on meeting the needs of the child first and foremost.

Because Pearl Buck believed that the basis of a family was motherly and fatherly love in an intimate setting, she was fundamentally against the institutionalization of orphans. Criticizing charities and religious groups that maintained orphanages, she argued that a child in any orphanage was there "not for his own sake but for the sake of some organization, and thereby deprived of his natural right to home and family."[121] The religious groups, according to Buck, seldom visited the children except on Christmas or Easter, but maintained the orphanages to "get a warm feeling of doing good."[122] She argued that despite adequate food and housing, the lack of individual care and the centralization of concern through a relationship to parents stunted the orphans' emotional growth.[123] While she acknowledged the temporary necessity of orphanages in war-torn countries, Buck contended that institutions prevented children from becoming whole human beings.

Global Friendship

In addition to missionaries' focus on global friendship, secular programs promoting international friendship started to arise in the 1930s. One of the largest international friendship programs, the International Friendship League, was founded in 1936 by Edna MacDonough. The International Friendship League was the largest international pen pal matching service supported by the federal government. In the Cold War era, the theme of global friendship became solidified in the political realm. In 1956, the Eisenhower administration made capital of the popularity of international friendship organizations to promote the rebranding of America's image. In the mid-1950s, Americans sent 330 million letters abroad annually.[124]

The most significant difference between missionaries and secular cultural ambassadors, such as war veterans or agents employed through the United States Information Agency, was missionaries' reason for the emphasis on cross-cultural friendship. The ecumenical missionaries' promotion of global friendship was a form of Christian witness against colonialism and racism. Amid Christian internationalist language, many ecumenical Christians started to advocate for developing global friendship across divisions as a statement of unity and diversity in the kingdom of God. This was a welcome antidote to the traditional mission practice, tinged as it was with cultural imperialism and religious hierarchy. Rather than viewing missions in terms of strategies or programs, ecumenists started to view missions as a life-long practice of global friendship and Christian witness.[125]

In this context, Pearl Buck yearned for the adoption of mixed-race children to eliminate prejudice and bring about global friendship based on universal colorblindness. She argued that the key to eliminating prejudice was to understand that in spite of differences, all human beings were basically the same: created in the image of God. She contended that when prejudice was unresolved, it bore fear—fear of the unknown and the "other" that prevented the communication essential to peace and reconciliation in any community. Arguing that the "world is only a community," Buck envisioned harmony between the U.S. and Asia through mixed-race children.[126] She believed that Amerasian children could be a positive bridge between the East and the West, alleviating the racial tension and ignorance so prevalent in the United States of her time.[127] For Buck, transnational adoption was not merely a personal act, but also a profoundly communal act that could actualize world friendship and reconciliation.

Buck also believed that transnational adoption could ultimately solve the problem of communism, because the bridge formed between the West and the East could alleviate the tension and could potentially win Asia over. She argued that incorporating mixed-race children into the national family would realize "a triumph of American democracy," betraying a common Cold War internationalist attitude.[128] One can argue that Buck's triumphalist and imperialist language was an unfortunate product of her time. But despite her view that a powerful United States could bring about global democracy, Buck urged Americans to learn from Asians. She acknowledged that the United States' benevolence could generate prejudice and a belief in American superiority. She particularly praised Asians for the way they valued their children and taught wisdom to the young. She further contended that Asians' wisdom and experience could save Americans from their parochial mindset.[129]

Buck knew that true friendship and reconciliation required the involvement of ordinary people on the grassroots level. Commenting on

Jessie Bennett Sams' *White Mother*, in which Sams described her experience as a black woman who had been raised by a white woman in the South, Buck argued that such an act could be a solution to racial conflict: "Were we all to follow in the footsteps of this one white mother, we would need not ask how to achieve peace on earth."[130] In this rather idealistic description of racial reconciliation, we see a gendered dimension of the adoption movement. Women, by developing personal friendships through transnational and transracial adoption, went beyond the walls of the home and fulfilled their civic duties as Americans and global citizens. While friendship had historically been associated with brotherhood and considered the province of men, women formed deep and meaningful relationships with their adopted children, drawing on their ability to nurture and care. The adoption movement connected women's responsibilities in the domestic and social spheres. The adoptive mothers were the kind of women Buck was looking for—those who did not make "their homes their graves," but actively lived out their calling within the home and beyond.

For Buck, one of the most rewarding aspects of managing Welcome House was seeing the change in the outlook of American citizens, not by force or compulsion but by a broadening of their perspective. Just as mothers gently guide their children in the right direction, the transnational adoption movement enabled Americans to see race and family differently through the enlargement of their hearts. Through interacting with mixed-race children, the small community in Pennsylvania became more global-minded. Through the children, the countries the local community had regarded as foreign became beloved friends and family. Drawing on such examples, Buck argued that prejudices can be broken, and that most people's prejudices were shallow unless they were reinforced by early hostility.[131]

Her vision for global friendship and union propelled her to collaborate with myriad adoption agencies, religious groups, and charities across the world. Because she considered the happiness of children the most important goal of her work, Buck was able to work with any agency that was willing to commit to her mission. She was gratified that agencies that in the past had never accepted mixed-race children were open to placing them after working with Welcome House.[132] Showing a positive view of religious pluralism, Buck believed that the spirit of true religion had no room for the religious division that was often combined with racial prejudice. She argued that the "divisive and possessive jealousies" of religious groups must be replaced with the spirit of true religion that granted the freedom to approach the Father God. She declared that all men were "brothers," that all humanity was God's children.[133] Emphasizing that all human beings were equally created in the image of God, she argued that everyone must be united in the spirit of service to humanity, whatever the subject. Buck further wrote that all professional social workers were "servants of humanity," and hence must be united as a community to get rid of the monstrous problems facing humanity.[134]

Pearl Buck, much like the other missionaries who advocated global friendship and Christian internationalism, argued that the battle should not be against certain races or nations—the struggle against racism and prejudice was, according to her, against those who did not uphold the principle of human equality. She wrote in her speech that the enemies were those who "judge a man by his skin, and not by what he is as an individual."[135] In the same speech, which she gave as a commencement address at Howard University (a historically black university) on June 5, 1942, Buck beseeched the young African American students in her audience to think of racism not as a local issue, but as a global issue that affects all of humanity: "We cannot fight for freedom unless we fight for freedom for all. We are not better than fascists if we fight for the freedom of one group, and not another, for the benefit of one race and not another, for the aggrandizement of a part and not the betterment of the whole!"[136]

Pearl Buck was arguably the initiator of special needs adoption and the first to normalize it. She believed that through adoption, which was both personal and public, a global community without prejudice or racism could be created. She promoted motherhood across racial and religious barriers as a step toward alleviating the global racial tensions of the postwar world. In other words, the "white mother" who embraced and unconditionally loved the non-white child became the symbol of anti-racist commitment and the vehicle for global friendship.[137] Her adoption endeavors were fundamentally based on her Christian belief that all human beings were equally created in the divine likeness. To Buck, then, transnational adoption was merely another extension of the Christian practice. Unlike the evangelical adoption evangelists, who catered to a conservative Christian audience, Pearl Buck normalized the notion of transracial adoption across America. Her promotion of an anti-racist, anti-imperialist, and global vision for friendship closely resembled the language of Cold War internationalism and resonated with a broader audience than the conservative missionaries could reach. Her powerful prose played an important role in eradicating the racial matching system and altering Americans' outlook on race issues.

4

Helen Doss's *The Family Nobody Wanted*

Adoption narratives—stories written by adoptive parents, birth parents, and, more recently, adoptees—have shaped adoption theory and practice throughout history. In 1954, Helen Doss published *The Family Nobody Wanted*, the first transnational adoption narrative written from a first-person perspective. This extraordinarily popular book emphasized how God's love triumphed over cultural and racial differences. With this tale, Helen Doss effectively translated the ideas of cultural critics such as Pearl Buck into narrative form.[1] Although Carl Doss, Helen's husband, was a Methodist minister and the family belonged to this mainline denomination, Helen's warm stories and compelling rhetoric spoke to both evangelicals and ecumenists, and to many who did not identify as Christians. While Pearl Buck used her ecumenist religious background to sharply criticize the American public, Helen Doss used the same background to move her readers' hearts and minds. Unlike Bertha Holt, who catered mostly to evangelicals, Doss spoke to a broader audience, as Buck did, and engaged directly with the issue of racism. But compared to Buck, Doss conveyed a perspective and drew on a theology that were decidedly moderate. Doss, for instance, never mentioned religious pluralism. As a balanced moderate, she proved capable of reaching conservatives and liberals alike.

Although less intensely than Pearl Buck, Helen Doss was also affected by the surge of interest in ecumenical Christianity and Christian internationalism. Doss's rhetoric closely resembled Buck's discourse about global friendship, racial equality, and anti-racial matching. Like Buck, she defended racial minorities and emphasized human equality based on the theology of *imago Dei* (divine likeness). Helen Doss's adoption narratives provided a much-needed corrective to an American culture infused with racism. Both scientific racism based on the eugenics movement and the racism that beleaguered American Christianity bred hatred and indifference toward children of mixed-race descent and children of color. Trained professionals and elites were deeply affected by the eugenics movement, which argued that human characteristics were largely determined by genetic and biological factors, such as race, biological fitness, and mental disorders. On the popular level, the enigmatic biblical narrative in Genesis 9 depicting the curse of Ham's descendants had justified slavery and racism in America.[2]

By making race issues familiar and relatable, Doss's account enabled ordinary Americans to see the innate value of children of color. Using common language and moving stories, Doss effectively countered the competing narratives that portrayed transnational and transracial adoption as perilous. Through her personal stories, she spoke directly against racism in America, thus linking transnational adoption to the broader anti-racism movement. Unlike her evangelical counterparts, she was unafraid to directly address the issue of racism, and as a result, she was able to translate the ecumenical Christians' anti-racist commitment into stories and language that evangelicals could relate to and embrace. This chapter explores Doss's narratives and situates her story within the broader framework of American adoption history. By 1950, confidentiality policies and sealed records had created a culture of secrecy and shame surrounding adoption practices. Firsthand accounts of adoption experiences were scarce, and testimonies and case files written by social workers and lawmakers were merely clinical. Amid the competing narratives that depicted transracial and transnational adoption as perilous and unorthodox, Doss's account opened up a new avenue through which other ordinary Americans could explore the idea of adopting mixed-race children. Her story functioned as a poignant antidote to the culture of secrecy and shame.

The Changing Adoption Landscape

American Racism Based on the Eugenics Movement

From 1900 to 1940, the notion of bad blood was a universally accepted principle in the domestic adoption landscape. Advocates of the eugenics movement believed that so-called bad blood (genetically inferior people in terms of physical attributes, illness, psychological disorders, and/or race) must be eliminated through sterilization and controlled breeding (negative eugenics). Thousands of women of color and those who suffered from illness and poverty were involuntarily sterilized during the first half of the twentieth century. Eugenicists argued that the reproduction of genetically superior people, by contrast, must be encouraged (positive eugenics).[3] The movement was widely supported by American intellectuals of virtually all political parties before the eugenics movement came to be negatively associated with Nazi Germany.

Fears and anxiety about bad blood spread widely beyond psychologists and biologists and were shared by social workers engaged in setting adoption policy. Albert Stoneman, the General Secretary of the Michigan Children's Aid Society, demonstrated this fear and the obsession with science as the only safe approach to adoption: "With our present knowledge of biology and heredity we seem justified in general not to offer for adoption the child of feebleminded parentage . . . The one thing we must do is to ban ignorance as disgraceful and to exalt accuracy and integrity."[4] This obsession with the notion of bad blood created a culture of fear and bigotry, particularly on the adoption scene.

The eugenics movement that circulated among the academic elites pointed to the larger American context of racism. Popular media and literature also echoed the idea that negative hereditary traits such as feeble-mindedness were innate. Moreover, middle-class Anglo-Saxon Americans believed that negative hereditary traits included race and ethnicity, betraying the racial attitudes of the time. In *The Bad Seed* (1954), a novel by William March, eight-year-old Rhoda Penmark was portrayed as a stereotypical "bad seed" who harbored criminal and sociopathic tendencies. Outwardly, she was a charming and polite young girl, but inwardly she was fundamentally twisted. She ended up secretly murdering her classmate and a maintenance man who worked at the Penmarks' house. Her mother Christine, who had learned that her daughter might be responsible for the murders, investigated the issue and discovered the secret of her own adoption; she learned that her biological mother, moreover, was a serial killer who had been executed in the electric chair. Fearing that she had inherited her mother's criminality and passed it to Rhoda, Christine attempted to painlessly kill Rhoda with a bottle of sleeping pills. Christine died by suicide soon afterward, but Rhoda, who was taken to the hospital, survived and was free to kill again.

The book was received with much acclaim and was later remade into a psychological horror film and several Broadway plays. Although the book was published in 1954, around the time most people were distancing themselves from the eugenics movement, the popular notion of bad blood was still subconsciously prevalent, and racism was certainly widespread. A small number of literary critics strongly opposed the idea of bad blood. August Derleth, a prominent American writer and anthologist, commented, "*The Bad Seed* would have been a stronger novel without this false premise—the granddaughter of a murderess is no more likely to be a murderess than the granddaughter of a seamstress, or anyone else."[5] However, the book demonstrated the persistence of the vigorous prejudice of the previous decade, which still haunted ordinary people's minds.

Racial Matching in Adoption

As demonstrated by the eugenics movement, racism had a deep and extensive impact on adoption policies. Social workers and policymakers believed it was a social crime to place inferior or defective children for adoption. Professionals used intelligence tests and investigated elaborate genealogies before placing children in adoptive homes. Although public discussion of eugenics ideology dissipated after Nazism's rigorous eugenics program, blood and genetics remained an important theme in adoption history in the following decades.

The eugenics movement's most direct and prolonged influence was exerted in the adoption practice of racial matching. Eugenicists' definition of "racial improvement" entailed not only discouraging the procreation of people of color but also filtering people in terms of ethnicity and religion. In 1924, majorities in the House and Senate passed the Immigration Act, which virtually eliminated the flow of immigrants into the United States. President Calvin Coolidge noted, "America must be kept American. Biological laws show . . . that Nordics deteriorate when mixed with other races." Eugenicists zealously acclaimed and supported the new law. The "other races," according to the eugenicists, meant not only people of color, but also Jews, southern Europeans, and other non-Nordic people.[6]

Especially prominent in the 1950s adoption landscape were anxieties about miscegenation in transracial and transnational adoption. Due to the eugenicists' prevailing view of the inferiority of people of

African descent, many adoption professionals believed that mixing the races in marriage would destroy the purity of each race and lead to "mongrelization."[7] Moreover, the fear of "race suicide," the notion that non-whites would come to outnumber whites, was reflected in various immigration laws and welfare reforms. Consequently, it was against the social welfare system's policies to place non-white children in white American homes. The scientific racism of trained adoption professionals and the everyday racism of ordinary people led to the perception that children of color had bad temperaments and were prone to feeble-mindedness, emotional instability, insanity, and violence. This environment led to the strict policy of racial matching, an attempt to create kinship without blood.

Deep fears concerning inferior races manifested themselves as subtle racism in the following decades in adoption agencies. The rhetoric assumed a politer, more nuanced form, but adoption professionals, prospective adoptive parents, and popular media continued to express a horror of race-mixing. Sheldon Reed, who coined the term "genetic counseling" to describe counseling about the passing of certain traits to offspring, consulted frequently with adoption professionals regarding racial matching. In his article "Skin Color," he noted that adoption agencies were primarily concerned with the heredity of skin color. Most people wanted children who could "pass for white" because their biggest question was about the skin color of the offspring of the children being considered for adoption. Influenced by a common myth about the reemergence of blackness in future generations, the potential adoptive parents were worried that their adopted children would marry white spouses but produce "black babies."[8]

The ideal form of matching entailed not only racial matching, but also a perfect match in terms of religious background, intelligence, and physical resemblance. In other words, adoptive parents typically wanted babies who could pass as their own children. In an attempt to artificially create kinship without blood, both adoptive parents and professionals produced a paradoxical result: ironically, matching validated the notion that blood was thicker than love, which inherently made adoption inferior to blood kinship. The 1950s obsession with the nuclear family turned adoption into a practice that served infertile couples' needs. Healthy white babies were in high demand. Prospective parents who wished for children who resembled them desperately attempted to prove their parental worthiness to adoption agencies.[9]

The Adoption Culture of Secrecy and Shame

In addition to the eugenics movement, another ideology that was consistent with racial matching was an adoption culture based on anonymity and shame. With the advent of the golden age of the American family, adoption agencies became more rigid and secretive in their pursuit of a pseudo-biological kinship based on near-perfect matching. Before World War II, caseworkers had endeavored to keep the channels of communication open between biological mothers and their children. Case workers understood that because emotional bonds had already been established, it was better for the children's emotional health to keep communication open. The relatively open prewar process changed radically with the inception of the baby boom.

The adoptive parents, who desired a tight-knit nuclear family, often preferred a completely closed adoption that prevented any communication between birth parents and adoptees. Confidentiality, a policy advocated by professionals and policymakers, helped to sever birth ties. When adoption decrees were issued, new birth certificates replaced the sealed originals containing the names of the biological parents. The initial aim of confidential records was to protect the children. The U.S. Children's Bureau stated that "it was imperative that the *child's original birth certificates be identified so that his complete birth record will be available to him when needed*."[10] During this time, confidential records were sealed from the public but remained accessible to the adoption triad—adoptees, adoptive parents, and biological parents.

However, during the height of the American obsession with nuclear families, children's needs became secondary to infertile couples' desire for children who could assimilate as if they were biological children. It was during this time that confidentiality morphed into secrecy.[11] Although by World War II, it was customary to make the court records of adoption proceedings and birth certificates confidential, the records were not deemed secretive. The sealed records that prevented even adult adoptees from accessing their original birth certificates created an oppressive adoption culture of secrecy and shame.[12] Moreover, by the early

1950s, psychologists and psychiatrists began to discourage the policy of open disclosure to adoptive parents. Most notably, in 1954, the psychiatric social worker Barbara Kohlsaat and the psychiatrist Adelaide M. Johnson argued that "because of the possibility of neurotic character traits in the adoptive parents, they and the child must be protected by keeping from them any knowledge about the child's background."[13]

To further complicate the issue, many adoptive parents avoided telling their children of their adopted status. Before the mid-twentieth century, professionals advocated "telling," a practice of telling children of their adopted status early in life. Despite social workers' consensus on the value of telling a child about their origin, many adoptive parents were reluctant to communicate this information to their children. Many parents kept the adoption a secret from everyone, including their relatives and neighbors. Due to America's cultural preference for blood families, these adoptive parents wanted children who matched them not only in terms of race but also in physical resemblance. Secrecy was crucial in the formation of this fictive genetic family; any memory or record of adoption had to be erased.

Some adoptive parents even went to the extent of publicly criticizing the policy of telling. For example, an adoptive mother wrote an article titled "To My Adopted Daughter: I Wish I Hadn't Told You" in McCall's magazine in 1959. The author detailed a list of problems her daughter had faced throughout her life because the mother had followed the recommendation of the professionals to tell her daughter about her adoption. The daughter experienced deep mental agony regarding her identity and struggled with a sense of rejection and abandonment and an exaggerated sense of obligation. The author concluded the essay by declaring, "The knowledge that one is adopted creates far more problems than the one it is supposed to solve." Adoptive parents' resistance to telling was supported by several psychoanalysts, including William Healy and Robert Knight, who identified various psychological problems associated with early and repeated telling.[14]

Adoption Narratives

Adoption practices based on secrecy provided a superficial solution to the problem of infertility and illegitimacy. For adoptive parents who desperately wanted a nuclear family, secretive adoption provided a fictive blood family. For children who otherwise would have been stigmatized as illegitimate, becoming a member of an artificial blood family erased the memory and reminder of inadequacy. However, the covert nature of adoption also fostered adoption practices based on shame. In this climate, it took courage to share about adoption stories, because adoption was a topic that involved sensitive issues such as illegitimacy, infertility, and unwed mothers. Although there were numerous fictional portrayals of adoption, true stories and firsthand accounts of adoption were scarce. Outcome Studies researchers compiled collective adoption biographies, but these were clinical; personal testimonies collected by lawyers were used merely to persuade judges of the psychological damage done by the culture of secrecy.

When magazine articles and books published personal adoption narratives written by adoptive parents, readers were often intrigued. Personal adoption narratives offered a strong antidote to the culture of secrecy. The stories often told of adoptees' struggles with identity formation, their longing for biological kin, and their profound desire for roots; at the same time, the joy of creating a new family and redefining the traditional nuclear family was often the capstone of these stories. Particularly prominent in the adoption narrative scene were female adoption evangelists, such as Pearl Buck and her powerful prose, and other writers who told their stories.

Helen Doss's popular narrative *The Family Nobody Wanted*, published in 1954, supplied the story component that Pearl Buck's essays lacked. While Buck's articles served as a corrective to American hypocrisy and racist rhetoric, Doss's narrative offered a strong antidote to the culture of secrecy by breaking the prolonged silence concerning transnational adoption. The book was so well received that Hollywood made two films out of it, and the Doss family appeared in numerous TV shows. Other than Helen Doss, Jean Paton, who established the Life History Study Center, was the first person to write a book containing first-person accounts of adult adoptees. Her book, *The Adopted Break Silence* (published in the same year as Doss's book), detailed adult adoptees' thoughts and emotions.

Helen Doss, like Bertha Holt, used compelling personal anecdotes and sentimentalism to communicate her vision of anti-racism to her readers. Rather than shunning emotions, she drew extensively on the personal experience and rhetoric of motherhood, pulling the heart-strings of many other women who identified deeply with her stories full of mundane and at times trite joys and struggles. In addition to writing her own stories, Helen Doss was often featured with her family in television shows and magazines as a beloved "international family" or a "United Nations family."[15]

The Family Nobody Wanted

The Family Nobody Wanted was the first memoir to offer a first-person transnational adoption narrative, and the book met with a significant amount of curiosity and enthusiasm. At a time when transnational adoption was just starting to gain momentum, Doss's book was a refreshing reminder that the traditional definition of the nuclear family could be expanded. The Dosses were the kind of Christians Pearl Buck was looking for—people who were not just willing but eager to adopt children who were labeled unadoptable by most adoption agencies. Transnational adoption to her represented a divine calling. As an adoption evangelist, she wrote in her book that it was her faith that motivated her to participate in God's mission—a mission to spread colorblind love based on the human equality found in the *imago Dei*.[16] Her timely memoir demystified secretive adoption practices and broke the stigma of transnational adoption. At the time, for all the reasons described above, a family consisting of children of different races was widely considered inferior to an adoptive family consisting of only white family members. By portraying a realistic picture of the joys, sorrows, challenges, and rewards of raising an international family, Helen Doss normalized the practice of transnational adoption.

The book contained many elements that reflected the family values of the 1950s. As prescribed by the zeitgeist, the young Helen Doss envisioned having a family. Her firsthand adoption account is replete with the post-war family values that marked the 1950s, often referred to as the "golden age" in American family history. She opened her book with a statement that epitomized the spirit of the time: "I didn't yearn for a career, or maids and a fur coat, or a trip to Europe. All in the world I wanted was a happy, normal little family." Throughout the book, readers can easily see her fascination with having children. Faced with the devastating news of infertility during an era when motherhood was synonymous with female contentment, Helen's initial reaction was self-pity and acute jealousy of women who could bear children. Carl, tired of hearing Helen lamenting, suggested adopting a baby. Although Carl was portrayed as engaged reluctantly with family life, he was an aloof figure when it came to family matters. He was more concerned about his pastoral ministry and making ends meet. Helen, convinced that motherhood was "compounded more of love than biology," eagerly sought out adoption.[17]

The young couple soon discovered that each agency had a long waiting list and that it would take two to three years for the social workers to find a child "whose background was a perfect match."[18] Moreover, due to their financial instability, the Doss couple was not welcomed by most agencies. However, Helen's poignant letters filled with longing moved one particular social worker's heart. After a home inspection, the social worker informed them that a Caucasian baby was available for adoption. Helen and Carl adopted Donald (Donny) at six weeks old. Finding a sibling for Donny was more difficult. Helen wrote, "We would never have had an interracial family if I had not been blocked by countless blind alleys in my search for a younger brother or sister for Donny. Asking to adopt another child was as futile as asking for the moon."[19] After finally convincing adoption agencies that race made no difference to them, the Doss couple adopted twelve children of color: Indian, Native American, Filipino, Hawaiian, Balinese, Malayan, and Mexican, in diverse combinations.

The public affectionately called Helen Doss's family the "United Nations Family" because it represented so many cultures and ethnicities. The Doss family's story was well-received because, despite the uniqueness of its multi-ethnic makeup, the family's experiences struck common chords and evoked a sense of ordinariness, commonality, and normalcy. Although the twelve children varied significantly in cultural background and race, they otherwise lived everyday lives in mid-twentieth-century America. Moreover, the baby boomer audience found the story of a mother raising twelve children a reinforcement of the value attributed to the nuclear family.

The family started with Helen's ordinary and natural desire to have a happy family, the norm of the time. When Helen adopted babies, she faced typical, ordinary problems that any young mother would face. In a witty style, she portrayed the everyday life of raising multiple children, from mediating fights between the children to struggles with cooking and cleaning. Virtually all parents in America could relate to these mundane elements, which created a sense of familiarity in the Doss family's story. Central to this story was the power of a love that superseded differences. Helen continuously attempted to normalize the experience of having mixed-race children. Throughout the book, she stressed that children were like Christmas gifts—what was inside the wrapping paper was what counted. The color of the wrapping did not matter.[20]

In an episode of a TV show called *You Bet Your Life* that aired on December 17, 1954, Helen exclaimed, "Children do not really realize [the racial differences] . . . they know they are theoretically different but [that] doesn't make any difference. For instance, my two oldest boys always play cowboy and Indian. But the blonde, blue-eyed boy plays the Indian and the Indian boy plays the cowboy."[21] According to Helen, the Doss children were truly colorblind. When Donny (Caucasian) was eight and Alex (Japanese, Burmese, and Korean mixed-race) was one year old, Donny said as he fondly glanced at Alex, "If he was seven years older, and if I had black hair, everybody would think that him and me was twins!"[22] Helen and Carl were proud that their children took it for granted that they were alike simply because they were a "really real family."[23] The children appeared exotic and different as separate people, but together they were a collection of silly, adorable, and seemingly ordinary American siblings.[24]

However, Doss's narrative was not just a story about a happy, ordinary family. Her adoption narrative spoke directly against competing narratives that depicted adoption in a negative light. Her book was a timely corrective to an American adoption landscape that was infused with remnants of eugenics and a culture of secrecy and shame. Rather than attacking the eugenics movement with rational arguments, Doss touched her readers' hearts and convinced them with her poignant stories and funny episodes. Instead of hiding, she openly communicated her adoption stories to her children, her relatives, and the public. She promoted colorblind love, but not racial essentialism that disregarded distinctiveness. She championed openness and was vocal about her stories and her faith, but with discernment and gentleness. Ordinary

Americans were drawn to Doss's stories because of these paradoxes—a family that was unique yet ordinary; colorblind yet distinct; bold yet humble.

Colorblind Love

Like Pearl Buck, Helen Doss advocated colorblind love and anti-racist rhetoric, but in a narrative form. By providing stories about an unconventional international family that was both ordinary and unique, Doss abated the stigma surrounding adoption and softened the dominant images of the American family that promoted only homogeneity. Stating that skin color was a superficial thing, Helen and Carl were eager to adopt mixed-race children. One social worker who indignantly opposed this idea exclaimed, "I would rather see a child raised in an orphanage, than by parents who look so *different*. Crossing racial lines is against all our *principles* of good social-work practice."[25] She was one of many social workers influenced by the residue of eugenics principles. In response to this comment, Helen wrote that all races were alike underneath, the same in "range of intellect and capacity for moral and spiritual growth."[26]

Helen and Carl continued to face problems as they sought to adopt mixed-race children. When they wanted to adopt Rita, a social worker compared the child with Susie, who had fairer skin: "Susie not only belongs to the dominant race, but also has beautiful blue eyes and blonde hair. How will poor little Rita feel, when the neighbor girls invite Susie to their birthday parties, their dances and slumber parties, and Rita isn't asked?"[27] Despite the new, softer language used by social workers, the principle of eugenics still governed the social worker's understanding of the dominant race. Helen wrote that their children did not regard themselves as different from one another: "Naturally they could see that there were minor and inconsequential variations, that Rita had 'the blackest, shiniest hair,' that Teddy could toast browner in the sun than the rest, but persons bearing such unearned distinctions were polite enough not to gloat."[28]

The beauty of Doss's stories was that they carried certain moral lessons without overtly criticizing the readers. Rather than *telling* the readers that racism was wrong, Helen *showed* why racial segregation and eugenics principles were absurd. Similarly, rather than directly condemning U.S. policies, she helped Americans accept their responsibility to the rest of the world. Her seemingly personal act of adopting and writing stories about her family was not only a private act of humanitarian work, but also an important corrective to the ingrained institutional racism in America. Part of the reason Doss's family-centered rhetoric was so effective was that the family already served as a model for a "free world" community in which various nations, both developed and underdeveloped, peacefully coexisted. The emotional unity and fluid yet structured hierarchies of age within a family were an ideal picture of what the global family should look like. There was an inevitable power imbalance in the child-mother relationship, and of course, children were not adopted by choice. Nevertheless, Doss's "United Nations family" provided an ideal model of postwar integration in which an international and interracial family was formed by choice, rather than force.

The scholar Christina Klein argues that in postwar America, the family became a framework where distinctiveness could be both celebrated and transcended. She goes further to argue that this framework offered "an imaginative justification for the permanent extension of U.S. power."[29] Although Helen Doss and the other adoption evangelists did not make a direct connection between their humanitarian mission and the extension of American global power, it is clear that their humanitarian works contributed to the positive remaking of America's image in the context of Cold War internationalism. By addressing the issue of racism within her family and community on the micro level, Doss filled in gaps that governments and policies could not reach.

Doss's narratives of forging connection and finding commonalities between the East and the West were effective in dismantling racism in both personal and institutional ways. Her moving stories, teeming with raw emotions such as empathy, love, anger, and disappointment, were an ideal tool for communicating about the sensitive topic of anti-racism, which many white Americans of the time avoided. While the U.S. government embraced the narrative of anti-imperialism and internationalism on the national level amid Cold War politics, it was the work of ordinary people like Doss that changed individuals' perception of race and family on the grassroots level. The sentimentalism of Doss's rhetoric in particular received some criticism for its saccharine nature, but it was undeniably effective at conveying the interconnectedness of humanity, since the sentimentalism functioned as a universalizing mode that transcended race and power dynamics between nations.[30] Indeed, the lived experience of adoption evangelists and their detailed, emotional stories extended beyond their own narratives, creating a sustainable and large-scale movement of transnational adoption across America.

Doss's efforts to tell stories continued with her writing of children's books dedicated to broadening children's perspective on race and ethnicity. In 1958 and 1959, she published *All the Children of the World* and *Friends around the World*, respectively, to teach children about the "wonderful variety to be found in God's world, and among all God's children."[31] In her first children's book, she emphasized the distinctiveness of the children, whereas her second book emphasized the commonality of all children. In *All the Children of the World*, she wrote that God planned all children to be different, some children with "pale, pink-colored skin," some with a "golden tan color" and "rich warm brown" skin. Still others were so "velvety brown that they look[ed] almost black." She concluded that whatever their skin color, it was "just right" for them. By using metaphors rather than directly addressing race or ethnicity, she creatively went beyond colorblindness and racial essentialism and showed that innate human dignity and value were tied to being an individual created by God. She then introduced the concept of adoption, stating that adoptive parents know that their "baby is just right," and that they are "glad that their baby is different from every other baby." She concluded the short storybook by emphasizing God's boundary-less love for all children, who are equally created in the image of God.[32]

In *Friends around the World*, however, Helen emphasized commonality over distinctiveness, as her goal was to promote global friendship among children. She wrote about various styles of living, food, work environments, and worship from India to Sweden. For example, in China, Pear Blossom "eats her rice and fish with chopsticks," and in Russia, Peter likes "a thick slice of dark wheat bread with his pork and cabbage soup."[33] In this way, Helen introduced various cultures around the world as distinctive and unique. She concluded that despite cultural differences, children were fundamentally alike inside. She encouraged cross-cultural friendship to children, ending the book with "These are your friends, all around the world."[34]

Both children's books acknowledged the distinctiveness and commonality of children, although with varying emphases. Her recognition of individuality was important, as many evangelical missionaries often overlooked racial and ethnic distinctiveness in an effort to communicate commonality. Doss's emphasis on individuality informed her Western readers that each child had a unique racial heritage, culture, history, and background; none of the children were labeled "helpless Asian orphans." In these books, Doss advocated the same principle promoted by ecumenists such as Pearl Buck: global friendship based on the understanding that all human beings were equally created in the image of God. Doss went even further than Buck in communicating the idea of global friendship directly to children, not with force but through sentimental stories. Instead of imposing, Doss gently invited the young readers to critically think about forging emotional and global ties with other children around the world. Doss, along with other organizations that championed global friendship such as the International Friendship League, collectively enlarged children's hearts and educated parents about America's shifting relationship to the world.

The greatest accomplishment of *The Family Nobody Wanted* was making race matters familiar, relatable, and believable. The characters in Helen's stories were common American people who could easily be anyone's neighbor—Rita's teacher, who assumed that Rita would *only* crave chili and hot tamales because of her Mexican heritage; neighbors who asked if Alex loved eating Asian chop suey; a white-haired lady who was surprised to find out about Helen's adoptive family after assuming that Susie (a blue-eyed, blonde-haired girl) was Helen's biological daughter.[35] These playful, innocuous episodes reminded the readers to reflect on their perspective and behavior and think again about race matters.

While Doss's books were characterized by sentimentalism and rose-tinted scenes of family life, there were moments where she somberly and directly criticized racism in the United States. In telling the story of Taro, a Japanese-Filipino foster child, Helen revealed the ugly face of her country. Taro stayed with the Doss family for one year as a foster child after his entire family except his father died in the Japanese American internment camps. During his stay, other boys made fun of Taro's face, calling him a "Jap." The little boys had seen the "prevalent cartoons of the Japanese military in the newspapers, distorted sketches with huge, toothy grins."[36] The story intensified when Taro's father arrived for Thanksgiving dinner severely injured. Taro's father had been beaten nearly to death by two assailants who believed that "the only good Jap's a dead one."[37] Taro's father was saved by Mike, a white serviceman married to a Japanese American woman. The soldier described how in Italy, a Nisei boy had saved his life at the cost of his own. Indignant at the apparent racism, he said, "A man's an American because of what he feels inside about his country. It burns me up to hear Americans of Japanese ancestry sneered at and called *Japs*. Plenty of those boys spilled good blood for our country."[38] Through the story, Helen displayed both the ugly reality of America and a glimpse of the hope of American democracy.

Furthermore, Doss spoke passionately against racism and eugenics in two incidents. The first episode occurred when a neighbor was talking to Carl in front of their front door. Rita, while playing in the driveway, flew off her trike and landed on her nose. Without making much fuss, Rita got up with Teddy's help. They giggled, hopped on their trikes and took off. After watching the entire episode unfold, the neighbor said, "Coming from such primitive stock, she couldn't possibly have felt it the way a *Caucasian* would have. I doubt if her nerve ends are very highly developed."[39] In regards to his comment, Helen wrote furiously how her children did not need the "studious anthropologists and ethnologists" to tell them that such a notion was laughable. She emphasized the commonalities among the children and pointed out that racial prejudice is one of the worst social tragedies and is difficult to cure.[40]

The anti-racist rhetoric climaxed in a story about Mrs. Pickles, a friend of the Doss family. When told about the Dosses' plan to adopt Gretchen, a half-African American and half-Caucasian girl, Mrs. Pickles remarked, "A nigger child? The good Lord made them to be slaves, and not on the same level with us."[41] After passionately preaching about how misled her biblical interpretation was, Carl said, "We Americans can't keep one-tenth of our population in an inferior position . . . and still be a healthy democracy. It isn't Christian and it isn't democratic, and most of us claim to be both."[42] The Dosses reminded the readers of the radical nature of Christianity. This was the same radical Christianity that shaped the antislavery movement; the radical Christianity that advocated ecumenism focusing on global friendship; the radical Christianity that spearheaded the anti-racist movement among a myriad of missionaries. Helen further wrote that Americans were no better than communist saboteurs if Americans continued to step on others because of the color of their skin.

When the Dosses informed their relatives of their plans to adopt Gretchen, Carl's mother said, "Just don't be bringing her visiting to my house . . . No nigger will call *me* Grandma!"[43] Helen grieved the fact that even her friends tried to stop her. One well-intentioned friend commented that most white communities would never accept "a girl of Negro blood into the heart of their social doings, especially after she gets to be in her teens and close to marrying age."[44] They even suggested that the Dosses disguise her African heritage and "label her as something else."[45] Helen responded, "We're teaching our other children to be proud of their whole heritage. Have we the right to make her ashamed to be what she is?"[46] The adoption of Gretchen eventually failed. Months passed after they filled out the releases and affidavits, but they never heard back from the agency. Lamenting the fact that prejudice was irrational and unpatriotic, they resented the bitter reality tainted with virulent racial hostility.[47]

Despite Doss' focus on colorblind love, the story about Gretchen revealed a strict racial hierarchy that placed African American children at the bottom. One of the negative effects of Doss' colorblind love was what has become known as "colorblind racism"—because the colorblind view of race denied the salience of racial differences, it also glossed over the institutional racism that many black communities faced. By claiming "racial neutrality," colorblind racism failed to address the systemic and persistent nature of racism that stratified society.[48] It is telling that the publication of Doss's book coincided with *Brown v. Board of Education of Topeka* (1954), a decision of the U.S. Supreme Court that put a halt to racial segregation in public schools.[49] While the Court ruled unanimously to end segregation in education, public reactions varied. Some Americans were enthusiastic about the decision, calling segregated education a "sorry heritage from slavery" and a "caste system."[50] Attorney Thurgood Marshall of New York argued that any kind of segregation was illegal under the Fourteenth Amendment to the U.S. Constitution.

Others disagreed sharply, arguing that the Amendment was designed to outlaw slavery, not to forbid segregated but "equal" schools.[51] Although many African American communities were in favor of school integration, white politicians, educators, and social workers maintained that integration would actually hurt black students, claiming that the so-called "intellectual gap" would be the biggest obstacle. They also argued that because the quality of education was equal in white and black schools, strict segregation should be maintained. However, Chief Justice Earl Warren declared that the "doctrine of separate but equal" had no place, since separate educational facilities were "inherently unequal."[52] Refuting the argument that integration would be harmful to black students, Warren stated that school segregation was detrimental to black children because it instilled in them a sense of inferiority, which in turn affected their motivation to learn.[53]

A prolonged period of violent resistance to educational integration ensued, much like the series of obstacles Gretchen experienced. Mobs gathered to protest school integration, and they often turned violent. In Baltimore, for example, a mob of approximately four hundred white adults and teenagers threatened three black students leaving Southern High School. One fourteen-year-old black student was punched in the face by one of the protesters. Many other black students were escorted home by the police after their parents expressed concern for their safety. One of the protesters proudly commented that the event was merely "the first step toward our ultimate goal of making sure that no Negroes attend white schools in the state."[54] "Old South" pro-segregation extremism continued to erupt, inflicting verbal harassment and physical violence on black communities.[55]

Those who supported school segregation promoted the "segregated but equal" doctrine. Much as colorblind racism ignored the United States' bitter racial hostilities, the "segregated but equal" doctrine glossed over the deep-seated, systemic racism within the educational system and justified continued inequality. The black students who were segregated in public schools, as Warren commented, received the message that they were inferior to white students. In a similar way, black families (or, in the case of adoption, black children) were regarded as responsible for the breakdown of the family, the problem of illegitimacy, and teenage criminality.[56] Although Doss was able to practice her idealistic form of colorblind love, it could not be denied that society perceived color.

Regrettably, Doss did not delve into the issue of systemic racism in her books, although she did provide anecdotes about the treatment that black children received, as in the case of Gretchen. Her failure to address the issue demonstrates the limitations of colorblindness: alleged racial neutrality could not solve the problem of longstanding, systemic racism against black American and mixed-race children with African heritage. As in the case of school segregation, even within the transnational adoption scene with its purported adherence to colorblindness, a "caste" system prevailed that disfavored black children. Unlike fully Asian or white mixed-race children, black mixed-race children could not be perceived as honorary whites, a situation that demonstrates the long-lasting effects of the eugenics movement and "one-drop" racial classification.

A Gendered Movement

Women missionaries' roles in the adoption movement at once reinforced and complicated traditional gender norms. While these women were still homemakers, they were participating in an important social and global movement in innovative ways. On one hand, Helen and Carl embodied the stereotypical gender roles of the 1950s. Tracking with the American obsession with nuclear families, gender roles became more polarized during this time. The ideology of the filiarchy, as discussed previously, became solidified as women took charge in the private, domestic sphere and retreated from the workplace. Women who once enjoyed relative financial freedom and vocational fulfillment were now expected to re-domesticate themselves as homemakers.

On the other hand, the adoption movement complicated traditional gender norms because women began to gain social power based on sentimental ideas about motherhood. In the 1930s, the concept of the "mother-child dyad" had been used by welfare workers to uplift and train mothers in the physical and psychological well-being of children. Katherine Lenroot, Chief of the United States Children's Bureau, promoted a view of the mother-child dyad in which motherhood guaranteed greater social and political authority.[57] Social workers during this time argued that the government must partner with mothers to raise emotionally and physically healthy children. By 1940s, the dyad rhetoric lost its power when public health and welfare workers shifted their discourse to emphasize a "scientific," rather than social, view of motherhood. Mothers' role diminished significantly as healthcare professionals defined motherhood in terms of biomedical needs. While on an individual level, sentimental motherhood was glorified during the golden age of family history, in the child welfare scene, the role of mothers decreased considerably. Doss's adoption practice complicated the matter because she fused glorified sentimental motherhood with child welfare, thereby privileging women in both the domestic and social spheres. Her direct role as a mother of adoptees went beyond the scientific boundaries of motherhood, as her child welfare "program" was specifically individualized to fit her role as a mother who nurtured, cared, protected, and provided. In a field where male social workers and physicians held the most power and authority, she brought the rhetoric of motherhood back to the child welfare system by *literally* becoming a mother.

Moreover, the adoption narrative functioned as a crucial vehicle by which female voices were heard. Stories written by adoptive fathers and male adoptees were scarce, and virtually nothing was published by birth fathers, who were usually absent from the children's lives. Mothers, who exerted power and authority in the domestic sphere, told their stories in a confessional and intimate style. This gendered aspect of the adoption narrative is important because adoption was a rare social phenomenon in which the hands and faces of the actions matched. In other words, women were the impetus that drove the adoption movement, and they were also the first to voice their opinions and stories.

The Family Everybody Wanted

In 1959, Helen Doss published *The Really Real Family*, an adoption narrative about Elaine and Diane, two girls from Hawaii who were adopted into the Doss family together. Compassionately and compellingly, Helen narrated the story from Elaine's perspective. Putting herself in Elaine's shoes, she wrote, "We didn't have any daddy, and we missed not having a mother or a daddy like other children . . . Wouldn't it be nice, to have a really *real* family, all our very own?"[58] In her typical storytelling fashion, Helen made the stories about sibling quarrels, the jealous sister, and funny episodes come alive. What Helen tried to portray throughout all her books was that her family was a *really real* family—neither superior nor inferior to the biological family, but *real* in every sense of the word. When asked if they would do the same thing—adopt the children—over again, the Dosses unabashedly replied that adopting the children was the single most enriching experience they had ever had.

Helen Doss's work is noteworthy in the broader adoption movement for several reasons. First, she had the ability to stir the public's emotions. Her book not only was the first transnational adoption narrative from a first-person perspective, but also become so popular that she was flooded with letters from all over the United States and around the world. An NBC radio show named them the "Christmas Family of the Year," and her book was dramatized and made into plays and a film. If Pearl Buck spoke through stern and sharp prose, Doss persuaded readers with her relatable stories and heartfelt pleas. Through the title *The Family Nobody Wanted*, Helen Doss ultimately pointed out that although outsiders imagined that their family was "made up of incompatible opposites," the Doss family emphatically consisted of children who were deeply wanted.[59] By speaking in the language of ordinary people, she convinced her readers that her family was indeed "a family everybody wanted," thus normalizing transnational adoption and reconceptualizing the notion of the "ideal family." Moreover, Doss was able to speak to both evangelical and ecumenical Christians due to her theologically neutral stance and adherence to traditional gender norms. Her role as a loving mother and a dedicated pastor's wife moved evangelicals' hearts; her rhetoric of global friendship and human solidarity based on *imago Dei* resonated with the ecumenists.

Second, within the existing adoption scene and the literary world, she popularized a new genre of adoption narratives. She revealed the fallacy of people's perception of adoption, criticizing the prevailing adoption culture based on secrecy and shame and denouncing the eugenics principles that were still widespread during her time. Her narratives were an effective antidote to the competing narratives and were met with great enthusiasm by parents, social workers, and teachers. Through narratives, not direct reprimands, she contributed to fighting the racial matching system that was prevalent in the social work of the time.

Finally, Helen Doss, along with other female Christians who led the transnational adoption movement, contributed to the remaking of America. The loving, maternal, and adoptive image of mothers nurturing an international family proved a popular alternative to combative discourses of masculinization and American imperialism in the Cold War context.[60] The expansionist discourse was softened by the imagery of women building a bridge across racial lines, all the while staying within the boundaries of the domestic sphere. Furthermore, the fact that female Christians vocalized their Christian faith seemed restorative after decades of war and blood. The once-held confidence in Christendom had been eradicated and the Christian West's morality had become dubious after decades of bloodshed. Amid this damage to the reputation of Western Christianity, missionaries' efforts in anti-imperialistic, anti-racist humanitarian projects offered hope to a cynical country.

Helen Doss reconceptualized the "ideal family," once defined as a traditional nuclear family, as a family based on real love and commitment. To her, colorblind love was sufficient to replace kinship based on blood and biology. By doing so, she also fought the racism that was deeply rooted in American society. The Doss family embodied several American qualities at their finest—sacrifice, familial love, patriotism, love for democracy, and equality for all. Their story touched so many Americans' hearts because their audiences recognized that they were what an ideal American family ought to symbolize. While this multicultural family was unusual for its time, the values it represented were increasingly shared by Americans of the 1950s.

Conclusion

Christianity, Race, Gender, and Family-Making

While the adoption evangelists discussed in this book detached themselves from the geopolitical agenda of the United States government, they worked in the context of Cold War democracy, often evoking the rhetoric of internationalism, American exceptionalism, and anti-communism. By doing so, they both purposely and inadvertently contributed to the broader project of Cold War internationalism and cross-cultural engagement. Furthermore, although their writings reveal the distinction between Christian Americanism and the Christian theology to which they subscribed, the media coverage of the adoption evangelists tended to blur the line between the two. The media combined the rhetoric of American patriotism and religious fervor to create a strong case for transnational adoption that appealed to the public.

It has become evident that transnational adoption represented something bigger than the phenomenon itself. What appeared as the seemingly private realm of family-making was part of the bigger social change initiated by adoption evangelists: anti-racism and the promotion of global friendship through kinship and familial intimacy. As John McLeod argues, transnational adoption was "central and not marginal to wider global tensions."[1] The family was the most fundamental social institution; it was the site where economic, social, and political relations developed. Adoption evangelists themselves emphasized in their writings that transnational adoption extended beyond the private realm, as it involved complex issues such as race, inequality, war politics, and foreign relations.

Adoption evangelists' transnational adoption activity was multifaceted, complicated and nuanced, with both positive and negative effects. On the positive side, adoption evangelists—through their anti-racist rhetoric and unconventional family-making—popularized and normalized the practice of adopting transracially. Their example empowered women to participate in a transnational movement in an unprecedented way. However, they also tended to neglect Asian children's racial and ethnic heritage and at times exhibited a sense of Western superiority and American exceptionalism. The transnational adoption movement also reinforced the idea that women's highest calling was to serve in the domestic sphere. Throughout the chapters of this book, some common themes in transnational adoption have emerged. First, the Christian faith played a vital role in shaping the foundation and methodology of both evangelical and ecumenical Christians. Second, adoption evangelists made significant contributions to the anti-racism movement, yet demonstrated paternalism despite their good intentions. Third, transnational adoption was a gendered movement, at once reinforcing and deconstructing traditional gender norms.

Evangelical and Ecumenical Christianity

As we have seen, evangelical and ecumenical Christians had different purposes, audiences, and methodologies regarding the practice of transnational adoption. First, evangelicals' self-identified purpose was spiritual in nature. Although meeting the physical needs of children was important to Pierce and Swanson, their primary goal was to bring spiritual salvation by educating the children. Similarly, the Holts' goal of "bringing the seed from the East" ultimately meant bringing the children to spiritual conversion. Through evangelical social activist films, World Vision and ESEA advertised the notion of evangelizing children through virtual adoption. Harry Holt reiterated multiple times in his newsletters that his final goal was to place abandoned children in Christian homes so that they might be converted. In contrast, ecumenical Christians' purpose was social. Pearl Buck, in particular, distanced herself from the rhetoric of spiritual conversion and emphasized cooperation among various religious traditions. Fighting institutional and systemic racism was her priority, and to achieve this end, she advocated religious pluralism and the peaceful collaboration of different faiths. With undivided attention, she sought to establish an anti-racist, anti-imperialist, and cosmopolitan outlook on a societal level. Similarly, although less explicitly, Helen Doss demonstrated that her goal was to fight racism and spread colorblind love. Through their potent prose and narratives, these two women mainline Christians contributed significantly to eradicating the matching system in the adoption landscape.

Second, the evangelical missionaries' main audience was their fellow conservative Christians. The recalcitrant fundamentalists who disengaged from mainstream society did not listen to them. However, to the emerging neo-evangelicals, who were already craving increased and meaningful social engagement, their message was powerful and effective. As a founding force of neo-evangelicalism, Pierce and Swanson made an important contribution to the evangelical niche by awakening the evangelical social conscience. The Holts solidified this social conscience and demanded an evangelical social commitment, all the while creating intense friction with social workers. Ironically, the conflict in some ways worked in their favor, as the persecution trope gave a stronger sense of purpose and determination to the conservative "Holt followers." Pearl Buck and Helen Doss, for their part, reached broader audiences thanks to their powerful prose and balanced rhetoric. As a prolific writer and social activist, Buck used her social platform to actively fight for Amerasian children. Doss, similarly, moved countless people's hearts and minds through her books and frequent television appearances. While her idea of global friendship and her perspective on racism closely resembled Buck's, Doss was able to translate her ecumenist stance into a theologically neutral language that appealed to a broad spectrum of readers.

Third, the methodology used to spread the adoption movement differed significantly between the evangelical and ecumenical Christians. Evangelicals relied heavily on religious jargon and insider language. Pierce, Swanson, and the Holts used dramatic founding myths to generate a unifying force that inspired evangelicals with a sense of purpose and "calling" due to its supernatural and spiritual nature. Due to their beliefs, they worked mainly with other evangelicals—Harry Holt, as we have seen, was famous for accepting applications from "born-again" Christian parents only. They also used vivid imagery, films, and narratives that emphasized the rhetoric of "us" versus "them." In many of their newsletters and films, the conservative missionaries contrasted poor, destitute, exotic, and foreign Asian countries with the wealthy, Christian, and civilized United States. Moreover, the evangelical missionaries stressed individual needs, distancing themselves from discussions of the systemic, structural issues of poverty and racism.

Pearl Buck, however, avoided religious jargon and was not reluctant to criticize the church for being self-serving. Buck wrote passionately about collaborating with other denominations, religions, and agencies to achieve the goal of extinguishing racism and racial matching. To that end, in her book *Children for Adoption*, Pearl Buck criticized the Holt's exclusive approach. She was unsettled by the Holts' "distinctly fundamentalist" questionnaire. After meeting Harry in person, she wrote that while she still disagreed with the approach the Holts' agency used, she understood that given the urgent circumstances of the mixed-race children, affording them a chance to live was the top priority.[2] It is noteworthy that she was able to relinquish her deep-seated disgust at fundamentalism in order to peacefully and effectively collaborate. In a similar way, Helen Doss stayed neutral in her religious language. Rather than focusing on evangelizing the children, her goal remained consistent: promoting global friendship and racial equality. Finally, the two female adoption evangelists fought poverty and racism on the structural and institutional levels. Although they were deeply involved with individual children, they also advocated for sustained social change.

Despite their differences, evangelical and ecumenical Christians together managed to reconstruct Americans' perception of race and family. The two groups' purposes, audiences, and methodologies differed, but their distinct forms of action and rhetoric contributed to the making of the transnational adoption movement. Both groups fought racism, albeit to different degrees; both groups proposed a "new type of family" for Americans obsessed with creating a postwar nuclear family; both groups reconceptualized Asians as innocuous and adoptable children; both groups appealed to the general public, not to the government. The evangelicals' social consciences, the ecumenists' anti-racist activity, and the latter's rhetoric of global friendship concertedly led to the inauguration of the transnational adoption movement.

Race Issues

The Christians involved in transnational adoption were both catalysts for and part of the broader movement of anti-racism. Robert Pierce and

Everett Swanson portrayed Korean children with vivid imagery, countering the violent images of Asians that had permeated America. Softening
the hearts of Americans was the key to the success of the adoption movement, because through this work, Asians came to be viewed no longer as
threats, but as objects of compassion and rescue. Harry and Bertha Holt,
likewise, emphasized that God's love triumphed over racial differences.
More implicitly, they advocated a colorblind society where all children
were viewed simply as God's creation. While the Holts did not make an
explicit connection between their adoption practice and the civil rights
movement, the spirit of human equality was the common denominator of
the two movements. The shift in the Christian attitude and the increased
opposition to racism helped pave the way for the early civil rights period.
The ecumenist Pearl Buck believed that through transracial adoption,
systemic racism could be eliminated. Doss also defended racial minorities and the principle of human equality based on the common human
dignity given by God. Doss translated Buck's ideas and ideology into anecdotes that moved ordinary Americans' hearts. They both advocated global
friendship across racial divisions as a statement of unity and solidarity.

Although both evangelical and ecumenical Christians contributed in
varying degrees in transforming American's outlook on race issues, their
methodology, as we have seen, was not above reproach. For example,
many of the conservative missionaries, influenced by Orientalist stereotypes, accentuated the differences and otherness of Asian children. In
evangelical humanitarian films, Korea was depicted as an exotic, strange,
and poverty-stricken country, in sharp contrast to the United States.
Moreover, the paternalistic nature of much of white American Christianity at the time made itself felt in the practice of transnational adoption. The missionaries' primary assumption was that life in America was
automatically better than life in Asia, even if children had to be separated from their homeland to reap the benefits of American life. Harry
and Bertha Holt used the language of "saving" and "rescuing" the children from calamity, often infused with the rhetoric of the white man's
burden. The emphasis was specifically on the Christian white man's burden, but the dichotomy between the Christian, civilized America and
the heathen, uncivilized Asia was the underlying assumption.

Another shortcoming was Pearl Buck's rhetoric of hybrid superiority
and the aspects of her narrative that strengthened the model minor-

ity stereotype. By recasting Asian Americans as law-abiding, harmless, and successful "model" immigrants and obscuring the country's systemic racism against black Americans, the model minority stereotype drove a racial wedge between Asian Americans and African Americans. Buck's narrative transformed Asian children from impoverished waifs to model adoptees who would flawlessly assimilate into white homes, treating the Asian children's ethnic heritage as largely inconsequential. Closely related to the model minority stereotype was the colorblindness trope that both evangelical and ecumenical Christians deployed. Colorblindness emphasizes what all humans have in common rather than directly addressing racial hierarchies. As we have seen, however, a racial hierarchy unquestionably existed in the transnational adoption scene. The language of colorblindness often glossed over preexisting racial inequalities. Moreover, the colorblind approach, like the model minority stereotype, focused on the assimilative potential of Asian children, often discounting their racial and ethnic roots. They were expected, in other words, to live as "honorary whites."

Despite their shortcomings, adoption evangelists made the transnational adoption movement possible. The impressive accomplishment of the evangelicals is their success at arousing the evangelical social conscience and nudging their co-religionists into social commitment. However modest, their anti-racist beliefs and rhetoric effected change for the better within the conservative Christian niche. Ecumenical Christians' most notable achievement was putting an end to the racial matching system. Buck and Doss, through their compelling writings, actively and directly fought against racial matching. Furthermore, they fostered cross-cultural engagement through their championing of global friendship and cosmopolitanism.

A Gendered Movement

The adoption evangelists' practice of transnational adoption simultaneously reinforced and departed from traditional gender norms. On one hand, the movement was consistent with the traditional Victorian view of family and gender roles. For example, male evangelical missionaries were portrayed as embodying stereotypical masculine qualities such as determination, strength, and tenacity. Evangelistic associations such as

Youth for Christ and the Christian Businessmen's Committee bred male evangelists and ecclesial leaders who carried on the legacy of male leadership. In contrast, women were discouraged from holding positions of ecclesial leadership and from entering the workforce, particularly during the postwar boom. At home, the language of male headship and female submission abounded, and many men worked as the sole breadwinners of their families while their wives were homemakers. The ideology of the "filiarchy" re-domesticated women amid the American obsession with nuclear families.

At times, traditional gender norms had less oppressive effects. For example, imagery related to mothers ameliorated the dominant combative discourses of masculinization and American imperialism in the Cold War context. Expansionist discourse was softened by the rhetoric of motherhood while staying within the socially accepted boundaries of the filiarchy. The language of personal commitment and motherhood was used by female Christians across denominational lines. They also exploited their ability to move people's hearts via powerful sentimentalism, a stereotypically feminine form of communication that proved remarkably effective at stirring their readers to action.

Furthermore, the adoption narrative was a crucial vehicle for disseminating women's voices. Stories written by adoptive fathers and male adoptees were scarce, and virtually nothing was published by birth fathers, who were usually absent from the children's lives. In adoption narratives, mothers, who exerted power and authority in the domestic sphere, told their stories in a confessional and intimate style. This gendered aspect of the adoption narrative is important because adoption was a rare social phenomenon in which the hands and faces of the actions matched. In other words, women were the impetus that drove the adoption movement, and they were also the first to voice their opinions and stories. These women's adoption narratives also functioned as an important restorative force in Christian mission. Through these narratives, mission was reframed in a Christian internationalist language, focusing on anti-racist, anti-imperialist humanitarian works and lifelong Christian witness instead of rigid indoctrination and Western imperialism. Finally, the transnational adoption movement offered a form of liberation from traditional gender norms by allowing women to be leaders in an important social movement. Buck, for example, exhorted women to participate in fighting racism, criticizing women who had retreated so far into domesticity that they were indifferent to pressing global and social issues.

Contemporary Transnational Adoption

Transnational adoption was part of the larger social movement of anti-racism and global friendship led by missionaries of the 1950s. America's postwar global influence coincided with the emergence of evangelicalism and a culture focused on familial values. Simultaneously, the black migration into the American industrial north and the transnational adoption movement created the preconditions for the anti-racist movement and civil rights movement. Missionaries played pivotal roles in breaking down racial barriers during the postwar era. What Robert Pierce and Everett Swanson did through their sponsorship program of Korean children was in sync with Billy Graham's mixed-race campaigns and anti-racist movement. Together, these conservative leaders created a neo-evangelicalism that meaningfully addressed the social needs of the world, providing a much-needed corrective to Christian fundamentalism.[3]

The upper-middle class cultural dominance of white evangelicals was challenged by Christians like Pearl Buck, who pointed out their hypocrisy. Pearl Buck and Helen Doss together reminded their readers of the radical nature of Christianity. Harry and Bertha Holt, by actively engaging in saving children, broke the conventional conservative Christian paradigm by introducing an alternative to the social gospel of the 1920s: they incorporated a social justice element that was lacking in evangelicalism. They protested against the war, racism, and inequality in many forms.[4] The adoption evangelists who brought the transnational adoption movement to the United States reshaped race and familial issues and remain important resources for investigations concerning international adoption today.

It is important to note that the historical context of the adoption evangelists differed vastly from our context today. In the 1950s, they initiated the movement as a direct relief response. The demand for children of mixed Asian heritage was much lower during their time, and they had to actively work to promote transnational adoption, an innovative practice motivated by their Christian beliefs. Their priority was the well-being of the mixed-race children, and the parents' needs were second-ary. In contrast, the demand for children on the part of infertile parents is significantly higher today. Moreover, due to rapid globalization, the willingness to adopt foreign children has increased during the past decade. Unfortunately, in this climate of increased demand and decreased supply of healthy babies, the international adoption movement has become a billion-dollar industry with countless forms of malpractice.

While both evangelical and ecumenical Christians' efforts were in many ways valuable, we see a consistent impulse to "use" the adoptees to achieve a broader goal—evangelicals saw adoption as a means to achieve evangelism; ecumenical dreamed of actualizing racial harmony and global friendship. Caught between such lofty goals, many adoptees had little chance to create their own narratives until recently. Listening to some of their voices helps us to examine the possibilities and limitations of Christian humanitarianism, and particularly how the adoption evangelists of the 1950s helped to redefine traditional family values and attitudes toward race in contemporary America. By connecting the dots between history and current trends in transnational adoption, child sponsorship programs, and evangelical missions, we can explore whether they had an enduring effect on contemporary American society as a whole.

Contemporary Evangelical Orphan Crisis

In recent years, the evangelical "orphan crisis" has come to the fore. Conservative Christians have urged action, citing 163 million orphans around the world who are in need of permanent homes. This commonly cited number comes from statistics collected by UNICEF that identify 163 million orphans worldwide. UNICEF's statistics include "single orphans," children who still have one living parent. In 2015, 15.1 million were "double orphans" who had lost both parents. Most single orphans live with a surviving parent or extended family, and ninety-five percent of all orphans are over the age of five, older than the typical age of adoption.[5] Rather than focusing on efforts to support the local families and communities that care for the orphans, many evangelical agencies misrepresent the statistics, claiming that there are 163 million orphans in need of adoptive families. To illustrate, Bethany Christian Services, America's largest adoption agency, announced triumphantly in 2011 that adoption placements through the organization had increased by nearly 13 percent from 2009 to 2010, claiming that "with more than 163 million orphans around the world, it is greatly encouraging to see so many people willing to provide a loving home to a child in need of one."[6]

In recent years, UNICEF has included a statement on its website correcting the misinterpretation and distinguishing single orphans from double orphans. Despite this effort, UNICEF's orphan statistics are constantly quoted to invoke a sense of urgency and strengthen the narrative of the "evangelical orphan crisis." The resulting adoption boom has been contested and criticized from many perspectives, including the view that characterizes such adoptions as child trafficking and child abuse. The complex issues of race, religion, Western imperialism, and identity formation also play important roles in the experiences of both parents and children. Horror stories of failed adoptions that have reached the international media have further complicated the issue.

Evangelical rhetoric about the orphan crisis bears striking similarities to Harry Holt's orphan salvation trope. At the heart of both Holt's adoption practice and orphan crisis rhetoric is the sense of divine mission. Russell Moore, president of the Ethics and Religious Liberty Commission of the Southern Baptist Convention, stresses just such a mission:

> Adoption is, on the one hand, *gospel*. In this, adoption tells us who we are as children of the Father. Adoption as gospel tells us about our identity, our inheritance, and our mission as sons of God. Adoption is also defined as *mission*. In this, adoption tells us our purpose in this age as the people of Christ. Missional adoption spurs us to join Christ in advocating for the helpless and the abandoned.[7]

Like Moore, many conservative proponents of adoption equate legal adoption to the gospel and the mission of God, much like Harry Holt's view of adoption as obedience to a direct command from God to bring "sons from the East." It can be inferred from Moore's statement that he is drawing a parallel between a theology of adoption and literal legal adoption. Such parallels are commonly found in other evangelical organizations as well. Elizabeth Styffe, the director of Global Orphan Care

Initiatives at Saddleback Church (one of the largest evangelical orphan care ministries), has commented that "when we were orphans, God adopted us."[8] Quoting from Ephesians 1:4–6, she uses the spiritual metaphor of theology of adoption to advocate the legal adoption movement to combat the orphan crisis, arguing that God's "spiritual adoption" must encourage Christians to pursue "physical adoption."[9] Many Christian advocates of the contemporary adoption movement perceive legal adoption as the primary means of understanding Christians' relationship with God, citing the vertical spiritual adoption of God's people.

The salvation narratives (both spiritual and physical) of the orphans in the 1950s continue to be a predominant impetus on the contemporary evangelical orphan scene. In a spiritual sense, contemporary evangelicals, like Holt, view adoption as a necessary means to communicate the gospel to the children. Stories of rescuing orphans from "heathen" (a term that today is implied rather than stated) countries and bringing them to salvation abound in Christian adoption testimonies.[10] In a physical sense, children are being rescued from developing countries and brought to white, upper-middle class, capitalist America, where food, shelter, and a nuclear family are provided. Sandra Patton-Imani argues that the focus on the nuclear family and the emphasis on rescuing the "fatherless" (that is, the children of single mothers) silences the birth mothers who are often left with no choice but to relinquish their children.[11] The contemporary orphan narrative reframes both single and double orphans as abandoned children in need of Western salvation from the horrors of war, physical and spiritual poverty, communism, and single motherhood.

The biblical basis for adoption has been one of the most controversial topics regarding the Christian responsibility to orphans. Many people who criticize Christians for the theology behind adoption argue that passages like "a father to the fatherless" (Psalms 68:5) cannot be applied literally to promote the adoption movement.[12] Moreover, the metaphorical "theology of adoption" that Paul outlines in the Book of Romans should not be exegeted in a way that advocates the legal adoption of children. The adoption metaphor Paul uses in describing salvation and Christians' relationship with God lacks any reference to the kind of adoption in practiced in the contemporary movement. The over-spiritualizing of adoption has created the unintended consequence of implying that the practice of non–family-related adoption will hasten God's kingdom. In this rhetoric, we once again discover the impulse to use children for the sake of accomplishing the greater goal of evangelism.

Another parallel between the adoption evangelists of the 1950s and advocates of the contemporary adoption boom is the use of sentimentalism and vivid imagery. The contemporary Christian adoption literature is permeated by a sense of triumphalism and optimism. Using sentimentalist rhetoric, these proponents of adoption passionately urge Christians to end the orphan crisis for good by providing permanent homes for the orphans. They predict that if every church member were actively involved in orphan ministries, the orphan crisis would be over.[13] World Vision and Compassion International continue to use vivid imagery and personalized photos of children to evoke compassion and a sense of burden. Such appeals to optimism and emotionalism, as we have seen, were commonly used by evangelical missionaries of the first half of the twentieth century and by the adoption evangelists who followed in their footsteps.

Combining the orphan salvation trope and sentimentalism, contemporary evangelicals echo their predecessors in effectively crafting a religious narrative of rescue. In this story of salvation, Christian Americans who hold deeply traditional family values are the solutions to family breakdown, single motherhood, teenage pregnancy, illegitimacy, institutionalization, and at-risk children. The problem with this religious narrative is the innate power inequality between the adoptive parents and the children, not merely within individual families, but also in the larger social and global context. Deeply embedded in the rescue narrative is what Khyati Joshi calls white Christian privilege, or the notion that Christian privilege and white privilege are entwined in American culture.[14] Evangelical salvation narratives assume Christian normativity and Western superiority and use the rhetoric of the white man's burden, conveying the desire to both civilize and Christianize the impoverished children at the cost of uprooting them from their native roots and dismantling their biological families (in the case of single orphans). Moreover, the emphasis on the white Christian burden diverts attention from the deeper issue of the socioeconomic circumstances of many countries in the global South that result in child relinquishment.[15]

Contemporary Colorblind Racism

One of the most noticeable themes found in the writings of Bertha Holt, Pearl Buck, and Helen Doss is the notion of colorblind love. To varying degrees, these Christian women embraced the ideology of colorblindness that became prominent in the 1950s and 1960s in the context of the civil rights movement and global anti-racist cosmopolitanism. They expressed the ideal of a nonracial society where skin color played no role for individuals or for society as a whole. As discussed before, however, colorblind racism often deemed Asian children's ethnic heritage inconsequential and glossed over the systemic racism that many children—particularly Afro-Asians—were facing. Because the adoption evangelists focused on human commonalities rather than distinctiveness, many parents who adopted children through missionary agencies were ill-equipped to address the issues pertaining to racial identity and inequality that their children faced in their communities.

Contemporary adoption literature, films, and documentaries offer poignant narratives of the consequences of colorblindness for adopted children's racial and ethnic identities. Adult adoptees who were adopted as children from the 1950s onward have begun to tell their own stories, countering the dominant narrative of rescue and charity. The stories demonstrate how the initial desirability and malleability of Asian adoptees had negative repercussions as the adoptees grew older and realized that society treated them differently. Many of those who, as honorary whites, did not face racism at home were perplexed when they went off to school or started working, for their parents and communities had not equipped them to navigate the reality of living as ethnic minorities. The narratives also capture the internal struggle many Asian and mixed-race adoptees experienced as they noticed they looked different from their white families. Many of the adoptees' parents, believing that love would conquer all, failed to address adoptees' developing identities as ethnic minorities growing up in a dominant culture.

In the documentary *Adopted* (2008), for example, Jennifer Fero vividly communicated her struggles with ethnic identity formation and constant need to overcompensate by seeking love and attention in order to feel that she belonged. During an interview, she remarked, "My family tells me many times, we see you as one of us. Well, one of us is a white working-class kid with blue eyes and big ears . . . like my family, I saw myself as a white . . . and that's why when I look myself in the mirror I would be surprised."[16] She went on to say that if her family truly acknowledged her identity as an Asian woman, she would know that they had really adopted her, not an "idea" of her. She expressed a deep desire for a core validation of who she was and where she belonged in the world. She admitted that she was constantly searching for her identity. Recollecting her childhood memories of being bullied for her "Asianness," she shared a sense of grief that none of her family members had helped her through the process.[17]

When Jennifer started to confront her family as an adult, her parents did not know how to react. Judy and Paul Fero, who had adopted Jennifer through the Holt adoption agency, used the rhetoric of colorblindness during their interview. Judy admitted that she had a hard time "with the race thing."[18] She commented that she was raised not to see race and that colorblindness was a virtue. They agreed that all they could do was love her, implying that the racism Jennifer faced was beyond their control. Recollecting her difficult time trying to bond with an Asian girl whose "little eyes were just flat brown," Judy, much like Harry and Bertha Holt, demonstrated a sense of divine calling: "I started praying and I assumed that God gave me the child I was supposed to have."[19] Despite the lack of initial emotional connection, Judy was confident that Jennifer had been brought by God and that she was supposed to see her through the lens of colorblindness. Eric Fero, Jennifer's brother, corroborated his parents' perspective by commenting that the family still thought it was wrong to see Jennifer as "anything else" than their daughter. The Feros, in their own way, were trying to protect Jennifer from being hurt by avoiding the topic of race altogether. Unfortunately, doing so only left Jennifer feeling misunderstood, neglected, and confused.

Another couple in the documentary, John and Jacqui Trainer, was planning to adopt a girl from China. Their interview reveals that colorblindness continues to be a persistent trait of white parents who adopt transnationally. John remarked, "We could've chosen Russia and we could've had a child that looked like us, but we didn't really want to do that, we really embrace diversity and that's what we want."[20] Jacqui also commented that skin color did not really matter to them because love transcends skin color, and race is an insignificant factor in familial love. The Trainers were also following the recent trend on the adoption scene of trying to incorporate "culture keeping," the notion that adopted children must be exposed to their birth culture.[21] This assumption is a dominant view held by many recent white middle-class adoptive parents. Unlike in the 1950s, contemporary adoptive parents have ample cross-cultural educational resources, and many adoption agencies provide cultural trainings for parents.

Despite the good intentions, there are two inherent problems with the ways adoptive parents practice culture keeping. First, since many parents focus on visible aspects of culture—holidays, clothing, food, and so on—the deeper, more nuanced aspects of culture are often ignored. The selective adaptation of visible cultural elements results in commodified versions of culture, or what the anthropologist Ann Anagnost calls "culture bites."[22] The bigger problem is that in many cases, a focus on commodified and decontextualized Asian cultural elements may result in a shallow understanding of multiculturalism, not unlike the superficial solution of colorblindness.[23] The focus on visible, decontextualized elements of Asian culture may give a false sense of security to parents who, as a result, may ignore the deep-rooted problems of racial identity or racial power relations. To have any value, visible culture keeping must be accompanied by sustained efforts to help the adoptees navigate the complex issues of race, power, white privilege (particularly white Christian privilege), and identity formation.

The Possibilities and Limitations of Adoption Evangelists

As we have seen, many evangelical adoption agencies and orphan care ministries use language that closely resembles the Holts' rhetoric about the spiritual and physical salvation of Asian children. Many of the evangelical organizations that focus their efforts on transnational adoption have inherited Holts' trope of the orphan crisis and their sense of divine mission. World Vision and Compassion International remain the two pillars of Christian child sponsorship programs. Although their religious language has faded over the decades, their mission and values remain grounded in religious conviction. Beginning in the 1970s, ecumenical Christians increasingly distanced themselves from transnational adoption and relinquished the task of facilitating it to social workers and secular adoption agencies. For example, instead of placing children for adoption, Pearl S. Buck International now provides intercultural education and humanitarian aid to children around the world, continuing Buck's legacy of philanthropy focused on global friendship.

Did the adoption evangelists have an abiding effect on the American racial and familial landscape in contemporary America? While the Western norm of the nuclear family is still intact, the adoption evangelists of the 1950s extended the definition of family to include children of different races. Whereas on the transnational adoption scene of the 1950s there existed a clear racial hierarchy with black children at the bottom, contemporary Christians—and evangelicals in particular—have become more open to adopting children from Africa. Moreover, there are various cross-cultural educational programs (Holt International in particular) for adoptive parents as well as numerous opportunities for adoptees to forge community bonds with each other. Post-adoption services also increasingly help parents navigate cultural issues. With the surge of negative testimonies and adoption narratives by adult adoptees, many international adoption organizations are concentrating their efforts on ensuring the cross-cultural competence of the potential adoptive parents.

While the adoption evangelists had modest enduring effects on the American racial landscape, the rhetoric of colorblindness continues to be problematic in transnational adoption circles. The language that many contemporary adoptive parents use bears striking similarities to the adoption evangelists' language of colorblind love, often obscuring the intractable, institutional nature of racism and failing to equip children of color to form healthy ethnic identities. The greatest peril of the colorblind love rhetoric continues to be the focus on individual efforts to fight racism. The adoption evangelists emphasized the relational aspect of racial reconciliation and argued that racial justice was the parents' individual responsibility rather than understanding race as a shaper of social outcomes. They tended to view racism as the result of individual prejudice, not as a longstanding system that unjustly benefits whites over ethnic minorities. Contemporary leaders of the evangelical orphan care movement also use similar language. Johnny Carr, in his book *Orphan Justice*, argues that racism is a "heart issue," not an institutional issue that can be remedied by government intervention. His solution to racism in

America is "confronting the racist in each one of us" by understanding the gospel.[24]

Many East Asian countries that have had to rely on foreign powers in regard to child welfare have started to see the negative consequences of transnational adoption. The ethnic identity crisis, a number of reported cases of abuse, and Asians' increasing openness to domestic adoption are some of the factors that have slowed down transnational adoption rates. In South Korea, for example, transnational adoption increased steadily after the Korean War erupted in 1950 and peaked during the turbulent decade of the 1970s. In recent years, due to the Korean government's effort to place children through domestic adoption, the rate of international adoption has decreased significantly. In 1999, 1,994 Korean children were adopted in the U.S. In 2018, there were only 206 adoptees.[25] Compared to the 1950s, this is a welcome change that enables Asian children to stay in their homeland, sparing them the agony of going through an ethnic identity crisis in addition to dealing with the sense of abandonment and the overcompensating need for love that are not uncommon among adoptees.

The adoption evangelists accomplished a great deal during their time by filling a gap that the government could not reach. However, the grassroots nature of their movement also produced adoptive parents and Christians in general who tended to view racial issues as exclusively an individual responsibility rather than as a systemic, governmental issue. Furthermore, while adoption evangelists genuinely wanted Asian and mixed-race children to find loving homes, they also strove to achieve the grander goals of evangelism and global friendship. However, to borrow Jennifer Fero's words, this was simply "too big of a burden" for young children who were already struggling to adapt to new surroundings and different-looking families.[26] The grassroots nature of the transnational adoption movement opened up far-reaching possibilities for adoption evangelists, but it also limited Christians' willingness and ability to fight the larger system that enabled individual prejudice against Amerasian children.

ACKNOWLEDGMENTS

This book is the result of countless people's collaborative efforts. I am deeply thankful for my advisor Dana Robert, who inspired me to become a better scholar and a teacher. Her academic passion and integrity have been a constant motivation and example. I am also grateful for Xiyi Yao for his wisdom and encouragement. His thoughtful guidance and attention to detail helped me immensely. Thanks goes to Carolyn Chen at UC Berkeley Department of Ethnic Studies for her openness and advice.

I received generous funding from the West Virginia and Regional History Center (WVRHC), University of Kassel, and Council of Christian Colleges & Universities for the book. I am thankful for archivists, librarians, and student workers at the WVRHC, the Social Welfare History Archives at the University of Minnesota, Randolph College, Swarthmore College, Presbyterian Historical Society, World Vision Central Records, University of Oregon, and Columbia University. Their help and support made countless hours at these various archives productive and enjoyable. Thanks goes to colleagues who inspired and helped me along the way. Special thanks belong to Allison Van Deventer, Daryl Ireland, Sung Deuk Oak, Heather Curtis, Russell Jeung, Rita Nakashima Brock, Teddy Hickman-Maynard, Jane Hong, Laura Briggs, and anonymous reviewers at New York University Press who gave thorough and thoughtful feedback. Jennifer Hammer at NYU Press was a strong advocate for me and provided invaluable advice and support throughout the revision process.

Portions of my book was published in my article "Mother of Transracial Adoption: Pearl Buck's Special Needs Adoption and American Self-Criticism," *Studies in World Christianity* 25, no. 3 (December 2019): 345–66. A revised version of chapter three appeared in "The Missiology of Pearl Sydenstricker Buck," *International Bulletin of Mission Research* 41, no. 2 (April 2017): 134–41. Thanks goes to anonymous reviewers who provided helpful comments and editors who made the publication process enjoyable.

I am indebted to my parents, Dong Geun Chung and Jung Hee Moon, for always guiding and enabling me to pursue my dream. I am grateful to my parents-in-law, John Lee and Joann Lee, for their unwavering support. Thanks goes to my brothers Samuel Chung and John Chung who helped me find my topic and sister-in-law Sharon Lee for encouraging me. Most of all, I am grateful for my husband Daniel Lee, who reminds me every day why I am called to academia.

NOTES

INTRODUCTION

1 The event was publicized in many newspapers at the time. See Gene Kramer, "'Pied Piper' Corrals 12 Korean Babies, Flies Them to America for Adoption," *Washington Post*, October 14, 1955.

2 The phrases *transnational adoption, international adoption*, and *intercountry adoption* denote an adoption between two countries. I use the term *transnational* to emphasize the transnational processes related to the global aspect of Christianity. In the 1950s, *intercountry adoption* was the dominant phrase used, as is reflected in direct quotes used in this book. Most of the transnational adoptions of the 1950s were also transracial adoptions. In Korea, the phrases *foreign adoption* (*kugoe ibyang*) and *overseas adoption* (*haeoe ibyang*) were commonly used. See Eleana J. Kim, *Adopted Territory: Transnational Korean Adoptees and the Politics of Belonging* (Durham, NC: Duke University Press, 2010), xiv.

3 The contemporary term used to indicate "any adoption across racial or ethnic lines, including what are probably the most frequent transracial adoptions in the United States—adoptions of Asian children by white parents" is "transracial adoption." However, in the 1950s, the term *mixed-race adoption* was frequently used. Mixed-race children were children born to parents of different races. In the context of the 1950s, *mixed-race children* almost exclusively referred to children born to American fathers and Asian mothers. In Korea, the convention of the time was to use the term *mixed-blood* (*honhyol*) children. *Full-blooded Korean* refers to a Korean child whose father and mother are both Korean. See Pamela Anne Quiroz, *Adoption in a Color-Blind Society* (Lanham, MD: Rowman & Littlefield Publishers, 2007), 42.

4 Susie Woo, *Framed by War: Korean Children and Women at the Crossroads of US Empire* (New York: New York University Press, 2019), 2.

5 David Peterson del Mar, *The American Family: From Obligation to Freedom* (New York: Palgrave Macmillan, 2011), 129.

6 Stephen A. Marglin and Juliet B. Schor, ed., *The Golden Age of Capitalism: Reinterpreting the Postwar Experience* (Oxford: Clarendon Press, 1992), 1; Robert Skidelsky, *Keynes: The Return of the Master* (New York: PublicAffairs, 2010), 116, 126.

7 Steven Mintz and Susan Kellogg, *Domestic Revolutions: A Social History of American Family Life* (New York: The Free Press, 1989), 182; Richard Reeves, *President Nixon: Alone in the White House* (New York: Simon & Schuster, 2002), 295.

8 Kellogg, *Domestic Revolutions*, 182.

9 Richard Rothstein, *The Color of Law: A Forgotten History of How Our Government Segregated America* (New York: Liveright Publishing Corporation, 2017).

10 James A. Kushner, "Urban Neighborhood Regeneration and the Phases of Community Evolution after World War II in the United States," *Indiana Law Review* 41, no. 3 (2008): 575–604.

11 del Mar, *The American Family*, 107.

12 Elaine Tyler May, *Barren in the Promised Land: Childless Americans and the Pursuit of Happiness* (New York: Basic Books, 1995), 138.

13 del Mar, *The American Family*, 105.

14 Quoted in Kellogg, *Domestic Revolutions*, 180; Betty Friedan, *The Feminine Mystique* (New York: W. W. Norton & Company, 1963), 42–43.

15 Carl R. Rogers, *On Becoming a Person: A Therapist's View of Psychotherapy* (Boston: Houghton Mifflin, 1961); del Mar, *The American Family*, 105.

16 Kellogg, *Domestic Revolutions*, 194; del Mar, *The American Family*, 105.

17 Kellogg, *Domestic Revolutions*, 184–185.

18 May, *Barren in the Promised Land*, 129.

19 Robert B. Westbrook, "'I Want a Girl, Just Like the Girl That Married Harry James': American Women and the Problem of Political Obligation in World War II," *American Quarterly* 42, no. 4 (1990), 587–614.

20 Joseph Adelson, "Is Women's Lib a Passing Fad?" *New York Times Magazine*, March 19, 1972.

21 Quoted in May, *Barren in the Promised Land*, 132; Louisa Randall Church, "Parents: Architects of Peace," *American Home*, November 1946, 18–19.

22 Ronald R. Rindfuss and James A. Sweet, *Postwar Fertility Trends and Differentials in the United States* (New York: Academic Press, 1977), 38

23 Kellogg, *Domestic Revolutions*, 180.

24 May, *Barren in the Promised Land*, 138–143.

25 Ellen D. Wu argues that World War II fostered the advent of racial liberalism: the growing belief in political circles that the country's racial diversity could be controlled through the assimilation of non-whites. This phenomenon caused Americans to undo the legal framework that relegated Asians outside the bounds of America. See Ellen D. Wu, *The Color of Success: Asian Americans and the Origins of the Model Minority* (Princeton, NJ: Princeton University Press, 2015), 3.

26 Quoted in Lon Kurashige, *Two Faces of Exclusion: The Untold History of Anti-Asian Racism in the United States* (Chapel Hill: University of North Carolina Press, 2016), 4; Congregational Record, 47th Cong., 1st sess., 1516 (March 1, 1882).

27 Yuki Yamazaki, "American Catholic Mission to Japanese in the United States: Their Intersection of Religion, Cultures, Generations, Genders, and Politics, 1910 to 1970" (Ph.D. dissertation, The Catholic University of America, 2011).

28 Ellen D. Wu, *The Color of Success: Asian Americans and the Origins of the Model Minority* (Princeton, NJ: Princeton University Press, 2014).

29 Kurashige, *Two Faces of Exclusion*, 229.

30 Jane Hong, *Opening the Gates of Asia: A Transpacific History of How America Repealed Asian Exclusion* (Chapel Hill: University of North Carolina Press, 2019), 3.

31 International Social Service–American Branch (ISS-USA), Box 10, "Children—Independent Adoption Schemes, Holt, Harry, vol. I, 1955–1957," Social Welfare History Archives (SWHA), University of Minnesota, Minneapolis, MN.

32 Ellen Herman, *Kinship by Design: A History of Adoption in the Modern United States* (Chicago: University of Chicago Press, 2009), 221.

33 International Social Service–American Branch (ISS-USA), Box 10, "Children—Independent Adoption Schemes, Holt, Harry, vol. I, 1955–1957," Social Welfare History Archives (SWHA), University of Minnesota, Minneapolis, MN.

34 "Operation Baby Lift," World Vision International Central Records.

35 Karen Dubinsky, *Babies Without Borders: Adoption and Migration across the Americas* (New York: New York University Press, 2010), 94.

36 Arissa Oh, *To Save the Children of Korea: The Cold War Origins of International Adoption* (Stanford, CA: Stanford University Press, 2015), 7.

37 U.S. Department of State–Bureau of Consular Affairs, https://travel.state.gov/content/travel/en/Intercountry-Adoption/adopt_ref/adoption-statistics.html.

38 Catherine Ceniza Choy, *Global Families: A History of Asian International Adoption in America* (New York: New York University Press, 2013), 49.

39 Elaine Tyler May, *Barren in the Promised Land: Childless Americans and the Pursuit of Happiness* (New York: Basic Books, 1995), 138. See also Steven Mintz and Susan Kellogg, *Domestic Revolutions: A Social History of American Family Life* (New York: The Free Press, 1989).

40 Kim, *Adopted Territory*, 24.

41 Kim, *Adopted Territory*, 45; Oh, *To Save the Children of Korea*, 1–2.

42 Unless directly quoting, I avoid using the term *orphan* unless it is clearly indicated that the child lost both parents. However, when referring to Korean children in general who needed a home, I use the term *orphans* in the plural form.

43 U.S. Department of State–Bureau of Consular Affairs. https://travel.state.gov/content/travel/en/Intercountry-Adoption/adopt_ref/adoption-statistics.html.

44 See, for example, Hyun Martin, *I Survived Childhood: A Memoir of Abandonment, Betrayal and Healing* (Be You Spa Inc., 2017); Thomas Park Clement, *Dust of the Streets: The Journey of a Biracial Orphan of the Korean War* (Bloomfield, IN: Truepenny Publishing Company, 2012); Julayne Lee, *Not My White Savior* (Los Angeles: Rare Bird Books, 2018); Jane Jeong Trenka, *Fugitive Visions: An Adoptee's Return to Korea* (Saint Paul, MN: Graywolf Press, 2009); Marijane Huang, *Beyond Two Worlds: A Taiwanese-American Adoptee's Memoir & Search for Identity* (Bloomington, IN: AuthorHouse, 2017).

45 Glenn Morey and Julie Morey, "Given Away: Korean Adoptees Share Their Stories," *New York Times*, July 23, 2019, www.nytimes.com/2019/07/23/opinion/korean-adoptees.html?fbclid=IwAR3Vn92w31BKi-4ZIFpPCBiidT_prBo7hytXyZX-heuhtOtxiWhojMsP_rPc.

46 There are countless articles and studies about the psychological damage involved in adoption. See, for example, Robert P. Knight, "Some Problems in Selecting and Rearing Adopted Children," *Bulletin of the Menninger Clinic* 5 (1941): 65–74; Elsie Stonesifer, "The Behavior Difficulties of Adopted and Own Children," *Smith College Studies in Social Work* 13 (1942): 161; Portia Holman, "Some Factors in the Aetiology of Maladjusted Children," *Journal of Mental Science* 99 (1953): 654–88; Bernice T. Eiduson and Jean B. Livermore, "Complications in Therapy with Adopted Children," *American Journal of Orthopsychiatry* 23 (1953): 795–802; Betty K. Ketchum, "An Exploratory Study of the Disproportionate Number of Adopted Children Hospitalized at Columbus Children's Psychiatric Hospital" (MA thesis, Ohio State University, 1962); Jeffrey J. Haugaard, "Is Adoption a Risk Factor for the Development of Adjustment Problems?," *Clinical Psychology Review* 18, no. 1 (1998): 47–69.

47 E. Wellisch, "Children Without Genealogy—A Problem of Adoption," *Mental Health* 13 (1952): 41–42. See also Marshall D. Schechter, "Observations on Adopted Children," *Archives of General Psychiatry* 3 (1960): 21–32.

48 For historical analyses of transnational adoption, see Christina Klein, *Cold War Orientalism: Asia in the Middlebrow Imagination, 1945–1961* (Berkeley: University of California Press, 2003); Eleana J. Kim, *Adopted Territory: Transnational Korean Adoptees and the Politics of Belonging* (Durham, NC: Duke University Press Books, 2010); Laura Briggs, *Somebody's Children: The Politics of Transracial and Transnational Adoption* (Durham, NC: Duke University Press, 2012); Choy, *Global Families*; Oh, *To Save the Children of Korea*; Woo, *Framed by War*; Kori A. Graves, *A War Born Family: African American Adoption in the Wake of the Korean War* (New York: New York University Press, 2020).

49 Dana Robert contends that most Pentecostal ministries of compassion were spearheaded by women missionaries and lay leaders. See Dana L. Robert, *American Women in Mission: The Modern Mission Era 1792–1992* (Macon, GA: Mercer University Press, 1997).

50 David A. Hollinger, *Protestants Abroad: How Missionaries Tried to Change the World but Changed America* (Princeton, NJ: Princeton University Press, 2017).

51 See Douglas A. Sweeney, "The Essential Evangelicalism Dialectic: The Historiography of the Early Neo-Evangelical Movement and the Observer-Participant Dilemma," *Church History* 60, no. 1 (1991): 70–84; Joel A. Carpenter, *Revive Us Again: The Reawakening of American Fundamentalism* (New York: Oxford University Press, 1999), 152.

52 Michael O. Emerson and Christian Smith, *Divided by Faith: Evangelical Religion and the Problem of Race in America* (New York: Oxford University Press, 2001), 2–3.

53 Dana L. Robert, "The First Globalization: The Internationalization of the Protestant Missionary Movement between the World Wars," *International Bulletin of Missionary Research*, 26, no. 2 (2002): 50.

54 The major archival collections that I have used are located at the West Virginia & Regional History Center (Morgantown, WV), Randolph College (Lynchburg,

VA), Union Theological Seminary (New York, NY), the Presbyterian Historical Society (Philadelphia, PA), Swarthmore College (Swarthmore, PA), the University of Minnesota (Minneapolis, MN), and the University of Oregon (Eugene, OR).

55 Eva Pascal traces the history of faith-based organizations. See Eva Pascal, "Do-It-Yourself Missions: The Rise of Independent Faith-Based Organizations and the Changing Contours of Missions," in *2010Boston: The Changing Contours of World Mission and Christianity*, ed. Todd M. Johnson et al. (Eugene, OR: Pickwick Publications, 2015), 193–212.

56 Eleana Kim, Report, US-Korea Institute at SAIS, 2009, accessed April 2020, www.jstor.org/stable/resrep11137.

See Bertha Holt, *The Seed from the East* (Los Angeles: Oxford Press, 1956), for detailed descriptions of the Holts' theology; Soojin Chung, "Transnational Adoption: A Noble Cause? Female Missionaries as Pioneers of Transnational Adoption, 1945–1965," *Evangelical Missions Quarterly* (2016): 52–58.

57 For more work on "matching," see Ellen Herman, "The Difference Difference Makes: Justine Wise Polier and Religious Matching in Twentieth-Century Child Adoption," *Religion and American Culture* 10 (2000): 57–98; Judith Modell and Naomi Dambacher, "Making a 'Real' Family: Matching and Cultural Biologism in American Adoption," *Adoption Quarterly* 1, no. 2 (1997): 3–33.

58 Non-matching adoption entailed adopting children who did not share a physical, religious, racial, or intellectual resemblance. Special needs adoption included adoption that was considered difficult, risky, and likely to fail due to race, physical or mental disability, or age.

59 Helen Doss, *The Family Nobody Wanted* (Boston: Northeastern University Press, 1954). Helen Doss demonstrated that there were no boundaries that God's love could not cross. At the same time, the story of the Doss family portrayed virulent racial realities. Their effort to adopt a half-black German war orphan met such resistance among friends and family members that they had to locate an African American couple to adopt the child.

60 Kim, *Adopted Territory*.

61 Kimberly D. McKee, "Monetary Flows and the Movements of Children: The Transnational Adoption Industrial Complex," *Journal of Korean Studies* 21, no. 1 (2016): 137–78.

62 After 1945, Lutherans, Catholics, and Seventh Day Adventists, and several other religious groups formed organizations such as the League for Orphan Victims in Europe (LOVE) and the American Joint Committee for Assisting Japanese-American Orphans.

1. THE FOUNDATION OF THE TRANSNATIONAL ADOPTION MOVEMENT

1 "About Us," World Vision, accessed January 12, 2018, www.worldvision.org/about-us; "About Us," Compassion International, accessed January 12, 2018, www.compassion.com/about/about-us.htm.

2 The Everett Swanson Evangelistic Association (ESEA) was officially incorporated in 1956, but Everett Swanson launched his overseas ministry in 1952.

3 The masculinized portrayal of East Asians permeated through most of 1800s and the first half of 1900s. In 1871, "yellow peril racism" led to the Chinese Massacre. The xenophobia against East Asians resulted in the Chinese Exclusion Act (1882), which was effective until 1943. Although Chinese were the main targets of yellow peril racism, Japanese and Korean farmers in California were also depicted as the hyper-masculine trope. See John Dower, *War Without Mercy: Race and Power in the Pacific War* (New York: Pantheon Books, 1986); Frank H. Wu, *Yellow: Race in America Beyond Black and White* (New York: Basic Books, 2002).

4 Kenneth S. Latourette, *A History of the Expansion of Christianity, vol 4: The Great Century in Europe and the United States of America* (Grand Rapids: Zondervan, 1970), 4.

5 Todd M. Johnson and Gina A. Zurlo, *World Christian Encyclopedia*, 3rd edition (Edinburgh: Edinburgh University Press, 2019), 917.

6 John R. Mott, *The Evangelization of the World in This Generation* (New York: Student Volunteer Movement for Foreign Missions, 1900).

7 Denton Lotz, "The Evangelization of the World in This Generation: The Resurgence of a Missionary Idea Among the Conservative Evangelicals" (Ph.D. dissertation, University of Hamburg, 1970), 35–36.

8 William R. Hutchison, *Errand to the World: American Protestant Thought and Foreign Missions* (Chicago: University of Chicago Press, 1993), 99.

9 Timothy Yates, *Christian Mission in the Twentieth Century* (Cambridge: Cambridge University Press, 1996), 11.

10 Dana L. Robert, "The First Globalization: The Internationalization of the Protestant Missionary Movement between the World Wars," *International Bulletin of Missionary Research* 26, no. 2 (2002), 50.

11 Dana L. Robert, *American Women in Mission: The Modern Mission Era 1792–1992* (Macon, GA: Mercer University Press, 1997), 307.

12 Bradley J. Longfield, "For Church and Country: The Fundamentalist-Modernist Conflict in the Presbyterian Church," *Journal of Presbyterian History* 78, no. 1 (2000): 37.

13 Harold Ockenga used the term "neo-evangelicals" in 1947. He wanted to separate the new evangelical movement from fundamentalism. See Douglas A. Sweeney, "The Essential Evangelicalism Dialectic: The Historiography of the Early Neo-Evangelical Movement and the Observer-Participant Dilemma," *Church History* 60, no. 1 (1991): 70–84; Joel A. Carpenter, *Revive Us Again: The Reawakening of American Fundamentalism* (New York: Oxford University Press, 1999), 152.

14 Axel R. Schafer, *Countercultural Conservatives: American Evangelicalism from the Postwar Revival to the New Christian Right* (Madison: University of Wisconsin Press, 2011), 10, 48.

15 Jon R. Stone, *On the Boundaries of American Evangelicalism: The Postwar Evangelical Coalition* (New York: St. Martin's Press, 1997).

16 David P. King, *God's Internationalists: World Vision and the Age of Evangelical Humanitarianism* (Philadelphia: University of Pennsylvania Press, 2019), 26.

17 Toward the end of Pierce's life, he founded a relief organization named Samaritan's Purse. After Pierce's death, Franklin Graham, the son of Billy Graham, took over the organization.

18 Joel A. Carpenter, "'Geared to the Times, but Anchored to the Rock': How Contemporary Techniques, Nationalism Helped Create an Evangelical Resurgence," *Christianity Today*, November 8, 1985, 44–47.

19 King, *God's Internationalists*, 26.

20 Lorie Henry Lee, "'Now That You Have Seen': A Historical Look at Compassion International 1952–2013" (Ph.D. dissertation, Southeastern Baptist Theological Seminary, 2014), 22.

21 Schafer, *Countercultural Conservatives*, 27; Matthew Avery Sutton, *American Apocalypse: A History of Modern Evangelicalism* (Cambridge: The Belknap Press of Harvard University Press, 2014), 327.

22 Marilee Pierce-Dunker, *Man of Vision* (Federal Way: World Vision Press, 2010), 22–23.

23 Most of the biographies of Robert Pierce are hagiographic accounts infused with insider language such as the "prodigal son." I borrowed these tropes from the stylized evangelical narratives to convey the unique Christian culture of the time.

24 Pierce-Dunker, *Man of Vision*, 33–53.

25 David P. King, "Seeking Global Vision: The Evolution of World Vision and American Evangelicalism" (Ph.D. dissertation, Emory University, 2012), 24.

26 Janet Moore Lindman, "The Manly Christian: Evangelical White Manhood," in *Bodies of Belief: Baptist Community in Early America* (Philadelphia: University of Pennsylvania Press, 2008), 164. See also Barry Hankins, *American Evangelicals: A Contemporary History of a Mainstream Religious Movement* (Lanham, MD: Rowman & Littlefield Publishers, 2008); Donald E. Hall, *Muscular Christianity: Embodying the Victorian Age* (New York: Cambridge University Press, 1994); Patrick Pasture, *Gender and Christianity in Modern Europe Beyond the Feminization Thesis* (Leuven, Belgium: Leuven University Press, 2012); Clifford Putney, *Muscular Christianity: Manhood and Sports in Protestant America* (Cambridge, MA: Harvard University Press, 2001); Charles Wilde, "Acts of Faith: Muscular Christianity and Masculinity Among the Gogodala of Papua New Guinea," *Oceania*, 75, no. 1 (2004): 32–48.

27 Barry Hankins, *American Evangelicals: A Contemporary History of a Mainstream Religious Movement* (Lanham, MD: Rowman & Littlefield, 2008), 108.

28 Thomas V. Frederick, "An Interpretation of Evangelical Gender Ideology: Implications for a Theology of Gender," *Theology & Sexuality* 16, no. 2 (2010): 183–192.

29 Franklin Graham and Jeanette Lockerbie, *Bob Pierce: This One Thing I Do* (Waco, TX: W Publishing Group, 1983), 50; Pierce-Dunker, *Man of Vision*, 56.

30 James C. Hefley, *God Goes to High School: An In-Depth Look at an Incredible Phenomenon* (Waco, TX: Word, 1970), 25; Carpenter, *Revive Us Again*, 161–164.

31 Pierce-Dunker, *Man of Vision*, 55–57.

32 Pierce-Dunker, *Man of Vision*, 85.

33 Ken Anderson, "Ambassador on Fire," *Youth for Christ* (1948), 16.

34 Pierce-Dunker, *Man of Vision*, 87–93.

35 Frank Phillips was a director of the Billy Graham crusade and of the Portland Youth for Christ. See Norman Rohrer, *Open Arms* (Wheaton, IL: Tyndale House Publishing, 1987), 55.

36 *World Vision Magazine*, August 1958, 38. World Vision International Central Records, Monrovia, CA.

37 Ibid.

38 National Association of Evangelicals (NAE) grew out of the New England Fellowship in 1929, spearheaded by J. Elwin Wright. It was an evangelical alternative to the Federal Council of Churches, an ecumenical organization. NAE was conservative in both theology and politics. NAE, along with Youth for Christ, played a significant role in creating evangelical momentum during the 1940s and 1950s. See Randall Ballmer, *Encyclopedia of Evangelicalism* (Louisville: Westminster John Knox Press, 2014), 483.

39 Rohrer, *Open Arms*, 56, 67.

40 Quoted in Pierce-Dunker, *Man of Vision*, 98.

41 Rohrer, *Open Arms*, 53.

42 Ibid.

43 Robert, *American Women in Mission*, xvii–xix.

44 Ibid., 253.

45 Graham and Lockerbie, *Bob Pierce*, 105.

46 Ibid.

47 Ibid., 70.

48 Ken Anderson, "Her Community Is Called Death," *Youth for Christ* (1949), 69.

49 Graham and Lockerbie, *Bob Pierce*, 69–75.

50 Quoted in Graham and Lockerbie, *Bob Pierce*, 74.

51 Quoted in Pierce-Dunker, *Man of Vision*, 84; Ken Anderson and Bob Pierce, *This Way to The Harvest* (Whitefish, MT: Kessinger Publishing, LLC, 2010).

52 Robert, *American Women in Mission*, 170.

53 Ibid., 197.

54 Gladys Aylward and Christine Hunter, *Gladys Aylward: The Little Woman* (Chicago: Moody Publishers, 1970).

55 Rohrer, *Open Arms*, 83; Alan Burgess, *The Small Woman* (Boston: E. P. Dutton, 1957).

56 Graham and Lockerbie, *Bob Pierce*, 113.

57 Dorothy L. Hodgson, *The Church of Women: Gendered Encounters between Massai and Missionaries* (Bloomington: Indiana University Press, 2005).

58 Lawrence Swanson, "Story of Everett Swanson," Compassion International Archives, Bellingham, WA.

59 Quoted in Lee, "Now That You Have Seen," 21.

60 Ibid., 22–24.

61 Peter Van Lierop, "A Tribute to Everett Swanson," *Compassion*, September/October 1977.

62 Everett Swanson, "Korea Calls," *The Standard*, July 25, 1952, 1–2.

63 Everett Swanson, "Spiritual Victories in Korea," *The Standard*, January 2, 1953, 2–5.

64 *One: Celebrating 50 Years of Compassion* (Seoul: Compassion International, 2002), 2–9.

65 Ibid.

66 Ibid., 10–11.

67 "Report from Korea," *The Standard*, September 4, 1953, 7.

68 "Korea: Shining Star for Christianity," *United Evangelical Action*, Feb. 1, 1954, 3.

69 Arissa Oh, *To Save the Children of Korea: The Cold War Origins of International Adoption* (Stanford, CA: Stanford University Press, 2015), 51; Soojin Chung, "Transnational Adoption: A Noble Cause? Female Missionaries as Pioneers of Transnational Adoption, 1945–1965," *Evangelical Missions Quarterly* (2016), 52–58.

70 "Marketing Korean Sponsor Promos, 1956–1960," World Vision International Central Records, Monrovia, CA.

71 Ibid.

72 Ibid.

73 Jim Hill, "Understanding Child Sponsorship: A Historical Perspective," World Vision International Central Records.

74 Everett Swanson, *Letter to Sponsors*, September 3, 1954, Compassion International Archive.

75 Ibid.

76 Bertha Holt, David Wisner, and Holt International Children's Services, *The Seed from the East* (Los Angeles: Oxford Press, 1956).

77 David Wisner, "Harry Holt Brings 8 Korean GI Orphans to United States," World Vision International Central Records.

78 "Operation Baby Lift," World Vision International Central Records.

79 Wisner, "Harry Holt Brings 8 Korean GI Orphans to United States." World Vision International Central Records.

80 "19 Korea War Orphans Flying Here from Japan," *Los Angeles Times*, June 12, 1956.

81 International Social Services-America Branch (ISS-USA), Box 10, Folder 28, "Swanson, Everett (Evangelistic Association, Inc.)," Social Welfare History Archives.

82 Among the charities they were involved with were the National Association for Retarded Children, the Children's Hospital Society of Los Angeles, the American Diabetes Association, the Exceptional Children's Foundation of Los Angeles, and World Vision. See Dan L. Thrapp, "Christianity Not Tough for Actors, Couple Find: Roy Rogers and Dale Evans Describe Impression of Religion on Their Lives," *Los Angeles Times*, April 24, 1965.

83 Dale Evans Rogers, *Dearest Debbie* (Grand Rapids, MI: Fleming H. Revell Co, 1965), 15.

84 "Roy Rogers' Child and 7 Are Killed in Crash of Bus," *New York Times*, August 18, 1964.

85 Lance Brisson and Richard Main, "Church Bus Hits 7 Cars; 8 Dead: Roy Rogers Adopted Girl Killed 60 Others Injured as Vehicles Crash Near San Clemente," *Los Angeles Times*, August 18, 1964; Ruth C. Ikerman, "Books for the Family: 'Dearest Debbie' Reflects Deep Faith," *Los Angeles Times*, April 25, 1965; "Last Rites Held for 2 Bus Crash Victims: Actress Dale Evans Mourns," *Los Angeles Times*, August 21, 1964.

86 "Roy Rogers' Child and 7 Are Killed in Crash of Bus," *New York Times*, August 18, 1964.

87 Dale Evans Rogers, *Angel Unaware* (Grand Rapids, MI: Fleming H. Revell Co, 1953).

88 Evans, *Dearest Debbie*, 9–11.

89 Ibid.

90 Evans, *Dearest Debbie*, 21–22.

91 See, for example, Hyun Martin, *I Survived Childhood: A Memoir of Abandonment, Betrayal and Healing* (Be You Spa Inc., 2017); Thomas Park Clement, *Dust of the Streets: The Journey of a Biracial Orphan of the Korean War* (Bloomfield, IN: Truepenny Publishing Company, 2012); Julayne Lee, *Not My White Savior* (Los Angeles: Rare Bird Books, 2018); Jane Jeong Trenka, *Fugitive Visions: An Adoptee's Return to Korea* (Saint Paul, MN: Graywolf Press, 2009); Marijane Huang, *Beyond Two Worlds: A Taiwanese-American Adoptee's Memoir & Search for Identity* (Bloomington, IN: AuthorHouse, 2017).

92 David M. Brodzinsky, Marshall D. Schechter, and Robin Marantz Henig, *Being Adopted: The Lifelong Search for Self* (New York: Anchor Book, 1992).

93 John D. Palmer, *The Dance of Identities: Korean Adoptees and Their Journey Toward Empowerment* (Honolulu: University of Hawaii Press, 2010), 7.

94 Evans, *Dearest Debbie*, 28.

95 B. Watson and M. Clarke, ed., *Child Sponsorship: Exploring Pathways to a Brighter Future* (Basingstoke: Palgrave Macmillan, 2014), 20.

96 Pierce-Dunker, *Man of Vision*, 101.

97 Hutchison, *Errand to the World*, 177–78.

98 Joel Carpenter, "The Fundamentalist Leaven and the Rise of an Evangelical United Front," in *The Evangelical Tradition in America*, ed. Leonard I. Sweet (Macon, GA: Mercer University Press, 1984), 257.

99 Gehman, *Let My Heart Be Broken*, 184; Grant Lee, "He Only Wants to Save the World," *Los Angeles Times*, January 22, 1975, G6. Quoted in David P. King, *God's Internationalists: World Vision and the Age of Evangelical Humanitarianism* (Philadelphia: University of Pennsylvania Press, 2019), 62.

100 Bob Pierce, "Marketing Korean Sponsor Promos, 1956–1960," World Vision International Central Records.

101 Robert Pierce, "Feed My Sheep," World Vision International Central Records.

102 Matthew 6:33; Matthew 5:6.

103 Quoted in Rohrer, *Open Arms*, 48–50.

104 Richard Gehman, *Let My Heart Be Broken with the Things That Break the Heart of God* (New York: McGraw-Hill, 1960), 34–35.

105 Robert Pierce, "Feed My Sheep," World Vision International Central Records.

106 "Marketing Sponsor/Childcare Historical Promotions 1950–1970," World Vision International Central Records.

107 Gary Vanderpol, "The Least of These: American Evangelical Parachurch Missions to the Poor, 1947–2005" (Ph.D. dissertation, Boston University, 2010).

108 "Marketing Sponsor/Childcare Historical Promotions 1950–1970," World Vision International Central Records.

109 Ibid.

110 Eleana J. Kim, *Adopted Territory: Transnational Korean Adoptees and the Politics of Belonging* (Durham: Duke University Press, 2010), 101.

111 Samuel L. Perry, *Growing God's Family: The Global Orphan Care Movement and the Limits of Evangelical Activism* (New York: New York University Press, 2017), 88–89.

112 Edward W. Said, *Orientalism* (New York: Vintage, 1979).

113 "Marketing Sponsor/Childcare Historical Promotions 1950–1970," World Vision International Central Records.

114 Ibid.

115 Robert Pierce, "Christmas Letter on December 1957," World Vision International Central Records.

116 "Would You Like to Adopt an Orphan Just Like Me?" World Vision International Central Records.

117 Bob Pierce and Ken Anderson, "China as We Saw It," *Youth for Christ*, September 1948, 65.

118 Robert Pierce, dir., *China Challenge* (1948).

119 *38th Parallel: The Story of God's Deadline in Korea*, directed by Robert Pierce, 1950.

120 *China Challenge*.

121 "Marketing Sponsor/Childcare Historical Promotions 1950–1970," World Vision International Central Records.

122 Gehman, *Let My Heart Be Broken*, 179.

123 ISS-USA Box 20, Folder 18, "Compassion International," SWHA.

124 ISS-USA Box 10, Folder 29, "World Vision International," SWHA.

125 Ibid.

2. HERO OR VILLAIN?

1 See, for example, SooJin Pate, *From Orphan to Adoptee: U.S. Empire and Genealogies of Korean Adoption* (Minneapolis: University of Minnesota Press, 2014).

2 Arissa Oh, *To Save the Children of Korea: The Cold War Origins of International Adoption* (Stanford, CA: Stanford University Press, 2015), 23; William F. Asbury, *Military Help to Korean Orphans: A Survey Made for the Commander-in-Chief, United Nations Forces, Far East, and for the Chief of Chaplains of the United States Army* (Richmond: Christian Children's Fund, 1954).

3 Bertha Holt, *The Seed from the East* (Los Angeles: Oxford Press, 1956), 24.

4 Soojin Chung, "Transnational Adoption: A Noble Cause? Female Missionaries as Pioneers of Transnational Adoption, 1945–1965," *Evangelical Missions Quarterly* (2016).

5 Holt, *The Seed from the East*, 25.

6 Chung, "Transnational Adoption: A Noble Cause?"; Oh, *To Save the Children of Korea*, 51.

7 Holt, *The Seed from the East*, 42.

8 Moxness, "Good Samaritan of Korea," 86.

9 Holt, *The Seed from the East*, 44.

10 Martin Luther, *Luther's Works: Lectures on Galatians, Chapters 1–4* (Saint Louis, MO: Concordia Publishing House, 1963).

11 Holt, *The Seed from the East*, 59.

12 Ibid.

13 Ibid.

14 The word "seed" has a biblical significance in both the Old Testament and New Testament. "Abraham's seed" (2 Chronicles 20:7) or "the holy seed" (Isaiah 6:13; Ezra 9:2) were used to refer to the Israelites. Paul used "seed" to show that the Abrahamic promise was fulfilled through Christ (Galatians 3:16).

15 Bertha Holt, *Bring My Sons from Afar* (Eugene, OR: Holt International Children's Services, 1986), 9.

16 David Wisner, "'The Bright Spot' in the Korean Orphan Situation," *Wesleyan Missionary*, December 1955.

17 Susan Pettiss, "Effect of Adoption of Foreign Children on U.S. Adoption Standards and Practices," *Child Welfare*, July 1958.

18 David Wisner, "Harry Holt Brings 8 Korean GI Orphans to United States," World Vision International Central Records.

19 Oh, *To Save the Children of Korea*, 92.

20 "Holt to Bring Eight Orphans to America," *World Vision News* 4, no. 4, September 1955.

21 "Holt to Bring Eight Orphans to America," *World Vision News*, September 1955.

22 "Holt to Bring Eight Orphans to America," *World Vision News*, September 1955.

23 "Operation Baby Lift," World Vision International Central Records.

24 Chung, "Transnational Adoption: A Noble Cause?"; Karen Dubinsky, *Babies without Borders: Adoption and Migration across the Americas* (New York: New York University Press, 2010), 94.

25 "Bertha Holt, the Mother of America," *Kyunghyang Newspaper*, October 8, 1966; "Bertha Holt Awarded," *Kyunghyang Newspaper*, October 18, 1995.

26 Chung, "Transnational Adoption: A Noble Cause?"; Shaila K. Dewan, "Bertha Holt, 96, a Leader in International Adoptions," *New York Times*, August 2, 2000.

27 Holt, *Seed from the East*, 194.

28 Moxness, "Good Samaritan of Korea," 84.

29 "Mr. Holt 'Moves the World,'" *Oregonian*, April 9, 1956. International Social Service–American Branch (hereafter ISS-US), Box 10, "Christian-Independent

Adoption Schemes, Harry Holt, 1955–1957, Vol. 1," Social Welfare History Archives (hereafter SWHA), University of Minnesota, Minneapolis, MN.

30 Ibid.

31 "Mr. Holt 'Moves the World,'" *Oregonian*, April 9, 1956. International Social Service–American Branch (hereafter ISS-US), Box 10, "Christian-Independent Adoption Schemes, Harry Holt, 1955–1957, Vol. 1," Social Welfare History Archives (hereafter SWHA), University of Minnesota, Minneapolis, MN.

32 Moxness, "Good Samaritan of Korea," 85.

33 Ibid., 85–86.

34 Ibid.

35 Barry Hankins, *American Evangelicals: A Contemporary History of a Mainstream Religious Movement* (Plymouth, UK: Rowman & Littlefield, 2009), 113.

36 Dana Robert, *American Women in Mission: A Social History of Their Thought and Practice* (Macon, GA: Mercer University Press, 1997), 4.

37 For critical scholarship on gender and Christian family, see J. Haggis, "White Women and Colonialism: Towards a Non-Recuperative History," in *Gender and Imperialism*, ed. C. Midgley (Manchester: Manchester University Press, 1998); J. Comaroff and J. Comaroff, *Of Revelation and Revolution: Christianity, Colonialism, and Consciousness in South Africa* (Chicago: University of Chicago Press, 1991); M. Labode, "From Heathen Kraal to Christian Home: Anglican Mission Education and African Christian Girls, 1850–1900," in *Women and Missions: Past and Present*, ed. F. Bowie, D. Kirkwood, and S. Ardener (Providence, RI: Berg, 1993).

38 Dana L. Robert, "The 'Christian Home' as a Cornerstone of Anglo-American Missionary Thought and Practice," in *Converting Colonialism: Visions and Realities in Mission History, 1706–1914, ed.* Dana L. Robert (Grand Rapids, MI: Curzon-Eerdmans, 2008), 134–165. See also Dana L. Robert, *American Women in Mission: A Social History of Their Thought and Practice* (Macon, GA: Mercer University Press, 1997), 56–75.

39 "He Brings 12 Korean Orphans," *Oregonian*, April 9, 1956. ISS-US, Box 10, "Christian-Independent Adoption Schemes, Harry Holt, 1955–1957, Vol. 1," SWHA.

40 Howard Brodie, "The Power of Faith," *Evening Star*, March 8, 1958.

41 Ibid.

42 Ibid.

43 Ibid.

44 "Bertha Holt, the Mother of America," *Kyunghyang Newspaper*, October 8, 1966.

45 David Wisner, "'The Bright Spot' in the Korean Orphan Situation," *Wesleyan Missionary*, December 1955.

46 Ibid.

47 Ibid.

48 "Holt to Bring Eight Orphans to America," *World Vision News*, September 1955.

49 Quoted in Oh, *To Save the Children of Korea*, 94.

50 "Last Member of Holt Dynasty Lives Up to Name," *Korea Herald*, December 11, 2011.

51 Chung, "Transnational Adoption: A Noble Cause?"

52 *Dear Friends*, December 27, 1956, ISS-US, Box 10, "Children-Independent Adoption Schemes, Harry Holt, 1955–1957, Vol. 1," SWHA.

53 Holt, *The Seed from the East*, 243.

54 "North Korea Attacks U.S. on Orphans," *Washington Post and Times Herald*, June 8, 1959.

55 "North Korea Attacks U.S. on Orphans," *Washington Post and Times Herald*, June 8, 1959.

56 Ibid.

57 Quoted in Oh, *To Save the Children of Korea*, 94; Holt, *Seed from the East*, 51.

58 "650 Korean Mixed-Race Children Adopted," *Dong-Ah Newspaper*, January 26, 1958.

59 Quoted in Oh, *To Save the Children of Korea*, 54.

60 Katherine Moon, *Sex among Allies: Military Prostitution in U.S.-Korea Relations* (New York: Columbia University Press, 1996); Brenda Stoltzfus and Saundra Pollock Sturdevant, *Let the Good Times Roll: Prostitution and the U.S. Military in Asia* (New York: New Press, 1992).

61 Quoted in Oh, *To Save the Children of Korea*, 60; William Asbury, "Military Help to Korean Orphanages: A Survey Made for the Commander-in-Chief, United Nations Forces, Far East, and for the Chief of Chaplains of the United States Army," 1954, George Drake Papers, University of Southern California, Los Angeles, CA.

62 "Embrology Related to International Marriage," *Kookminbo*, October 8, 1958.

63 Pearl Buck, "Other/Children, American-Asian," 4052, Box 64, Folder 258.13 IX. The Pearl S. Buck Literary Manuscripts Collection, West Virginia & Regional History Center, Morgantown, WV.

64 *Dear Friends*, December 27, 1956, ISS-US, Box 10, "Children-Independent Adoption Schemes, Harry Holt, 1955–1957, Vol. 1," SWHA.

65 Ibid.

66 Ibid.

67 Ibid.

68 Ibid.

69 From William T. Kirk to Rev. Eugene Carson Blake, D.D. The Presbyterian Church in the United States of America. June 17, 1958, ISS-US, Box 10, "Children-Independent Adoption Schemes, Harry Holt, 1958–1959, Vol. 2," SWHA.

70 From Raymond W. Riese (Child Welfare Director) to Paul H. Martin, M.D. May 13, 1958, ISS-US, Box 10, "Children-Independent Adoption Schemes, Harry Holt, 1958–1959, Vol. 2," SWHA.

71 From Margaret A. Valk (Senior Case Consultant) to Dr. Ursula Mende (ISS Germany), March 20, 1959, ISS-US, Box 10, "Children-Independent Adoption Schemes, Harry Holt, 1958–1959, Vol. 2," SWHA.

72 From Harry Holt to Wright County Welfare, November 24, 1959, ISS-US, Box 10, "Children-Independent Adoption Schemes, Harry Holt, 1958–1959, Vol. 2," SWHA.

73 From Harry Holt to Joseph H. Reid (Executive Director of Child Welfare League of America), Jul 20, 1959, ISS-US, Box 10, "Children-Independent Adoption Schemes, Harry Holt, 1958–1959, Vol. 2," SWHA.

74 Ibid.

75 From J. Calvitt Clarke (CCF) to Harry Holt, April 30, 1959, ISS-US, Box 10, "Children-Independent Adoption Schemes, Harry Holt, 1958–1959, Vol. 2," SWHA.

76 Ibid.

77 Ibid.

78 From Joseph H. Reid (Executive Director ISS) to Harry Holt, undated, ISS-US, Box 10, "Children-Independent Adoption Schemes, Harry Holt, 1958–1959, Vol. 2," SWHA.

79 Ibid.

80 From Joseph H. Reid (Executive Director ISS) to Harry Holt, undated, ISS-US, Box 10, "Children-Independent Adoption Schemes, Harry Holt, 1958–1959, Vol. 2," SWHA.

81 Ibid.

82 Arnold Lyslo, "A Few Impressions on Meeting the Harry Holt Plane, the 'Flying Tiger,' Which Arrived in Portland, Oregon, December 27, 1958," ISS-US, Box 10, "Children— Independent Adoption Schemes, Holt, Harry, Vol. 2 1958– 1959," SWHA.

83 Arnold Lyslo, "A Few Impressions on Meeting the Harry Holt Plane, the 'Flying Tiger,' Which Arrived in Portland, Oregon, December 27, 1958," ISS-US, Box 10, "Children— Independent Adoption Schemes, Holt, Harry, Vol. 2 1958– 1959," SWHA.

84 Ibid.

85 Ibid.

86 Oh, *To Save the Children of Korea*, 107.

87 Ellen Herman, "Proxy Adoptions," The Adoption History Project, accessed May 10, 2018, http://pages.uoregon.edu/adoption/topics/proxy.htm.

88 From Mrs. Edward Gresham (Director of Bureau of Child Welfare) to Mr. Laurin Hyde (Study Consultant of Joint Study of Proxy Adoptions), May 27, 1958, ISS-US, Box 10, "Children—Proxy Adoptions, 1957–1966," SWHA.

89 From William T. Kirk to Rev. Eugene Carson Blake, June 17, 1958, ISS-US, Box 10, "Children—Independent Adoption Schemes, Holt, Harry, Vol. 2 1958– 1959," SWHA.

90 Ibid.

91 Susan Pettiss, "Adoption by Proxy," *Child Welfare*, October 1955, ISS-US, "Children: Proxy Adoptions 1954–1956," SWHA.

92 Susan Pettiss, "Effect of Adoption of Foreign Children on U.S. Adoption Standards and Practices, Child Welfare," July, 1958, ISS-US, Box 10, "Children-Proxy Adoptions, 1957–1966," SWHA.

93 Ibid.

94 Ibid.

95 Ibid.

96 From Susan T. Pettiss to Joseph E. Alloway (Executive Director of State of New Jersey Board of Child Welfare), April 18, 1958, ISS-US, Box 10, "Children— Independent Adoption Schemes, Holt, Harry, Vol. 1, 1958– 1959," SWHA; From Susan T. Pettis (Assistant Director of ISS) to Christine C. Reynolds, June 30, 1958, ISS-US, Box 10, "Children— Independent Adoption Schemes, Holt, Harry, Vol. 1, 1958– 1959," SWHA.

97 From Helen E. Boardman (RSW, Director, Social Service) to Bernice Copland (State Department of Social Welfare), June 9, 1958, ISS-US, Box 10, "Children-Proxy Adoptions 1957–1966," SWHA.

98 From Wilmer H. Tolle to Harry Holt. March 20, 1958, ISS-US, Box 10, "Children— Independent Adoption Schemes, Holt, Harry, Vol. 1, 1958– 1959," SWHA.

99 Ibid.

100 Ibid.

101 From Dorothy K. Frost to unknown, Subject: Mr. and Mrs. John Chambers, November 25, 1958, ISS-US, Box 10, "Children— Independent Adoption Schemes, Holt, Harry, Vol. 1, 1958– 1959," SWHA.

102 "Indict Woman in Tot's Death," *New York Journal American*, July 24, 1957.

103 Ibid.

104 Ibid.

105 "Holt Sees Ott Difficulties as Attempt by Welfare Officials to Attack Him," ISS-US, Box 10, "Children-Proxy Adoptions, 1957–1966," SWHA.

106 Ibid.

107 "Holt Sees Ott Difficulties as Attempt by Welfare Officials to Attack Him," ISS-US, Box 10, "Children-Proxy Adoptions, 1957–1966," SWHA.

108 "Oregon Woman Indicted on Child-Killing Charge," *Oregon Statesman*, July 24, 1957.

109 "Holt Sees Ott Difficulties as Attempt by Welfare Officials to Attack Him," ISS-US, Box 10, "Children-Proxy Adoptions, 1957–1966," SWHA.

110 From Raymont W. Riese (Child Welfare Director) to William T. Kirk (General Director American Branch, ISS), March 3, 1958, ISS-US, Box 10, "Children— Independent Adoption Schemes, Holt, Harry, Vol. 1, 1958– 1959," SWHA.

111 Ibid.

112 Ibid.

113 Ibid.

114 From Roberta Rindfleisch (Director of Child Welfare Division) to Susan T. Pettiss (Assistant Director of ISS), November 19, 1958, ISS-US, Box 10, "Children— Independent Adoption Schemes, Holt, Harry, Vol. 1, 1958– 1959," SWHA; From

Lawrence E. Laybourne to Virginia Smucker, January 14, 1958, ISS-US, Box 10, "Children— Independent Adoption Schemes, Holt, Harry, Vol. 1, 1958–1959," SWHA.

115 Ibid.

116 Ibid.

117 Holt, *Seed from the East*, 171, 185.

118 Ibid., 187.

119 Ibid., 241.

120 Ibid., 197, 222, 236.

121 Richard T. Shaefer, *Encyclopedia of Race, Ethnicity, and Society* (Thousand Oaks, CA: Sage Publications, Inc., 2008), 320.

122 Holt, *Seed from the East*, 191, 220.

123 Ibid.

124 Ibid., 189.

125 Richard T. Shaefer, *Encyclopedia of Race, Ethnicity, and Society* (Thousand Oaks, CA: Sage Publications, Inc., 2008), 321. See also Eduardo Bonilla-Silva, *Racism without Racists: Colorblind Racism and the Persistence of Racial Inequality in America* (Lanham, MD: Rowman & Littlefield, 2014); Amy Ansell, "Casting a Blind Eye: The Ironic Consequences of Color-Blindness in South Africa and the United States," *Critical Sociology* 32, no. 2 (2006): 333–56; Kwame Appiah and Amy Gutmann, *Color Conscious: The Political Morality of Race* (Princeton, NJ: Princeton University Press, 1998); Michael J. Brown et al., *Whitewashing Race: The Myth of a Color-Blind Society* (Berkeley, CA: University of California Press, 2003).

126 Holt, *Seed from the East*.

127 *World Vision News* 4, no. 5, December 1955.

128 Glenn Morey and Julie Morey, "Given Away: Korean Adoptees Share Their Stories," *New York Times*, July 23, 2019.

129 Ibid., 209.

130 Ibid., 240.

3. MOTHER OF TRANSRACIAL ADOPTION

1 Soojin Chung, "Transnational Adoption: A Noble Cause? Female Missionaries as Pioneers of Transnational Adoption, 1945–1965," *Evangelical Missions Quarterly* (2016): 52–58.

2 Michael G. Thompson, "Sherwood Eddy, the Missionary Enterprise, and the Rise of Christian Internationalism in 1920s America," *Modern Intellectual History* 12 (2014): 65–93.

3 Hosu Kim, *Birth Mothers and Transnational Adoption Practice in South Korea: Virtual Mothering* (Berlin: Springer, 2016), 44.

4 Peter Conn, *Pearl S. Buck: A Cultural Biography* (New York: Cambridge University Press, 1996), 3.

5 Soojin Chung, "The Missiology of Pearl Sydenstricker Buck," *International Bulletin of Mission Research* 41, no. 2 (2017): 134–41.

6   Conn, *Pearl S. Buck*, 18.
7   Chung, "The Missiology of Pearl Sydenstricker Buck," 134–41.
8   Pearl S. Buck, *My Several Worlds* (New York: John Day, 1954), 97.
9   Chung, "The Missiology of Pearl Sydenstricker Buck," 134–41.
10 Conn, *Pearl S. Buck*, 73.
11 Soojin Chung, "Transnational Adoption: A Noble Cause? Female Missionaries as Pioneers of Transnational Adoption, 1945–1965," *Evangelical Missions Quarterly* (2016): 52–58; Chung, "The Missiology of Pearl Sydenstricker Buck," 134–41.
12 Theodore F. Harris, *Pearl S. Buck: A Biography* (New York: John Day, 1969), 298.
13 Conn, *Pearl S. Buck*, 354.
14 Chung, "The Missiology of Pearl Sydenstricker Buck," 134–41.
15 Bradley J. Longfield, "For Church and Country: The Fundamentalist-Modernist Conflict in the Presbyterian Church," *Journal of Presbyterian History* 78, no. 1 (2000): 37.
16 Chung, "The Missiology of Pearl Sydenstricker Buck," 134–41; William Ernest Hocking, *Re-thinking Missions: A Laymen's Inquiry after One Hundred Years* (New York: Harper & Brothers, 1932), 32–33, 327.
17 Timothy Yates, *Christian Mission in the Twentieth Century* (Cambridge: Cambridge University Press, 1996), 72. See also William R. Hutchison, *Errand to the World: American Protestant Thought and Foreign Missions* (Chicago: University of Chicago Press, 1993), 165.
18 Jeffrey K. Hadden, "H. Paul Douglass: His Perspective and His Work," *Review of Religious Research* 22, no. 1 (1980): 78.
19 Longfield, "For Church and Country," 47.
20 Chung, "The Missiology of Pearl Sydenstricker Buck," 134–41; Pearl S. Buck, "The Laymen's Mission Report," *Christian Century* (1932): 1434.
21 Pearl S. Buck, "Is There a Case for Foreign Missions?," *Harpers Magazine* (January 1933), 150.
22 Dallas M. Roark, "J. Gresham Machen: The Doctrinally True Presbyterian Church," *Journal of Presbyterian Historical Society* 43, no. 2 (1965), 135; Chung, "The Missiology of Pearl Sydenstricker Buck," 134–41.
23 James A. Patterson, "Robert E. Speer, J. Gresham Machen, and the Presbyterian Board of Foreign Missions," *Journal of Presbyterian Historical Society* 64, no. 1 (1986): 63.
24 Chung, "The Missiology of Pearl Sydenstricker Buck," 134–41; Quoted in Charles Silver, "Pearl Buck, Evangelism, and Works of Love: Images of the Missionary in Fiction," *Journal of Presbyterian History* 51, no. 2 (1973): 220.
25 "Mrs. Buck Resigns Her Mission Post," *New York Times*, May 2, 1933, 15.
26 Quoted in Patterson, "Robert E. Speer, J. Gresham Machen, and the Presbyterian Board of Foreign Missions," 64.
27 Chung, "The Missiology of Pearl Sydenstricker Buck," 134–41; D. G. Hart, "After the Breakup, Heartbreak: Conservative Presbyterians without a Common Foe," *Journal of Presbyterian History* 86, no. 2 (2008): 64.

28 "What Mrs. Buck Said about Missionaries," *Milwaukee Journal*, May 3, 1933.

29 Chung, "The Missiology of Pearl Sydenstricker Buck," 134–41.

30 Chung, "Transnational Adoption: A Noble Cause?"

31 Pearl S. Buck, *Children for Adoption* (New York: Random House, 1965), 76.

32 Chung, "Transnational Adoption: A Noble Cause?" The name of the baby is inconsistent in Pearl Buck's writings. In *Children for Adoption*, she used the name Robbie, while in other unpublished manuscripts she called him Ved or David. She may have used a pseudonym to protect the child's identity.

33 Chung, "Transnational Adoption: A Noble Cause?"

34 Pearl Buck, "Other/'A Case Study: Welcome Home,'" 4052, Box 64, Folder 265.12 XIX, The Pearl S. Buck Literary Manuscripts Collection, West Virginia & Regional History Center, Morgantown, WV; Buck, *Children for Adoption*, 79.

35 Pearl Buck, "I Am the Better Woman for Having My Two Black Children," *Today's Health*, January 1972; Buck, Children for Adoption, 80; Buck, "Other/'A Case Study: Welcome Home.'"

36 Ibid.

37 Here, too, the name is inconsistent. In *Children for Adoption*, Buck called him Peter; all other unpublished manuscripts named him Lennie. Pearl Buck, "Other/Welcome House INC." 4052, Box 65, Folder 266.10 IX, The Pearl S. Buck Literary Manuscripts Collection, West Virginia & Regional History Center, Morgantown, WV.

38 Buck, "Other/'A Case Study: Welcome Home,'" The Pearl S. Buck Literary Manuscripts Collection.

39 Buck, *Children for Adoption*, 83.

40 Pearl Buck, "Other/'Welcome Home, Inc.'" 4052, Box 65, Folder 266.10 IX, The Pearl S. Buck Literary Manuscripts Collection, West Virginia & Regional History Center, Morgantown, WV.

41 Pearl Buck, "Other/Letters to Welcome House." 4052, Box 65, Folder 266.16 XV. The Pearl S. Buck Literary Manuscripts Collection, West Virginia & Regional History Center, Morgantown, WV.

42 Ibid.

43 Buck, *Children for Adoption*, 86–87. Buck, "Other/'A Case Study: Welcome Home,'" The Pearl S. Buck Literary Manuscripts Collection.

44 Chung, "Transnational Adoption: A Noble Cause?"; Buck, "Other/'Welcome Home, Inc.'"; Buck, "Other/'A Case Study: Welcome Home,'" The Pearl S. Buck Literary Manuscripts Collection.

45 For more work on "matching," see Ellen Herman, "The Difference Difference Makes: Justine Wise Polier and Religious Matching in Twentieth-Century Child Adoption," *Religion and American Culture* 10 (2000), 57–98; Judith Modell and Naomi Dambacher, "Making a 'Real' Family: Matching and Cultural Biologism in American Adoption," *Adoption Quarterly* 1, no. 2 (1997): 3–33.

46 Emily Cheng, "Pearl S. Buck's 'American Children': US Democracy, Adoption of the Amerasian Child, and the Occupation of Japan in *The Hidden Flower*," *Frontiers: A Journal of Women Studies* 35, no. 1 (2014): 181–210.

47 Hosu Kim, *Birth Mothers and Transnational Adoption Practice in South Korea: Virtual Mothering* (Berlin: Springer, 2016), 44; SooJin Pate, *From Orphan to Adoptee: U.S. Empire and Genealogies of Korean Adoption* (Minneapolis: University of Minnesota Press, 2014), 36.

48 David S. Foglesong, "Roots of 'Liberation': American Images of the Future of Russia in the Early Cold War, 1948–1953," *International History Review* 21 (1999): 57–79; Emily S. Rosenberg, *Spreading the American Dream: American Economic and Cultural Expansion, 1890–1945* (New York: Hill and Wang, 1982).

49 Susan Zeiger, *Entangling Alliances: Foreign War Brides and American Soldiers in the Twentieth Century* (New York: New York University Press, 2010), 7.

50 Harry Truman, American Education Week Announcements, 1946 and 1949, HST Papers, Staff Member and Office Files: White House Office of the President's Correspondence Secretary Files, box 1, Education, TL. Quoted in Jennifer Helgren, *American Girls and Global Responsibility: A New Relation to the World during the Early Cold War* (Newark, NJ: Rutgers University Press, 2017), 23.

51 Chung, "Transnational Adoption: A Noble Cause?"

52 Robert Shaffer, closely examining Pearl Buck's East and West Association, similarly argues that Buck's fundamental commitment to the equality of countries led to a critical perspective toward American culture and politics. See Robert Shaffer, "Pearl S. Buck and the East and West Association: The Trajectory and Fate of 'Critical Internationalism,' 1940–1950," *Peace & Change* 28, no. 1 (2003): 1–36.

53 Chung, "Missiology of Pearl S. Buck."

54 Chung, "Missiology of Pearl S. Buck"; William R. Hutchison, *Errand to the World: American Protestant Thought and Foreign Missions* (Chicago: University of Chicago Press, 1993), 180; Timothy Yates, *Christian Mission in the Twentieth Century* (Cambridge: Cambridge University Press, 1996), 65–66. Anti-racist rhetoric will be examined later.

55 Chung, "Missiology of Pearl S. Buck."

56 Ibid.; Buck, "Is There a Case for Foreign Missions?" 152.

57 Chung, "Missiology of Pearl S. Buck."

58 Buck, *Children for Adoption*, 8.

59 Chung, "Missiology of Pearl S. Buck."

60 Ibid.

61 Buck, "Is There a Case for Foreign Missions?" 152.

62 Address by Marshall Field to the National Conference on Adoptions, January 26, 1955, Box 16, Folder 8, Child Welfare League of America Papers, Social Welfare History Archives, University of Minnesota, Minneapolis, MN.

63 Ellen D. Wu argues that World War II fostered the advent of racial liberalism: the growing belief in political circles that the country's racial diversity could be controlled through the assimilation of non-whites. This phenomenon caused Americans to undo the legal framework that relegated Asians to outside the bounds of America. See Ellen D. Wu, *The Color of Success: Asian Americans and the Origins of the Model Minority* (Princeton, NJ: Princeton University Press, 2015), 3.

64 Kirsteen Kim and Andrew Anderson, *Edinburgh 2010: Mission Today and Tomorrow* (Eugene, OR: Wipf and Stock Publishers, 2011), 305.

65 Quoted in Dana Robert, "'Rethinking Missionaries' from 1910 to Today," *Methodist Review* 4 (2012), 2.

66 Yates, *Christian Mission in the Twentieth Century*, 65–66; Hutchison, *Errand to the World*, 180.

67 W. Wilson Cash, "The Jerusalem Meeting of the International Missionary Council," *Churchman* 42, no. 4 (1928).

68 International Missionary Council, *The Christian Mission in the Light of Race Conflict* (New York: International Missionary Council, 1928), 187–195.

69 Edmund Davison Soper, *Racism: A World Issue* (New York & Nashville: Abingdon-Cokesbury Press, 1947).

70 Dana Robert, "'Rethinking Missionaries' from 1910 to Today," 2–4; Wilbert R. Shenk, *Earthen Vessels: American Evangelicals and Foreign Missions, 1880–1980*, ed. Joel Carpenter (Eugene: Wipf & Stock Pub, 2012), 296–297.

71 International Missionary Council, *The Christian Mission in the Light of Race Conflict*, 192.

72 Pearl Buck, "Welcome House," *Reader's Digest*, July 1958, 48.

73 Chung, "Transnational Adoption: A Noble Cause?"

74 Buck, *Children for Adoption*, 90, 91.

75 Pearl Buck, "Save the Children for What?" *Journal of Educational Sociology* 17, no. 4 (1943).

76 Pearl Buck, "Other/Children, American-Asian," 4052, Box 64, Folder 258.13 IX. The Pearl S. Buck Literary Manuscripts Collection, West Virginia & Regional History Center, Morgantown, WV.

77 Ibid.

78 Kori A. Graves, *A War Born Family: African American Adoption in the Wake of the Korean War* (New York: New York University Press, 2020), 189, 198.

79 Ellen D. Wu, *The Color of Success: Asian Americans and the Origins of the Model Minority* (Princeton, NJ: Princeton University Press, 2014).

80 Graves, *A War Born Family*, 199.

81 For more work on eugenics, see Daniel J. Kevles, *In the Name of Eugenics: Genetics and the Uses of Human Heredity* (Cambridge: Harvard University Press, 1995); Wendy Kline, *Building a Better Race: Gender, Sexuality, and Eugenics from the Turn of the Century to the Baby Boom* (Berkeley: University of California Press, 2001); Edward J. Larson, *Sex, Race, and Science: Eugenics in the Deep South* (Baltimore: Johns Hopkins University Press, 1995).

82 Pearl Buck, "Children Waiting," 727, Box 1, Folder 8. The Pearl S. Buck Literary Manuscripts Collection, West Virginia & Regional History Center, Morgantown, WV.

83 Ibid.

84 Catherine Ceniza Choy, *Global Families: A History of Asian International Adoption in America* (New York: New York University Press, 2013).

85 Ibid.

86 Quoted in Arissa Oh, *To Save the Children of Korea: The Cold War Origins of International Adoption* (Stanford, CA: Stanford University Press, 2015), 53–54.

87 Ellen Herman, *Kinship by Design: A History of Adoption in the Modern United States* (Chicago: University of Chicago Press, 2008), 17.

88 Susie Woo, *Framed by War: Korean Children and Women at the Crossroads of US Empire* (New York: New York University Press, 2019), 124.

89 Woo, *Framed by War*, 124.

90 Woo, *Framed by War*, 125.

91 Graves, *A War Born Family*, 212.

92 Conn, *Pearl S. Buck*, 375.

93 Pearl Buck, "I Am the Better Woman for Having My Two Black Children," *Today's Health*, January 1972, 22.

94 Buck, *Children for Adoption*, 167; "Author Pearl Buck to Adopt Part-Negro Orphan," Chicago Defender, 5 April 1958.

95 Rochelle Girson, "Welcome House," *Saturday Review*, July 1952, 21; Christina Klein, *Cold War Orientalism: Asia in the Middlebrow Imagination, 1945–1961* (Berkeley: University of California Press, 2003), 147.

96 Chung, "Transnational Adoption: A Noble Cause?"; Pearl Buck, "Breaking the Barriers of Race Prejudice," *Journal of Negro Education* 11., no. 4 (1942).

97 Pearl Buck, "Men as Beasts," 727, Box 1, Folder 42. The Pearl S. Buck Literary Manuscripts Collection, West Virginia & Regional History Center, Morgantown, WV.

98 Buck, "Men as Beasts," The Pearl S. Buck Literary Manuscripts Collection.

99 James D. Hart, *The Popular Book: A History of America's Literary Taste* (Berkeley: University of California Press, 1950), 253.

100 Conn, *Pearl S. Buck*, 382.

101 Pearl S. Buck, *Of Men and Women* (New York: John Day Company, 1941), 116.

102 https://hrc.contentdm.oclc.org/digital/collection/p15878coll9o/id/46/rec/53.

103 Buck, "Children, American-Asian," The Pearl S. Buck Literary Manuscripts Collection.

104 Buck, *Children for Adoption*, 29.

105 Buck, "Men as Beasts," The Pearl S. Buck Literary Manuscripts Collection.

106 Susan Zeiger, *Entangling Alliances: Foreign War Brides and American Soldiers in the Twentieth Century* (New York: New York University Press, 2010).

107 Buck, "Men as Beasts," The Pearl S. Buck Literary Manuscripts Collection.

108 Buck, *Children for Adoption*, 30.

109 Pearl Buck, "American Unity," 727, Box 8, Folder 1. The Pearl S. Buck Literary Manuscripts Collection, West Virginia & Regional History Center, Morgantown, WV.

110 Pearl Buck, "Breaking the Barriers of Race Prejudice," *Journal of Negro Education* 11, no. 4 (1942): 444–453.

111 Buck, "Men as Beasts," The Pearl S. Buck Literary Manuscripts Collection.

112 Buck, "Children, American-Asian," The Pearl S. Buck Literary Manuscripts Collection.

113 Buck, "Children Waiting," The Pearl S. Buck Literary Manuscripts Collection.

114 Buck, "Articles about Adoption," The Pearl S. Buck Literary Manuscripts Collection.; Buck, "Men as Beasts," The Pearl S. Buck Literary Manuscripts Collection.

115 Buck, "Children Waiting," The Pearl S. Buck Literary Manuscripts Collection.

116 Buck, "To an Amerasian Child," The Pearl S. Buck Literary Manuscripts Collection.

117 Chung, "Transnational Adoption: A Noble Cause?"

118 Helgren, American Girls and Global Responsibility, 128.

119 Quoted in Harriet Hyman Alonso, Peace as a Women's Issue: A History of the U.S. Movement for World Peace and Women's Rights (Syracuse, NY: Syracuse University Press, 1993), 84.

120 Buck, "Children Waiting," The Pearl S. Buck Literary Manuscripts Collection.

121 Buck, Children for Adoption, 53.

122 Buck, "Children Waiting," The Pearl S. Buck Literary Manuscripts Collection.

123 Buck, Children for Adoption, 54.

124 Helgren, American Girls and Global Responsibility, 59.

125 Dana L. Robert, Faithful Friendships: Embracing Diversity in Christian Community (Grand Rapids, MI: William B. Eerdmans, 2019).

126 Pearl Buck, "A Case Study: Welcome House," Box 64, folder 265.12, Buck, Literary Manuscripts, West Virginia and Regional History Collection, Morgantown, WV.

127 Chung, "Transnational Adoption: A Noble Cause?"

128 Pearl Buck, "Should White Parents Adopt Brown Babies?" Ebony, June 1958.

129 Buck, "Children Waiting," The Pearl S. Buck Literary Manuscripts Collection.

130 Quoted in Christina Klein, Cold War Orientalism: Asia in the Middlebrow Imagination, 1945–1961 (Berkeley: University of California Press, 2003), 178.

131 Buck, "A Case History: Welcome House," The Pearl S. Buck Literary Manuscripts Collection.

132 Buck, "A Case History: Welcome House," The Pearl S. Buck Literary Manuscripts Collection.

133 Buck, "Men as Beasts," The Pearl S. Buck Literary Manuscripts Collection.

134 Ibid.

135 Buck, "Breaking the Barriers of Race Prejudice," The Pearl S. Buck Literary Manuscripts Collection.

136 Ibid.

137 Quoted in Klein, Cold War Orientalism, 178; Pearl S. Buck, "The 1957 Anisfield-Wolf Awards," Saturday Review, 28 June 1958, 22.

4. HELEN DOSS'S THE FAMILY NOBODY WANTED

1 Helen Doss, The Family Nobody Wanted (Boston: Northeastern University Press, 1954).

2 Sylvester A. Johnson, *The Myth of Ham in Nineteenth-Century American Christianity: Race, Heathens, and the People of God* (New York: Palgrave Macmillan, 2004).

3 Pamela Anne Quiroz, "From Race Matching to Transnational Adoption: Race and the Changing Discourse of US Adoption," *Critical Discourse Studies* 5, no. 3 (2008): 250.

4 Albert H. Stoneman, "Adoption of Illegitimate Children: The Peril of Ignorance," *Child Welfare League of America Bulletin* 5, February 15, 1926, 8.

5 Elaine Showalter, *Insights, Interviews & More* (New York: HarperCollins Publishers, 1997), 6.

6 Daniel J. Kevles, *In the Name of Eugenics: Genetics and the Uses of Human Heredity* (Berkeley: University of California Press, 1985).

7 May, *Barren in the Promised Land*, 103–110.

8 Sheldon C. Reed, "Skin Color," in *Counseling in Medical Genetics* (Philadelphia: W. B. Saunders Company, 1955): 153–160.

9 May, *Barren in the Promised Land*, 144–145.

10 U.S. Children's Bureau was the first governmental bureau governed by women. See U.S. Children's Bureau, *The Confidential Nature of Birth Records, Including the Special Registration Problems of Children Born out of Wedlock, Children of Unknown Parentage, Legitimated Children, and Adopted Children* (Washington, DC: Government Printing Office, 1949), 5–7.

11 Ellen Herman, "Confidentiality and Sealed Records," The Adoption History Project, accessed March 10, 2018, http://pages.uoregon.edu/adoption/topics/confidentiality.htm.

12 E. Wayne Carp argues that there were multiple reasons for this shift from confidentiality to secrecy. Some of the reasons included "a desire to defend the adoptive process, protect the privacy of unwed mothers, increase their own influence and power, and bolster social work professionalism; these motivations in turn reflected profound changes in client demography and an intellectual paradigm shift in social work." See E. Wayne Carp, *Family Matters: Secrecy and Disclosure in the History of Adoption* (Cambridge, MA: Harvard University Press, 1998), 102.

13 Quoted in Carp, *Family Matters*, 121; Barbara Kohlsaat and Adelaide M. Johnson, "Some Suggestions for Practice in Infant Adoptions," *Social Casework* (1954): 93–94.

14 Carp, *Family Matters*, 126–27; May, *Barren in the Promised Land*, 138–43.

15 "Life Visits a One Family U.N.: Methodist Minister and His Wife Adopt Children of All Races," *LIFE Magazine*, November 12, 1951.

16 Ibid., 14.

17 Helen Doss, *The Family Nobody Wanted* (Boston: Northeastern University Press, 2001), 3–4.

18 Doss, *The Family Nobody Wanted*, 5.

19 Ibid., 23.

20 Ibid., 29.

21 Groucho Marx, *You Bet Your Life* #54–14, December 16, 1954.

22 Doss, *The Family Nobody Wanted*, 164, 119; Ellen Herman, *Kinship by Design: A History of Adoption in the Modern United States* (Chicago: University of Chicago Press, 2009), 213.

23 Ibid.

24 Ibid.

25 Doss, *The Family Nobody Wanted*, 29–31.

26 Ibid.

27 Ibid.

28 Ibid, 61, 164.

29 Christina Klein, *Cold War Orientalism: Asia in the Middlebrow Imagination, 1945–1961* (Berkeley: University of California Press, 2003), 146.

30 Klein, *Cold War Orientalism*, 14.

31 Helen Doss, *All the Children of the World* (Nashville: Abingdon Press, 1958).

32 Ibid.

33 Helen Grigsby Doss, *Friends around the World* (Nashville: Abingdon Press, 1959).

34 Ibid.

35 Ibid., 166, 42.

36 Doss, *The Family Nobody Wanted*, 80–95.

37 Ibid.

38 Doss, *The Family Nobody Wanted*, 80–95.

39 Ibid., 167–168.

40 Ibid.

41 Ibid., 187–188.

42 Ibid.

43 Ibid., 188–190.

44 Ibid.

45 Ibid.

46 Ibid.

47 Ibid.

48 Sandra Patton, *BirthMarks: Transracial Adoption in Contemporary America* (New York: NY, New York University Press, 2000), 22.

49 "Text of Supreme Court Decision Outlawing Negro Segregation in the Public Schools," *New York Times*, May 18, 1954.

50 "Court Argument Starts on School Segregation: John W. Davis Says Mingling of Students Might Cost Negroes More Than They Gain," *Los Angeles Times*, Dec. 8, 1953.

51 Ibid.

52 "Kill Jim Crow Schools: U.S. Supreme Court Rules Unanimously in Ending Segregation in Education," *Chicago Defender*, May 22, 1954.

53 Ibid.

54 "Mobs Push Ban on Negro Pupils in Public Schools," *Daily Boston Globe*, Oct. 2, 1954.

55 John N. Popham, "School Integration Brings Varied Reaction in Nation," *New York Times*, Oct. 3, 1954.

56 Patton, *BirthMarks*, 5.

57 Nichole Sanders, "The Medicalization of Childhood in Mexico during the Early Cold War, 1945–1960," in *Gender, Sexuality, and the Cold War: A Global Perspective*, ed. Philip E. Muehlenbeck (Nashville, TN: Vanderbilt University Press, 2017), 140. See also Judith Bennett, *History Matters: Patriarchy and the Challenge of Feminism* (Philadelphia: University of Pennsylvania Press, 2006).

58 Helen Doss, *The Really Real Family* (Boston: Little, Brown, and Company, 1959).

59 Doss, *The Family Nobody Wanted*, 165.

60 Klein, *Cold War Orientalism*, 189.

CONCLUSION

1 John McLeod, Bryan Cheyette, and Martin Paul Eve, *Life Lines: Writing Transcultural Adoption*, Reprint edition (London: Bloomsbury Academic, 2017), 86.

2 Chung, "Transnational Adoption: A Noble Cause?"; Buck, *Children for Adoption*, 152.

3 See Carl F. H. Henry, *The Uneasy Conscience of Modern Fundamentalism*, foreword by Richard J. Mouw (Grand Rapids: Wm. B. Eerdmans Publishing, 2003).

4 Mark Hutchinson and John Wolffe, *A Short History of Global Evangelicalism* (Cambridge: Cambridge University Press, 2012), 205.

5 "Orphans," UNICEF, accessed May 2020, www.unicef.org/media/media_45279.html.

6 "Bethany Christian Services Reports Increased Adoption Placements in 2010," CISION: PR Newswire, accessed May 2020, www.prnewswire.com/news-releases/bethany-christian-services-reports-increased-adoption-placements-in-2010-115476794.html.

7 Russell Moore, *Adopted for Life: The Priority of Adoption for Christian Families and Churches* (Wheaton, IL: Crossway, 2009), 13–14.

8 Elizabeth Styffe, "Orphan-Care Ministries Aim to Eradicate Global Problems," Charisma Leader, accessed May 2020, https://ministrytodaymag.com/outreach/missions/19805-how-we-can-end-the-orphan-crisis.

9 Ibid.

10 See, for example, Daniel J. Bennett, *A Passion for the Fatherless: Developing A God-Centered Ministry to Orphans* (Grand Rapids, MI: Kregel, 2011); Dan Cruver et al., *Reclaiming Adoption: Missional Living through the Rediscovery of Abba Father* (Minneapolis, MN: Cruciform Press, 2011); Tony Merida and Rick Morton, *Orphanology: Awakening to Gospel Centered Adoption and Orphan Care* (Birmingham, AL: New Hope Publishers, 2011).

11 Sandra Patton-Imani, "Orphan Sunday: Narratives of Salvation in Transnational Adoption," *Dialog: A Journal of Theology* 51, no. 4 (Winter 2012): 294–304.

12 David M. Smolin, "Of Orphans and Adoption, Parents and the Poor, Exploitation and Rescue: A Scriptural and Theological Critique of the Evangelical Christian

Adoption and Orphan Care Movement," *Regent Journal of International Law* 8, no. 2 (2012): 267–324.

13 Styffe, "Orphan-Care Ministries," Chrisma Leader. https://ministrytodaymag.com/outreach/missions/19805-how-we-can-end-the-orphan-crisis.

14 Joshi, Khyati Y. *White Christian Privilege: The Illusion of Religious Equality in America* (New York: New York University Press, 2020).

15 Sandra Patton, *BirthMarks: Transracial Adoption in Contemporary America* (New York: New York University Press, 2000); Patton-Imani, "Orphan Sunday," 294.

16 Barb Lee, dir., *Adopted: The Movie* (Point Made Films, 2008).

17 Ibid.

18 Ibid.

19 Ibid.

20 Ibid.

21 Andrea Louise, *How Chinese Are You? Adopted Chinese Youth and Their Families Negotiate Identity and Culture* (New York: New York University Press, 2015), 18.

22 Ibid., 23.

23 Ibid., 23.

24 Quoted in Samuel L. Perry, *Growing God's Family: The Global Orphan Care Movement and the Limits of Evangelical Activism* (New York: New York University Press, 2017), 214–15; Johnny Carr, *Orphan Justice: How to Care for Orphans beyond Adopting* (Nashville: B&H Publishing Group), 134.

25 "Adoption Statistics," U.S. Department of State—Bureau of Consular Affairs, accessed May 2020, https://travel.state.gov/content/travel/en/Intercountry-Adoption/adopt_ref/adoption-statistics1.html?wcmmode=disabled.

26 Barb Lee, dir., *Adopted: The Movie* (Point Made Films, 2008).

BIBLIOGRAPHY

PRIMARY SOURCES

Archival Material
Presbyterian Historical Society. Philadelphia, PA.
Randolph College. Nora Stirling Pearl Buck Collection. Lynchburg, VA.
Swarthmore College. Swarthmore College Peace Collection (SCPC). Swarthmore, PA.
University of Minnesota. Social Welfare History Archives. Minneapolis, MN.
University of Oregon. Richard Neuberger Papers, 1930–1960. Eugene, OR.
West Virginia & Regional History Center. Pearl S. Buck Literary Manuscripts Collection Morgantown, WV.
World Vision Central Records. World Vision International. Monrovia, CA.

Periodicals
Asia Magazine, 1945–1946.
Christianity Today, 1956–1960.
Churchman, 1928.
Dong-A Il Bo (Dong-A Newspaper), 1945–1960.
Eugene Register Guard, 1957.
Kyung Hyang Shin Moon (Kyung Hyang Newspaper), 1945–1966; 1995.
Los Angeles Times, 1945–1960.
Milwaukee Journal, 1933.
New York Journal American, 1957.
Pacific Stars and Stripes, 1950–1955.
Saturday Review, 1952.
The New York Times, 1945–1960.
The Standard (official publication of the Baptist General Conference), 1952–1958.
The Washington Post and Times Herald, 1959.
United Evangelical Action, 1954.
World Vision Magazine, 1957–1960.
World Vision News, 1952–1956.

Documentaries/TV Show
China Challenge, 1948.
38th Parallel: The Story of God's Deadline in Korea, 1950.

Marx, Groucho. *You Bet Your Life* #54–14, December 16, 1954.

Articles and Books

Anderson, Ken. "Ambassador on Fire," *Youth for Christ*, June 1948.

Anderson, Ken. "Her Community Is Called Death," *Youth for Christ*, April 1949.

Anderson, Ken, and Bob Pierce. *This Way to the Harvest.* Kessinger Publishing, 2010.

Aylward, Gladys, and Christine Hunter. *Gladys Aylward: The Little Woman.* Chicago: Moody Publishers, 1970.

Buck, Pearl S. "Breaking the Barriers of Race Prejudice." *Journal of Negro Education* 11, no. 4 (1942): 444–53.

Buck, Pearl S. *A Bridge for Passing.* New York: John Day Company, 1962.

Buck, Pearl S. *Children for Adoption.* New York: Random House, 1965.

Buck, Pearl S. "China and the West." *Annals of the American Academy of Political and Social Science* (1933): 118–31.

Buck, Pearl S. "The Future of the White Man in the Far East." *Foreign Affairs* 19, no. 1 (1940).

Buck, Pearl S. "I Am the Better Woman for Having My Two Black Children." *Today's Health*, January 1972.

Buck, Pearl S. "Is There a Case for Foreign Missions?" *Harper's Monthly Magazine* 166 (1933): 143–146.

Buck, Pearl S. "The Laymen's Mission Report." *Christian Century* (1932).

Buck, Pearl S. *My Several Worlds.* New York: John Day Company, 1954.

Buck, Pearl S. *Of Men and Women.* New York: John Day Company, 1941.

Buck, Pearl S. "Save the Children for What?" *Journal of Educational Sociology* 17, no. 4 (1943): 195–99.

Buck, Pearl S. "Should White Parents Adopt Brown Babies?" *Ebony* (1958): 26–30.

Buck, Pearl S. "Welcome House," *Reader's Digest* (1958): 47–50.

Child Welfare League of America. *Standards for Adoption Service.* New York: Child Welfare League of America, 1958.

Doss, Helen Grigsby. *All the Children of the World.* New York: World's Work, 1963.

Doss, Helen Grigsby. *The Family Nobody Wanted.* Boston: Northeastern University Press, 2001.Doss, Helen Grigsby. *Family of Children.* Nashville: Perigee, 1979.

Doss, Helen Grigsby. *Friends around the World.* Nashville: Abingdon Press, 1959.

Doss, Helen Grigsby. "Our International Family," *Reader's Digest* (1949): 58–59.

Doss, Helen Grigsby. *The Really Real Family.* Boston: Little, Brown, 1959.

Gehman, Richard. *Let My Heart Be Broken with the Things That Break the Heart of God.* New York: McGraw-Hill, 1960.

Hartog, Jan De. *Adopted Children.* Revised edition. New York: Adama Books, 1987.

Hartog, Jan De. *The Children: A Personal Record for the Use of Adoptive Parents.* New York: Atheneum, 1969.

Hocking, William Ernest. *Re-thinking Missions: A Laymen's Inquiry after One Hundred Years.* New York: Harper & Brothers, 1932.

Holt, Bertha. *Bring My Sons from Afar*. Eugene, OR: Holt International Children's Services, 1986.

Holt, Bertha. *Outstretched Arms: A Summary of Happenings Since "The Seed from the East."* Eugene, OR: Holt International Children's Services, 1972.

Holt, Bertha. *The Seed from the East*. Los Angeles: Oxford Press, 1956.

Holt International Children's Services, and John Aeby. *Years of Love: A Collection of Articles and Letters about Adoption and Helping Homeless Children*. Eugene, OR: Holt International Children's Services, 1992.

International Missionary Council. *The Christian Mission in the Light of Race Conflict*. New York, International Missionary Council, 1928.

Lierop, Peter Van. "A Tribute to Everett Swanson," *Compassion*, September/October 1977.

Moxness, Ron. "Good Samaritan of Korea," *American Mercury*, October 1956, 85.

Pettiss, Susan. "Effect of Adoption of Foreign Children on U.S. Adoption Standards and Practices," *Child Welfare* (July 1958).

Pierce, Bob. *Orphans of the Orient: Stories That Will Touch Your Heart*. Grand Rapids, MI: Zondervan Publishing House, 1964.

Pierce, Bob. *The Untold Korean Story*. Grand Rapids, MI: Zondervan Publishing House, 1951.

Pierce, Bob, and Ken Anderson. "China as We Saw It," *Youth for Christ*, September 1948.

Reed, Sheldon C. "Skin Color," in *Counseling in Medical Genetics*. Philadelphia: W. B. Saunders Company, 1955.

Rogers, Dale Evans. *Dearest Debbie*. Grand Rapids, MI: Fleming H. Revell Co, 1965.

Swanson, Everett. "Korea Calls," *The Standard*, July 25, 1952, 1–2.

Swanson, Everett. "Spiritual Victories in Korea," *The Standard*, January 2, 1953, 2–5.

U.S. Children's Bureau. "The Confidential Nature of Birth Records, including the special registration problems of children born out of wedlock, children of unknown parentage, legitimated children, and adopted children," Washington DC: Government Printing Office, 1949.

Wisner, David. "'The Bright Spot' in the Korean Orphan Situation," *Wesleyan Missionary*, December 1955.

SECONDARY SOURCES

Articles and Books

Adelson, Joseph. "Is Women's Lib a Passing Fad?" *New York Times Magazine*, March 19, 1972.

Alonso, Harriet Hyman. *Peace as a Women's Issue: A History of the U.S. Movement for World Peace and Women's Rights*. Syracuse, NY: Syracuse University Press, 1993.

Alstein, Howard, and Rita Simon. *Intercountry Adoption: A Multinational Perspective*. New York: Praeger, 1990.

Anderson, David C. *Children of Special Value: Interracial Adoption in America*. New York: St. Martin's Press, 1971.

Aronson, Howard G. "The Problem of Rejection of Adoptive Applicants," *Child Welfare* 39 (1960): 21–26.

Ashby, LeRoy. *Endangered Children: Dependency, Neglect, and Abuse in American History*. New York: Twayne Publishers, 1997.

Askeland, Lori, ed. *Children and Youth in Adoption, Orphanages, and Foster Care: A Historical Handbook and Guide*. Westport, CT: Greenwood Press, 2006.

Baek, Chun Seong. *Chosun's Little Jesus: Seo Seo-Peong*. Seoul: Duranno International Press, 2017.

Baer, Janine M. *Growing in the Dark: Adoption Secrecy and Its Consequences*. Bloomington, IN: Xlibris Corporation, 2004.

Ballmer, Randall. *Encyclopedia of Evangelicalism*. Louisville, KY: Westminster John Knox Press, 2014.

Bartholet, Elizabeth. *Family Bonds: Adoption and the Politics of Parenting*. Boston: Houghton Mifflin, 1993.

Bartholet, Elizabeth. *Nobody's Children: Abuse and Neglect, Foster Drift, and the Adoption Alternative*. Boston: Beacon Press, 1999.

Bartholet, Elizabeth. "Where Do Black Children Belong? The Politics of Race Matching in Adoption," *University of Pennsylvania Law Review* 139 (1991): 1163–1256.

Bates, J. Douglas. *Gift Children: A Story of Race, Family, and Adoption in a Divided America*. New York: Ticknor & Fields, 1993.

Bennett, Amanda, and Sara Brinton. *In Defense of the Fatherless: Redeeming International Adoption & Orphan Care*. Fearn, United Kingdom: Christian Focus, 2015.

Bennett, Scott H. *Radical Pacifism: The War Resisters League and Gandhian Nonviolence in America, 1915–1963*. Syracuse, Syracuse University Press, 2003.

Berebitsky, Julie. *Like Our Very Own: Adoption and the Changing Culture of Motherhood, 1851–1950*. Lawrence: University Press of Kansas, 2000.

Bernstein, Nina. *The Lost Children of Wilder: The Epic Struggle to Change Foster Care*. New York: Pantheon Books, 2001.

Billingsley, Andrew, and Jeanne M. Giovannoni. *Children of the Storm: Black Children and American Child Welfare*. New York: Harcourt, Brace, Jovanovich, 1972.

Brian, Kristi. *Reframing Transracial Adoption: Adopted Koreans, White Parents, and the Politics of Kinship*. Philadelphia: Temple University Press, 2012.

Briggs, Laura. "Mother, Child, Race, Nation: The Visual Iconography of Rescue and the Politics of Transnational and Transracial Adoption," *Gender & History* 15 (2003): 179–200.

Briggs, Laura. *Somebody's Children: The Politics of Transracial and Transnational Adoption*. Durham, NC: Duke University Press, 2012.

Brodie, Howard. "The Power of Faith," *Evening Star*, March 8, 1958.

Brouwer, Ruth Compton. *Modern Women Modernizing Men: The Changing Missions of Three Professional Women in Asia and Africa, 1902–69*. Vancouver: University of Washington Press, 2002.

Brown, Florence G. "Adoption of Children with Special Needs." New York: Child Welfare League of America, March 1958.

Byun, Eddie. *Justice Awakening: How You and Your Church Can Help End Human Trafficking*. Downers Grove, IL: InterVarsity Press, 2014.

Caldwell, Mardie, Heather Featherston, and Terry Meeuwsen. *Called to Adoption: A Christian's Guide to Answering the Call*. Nevada City: American Carriage House Publishing, 2011.

Carp, E. Wayne, ed. *Adoption in America: Historical Perspectives*. Ann Arbor: University of Michigan Press, 2002.

Carp, E. Wayne. *Family Matters: Secrecy and Disclosure in the History of Adoption*. Cambridge, MA: Harvard University Press, 1998.

Carp, E. Wayne. "Professional Social Workers, Adoption, and the Problem of Illegitimacy, 1915–1945," *Journal of Policy History* 6 (1994): 161–184.

Carpenter, Joel A. "The Fundamentalist Leaven and the Rise of an Evangelical United Front," in *The Evangelical Tradition in America*, ed. Leonard I. Sweet. Macon, GA: Mercer University Press, 1984.

Carpenter, Joel A. "'Geared to the Times, but Anchored to the Rock': How Contemporary Techniques, Nationalism Helped Create an Evangelical Resurgence," *Christianity Today*, November 8, 1985, 44–47.

Carpenter, Joel A. *Revive Us Again: The Reawakening of American Fundamentalism*. New York: Oxford University Press, 1999.

Carr, Johnny. *Orphan Justice: How to Care for Orphans beyond Adopting*. Nashville: B&H Publishing Group.

Chandra, Anjani, et al. "Adoption, Adoption Seeking, and Relinquishment for Adoption in the United States," *Advance Data from Vital and Health Statistics of the Centers for Disease Control and Prevention/National Center for Health Statistics*, no. 306 (1999): 1–16.

Cheng, Emily. "Pearl S. Buck's 'American Children': US Democracy, Adoption of the Amerasian Child, and the Occupation of Japan in *The Hidden Flower*," *Frontiers: A Journal of Women Studies* 35, no. 1 (2014): 181–210.

Chesnutt, Charles W. *The Quarry*. Princeton, NJ: Princeton University Press, 1999.

Choi, Hyæweol. *Gender and Mission Encounters in Korea: New Women, Old Ways: Seoul-California Series in Korean Studies, Volume 1*. Berkeley: University of California Press, 2009.

Choi, Myung Keun. *Changes in Korean Society between 1884–1910 as a Result of the Introduction of Christianity*. New York: Peter Lang International Academic Publishers, 1997.

Choy, Catherine Ceniza. *Global Families: A History of Asian International Adoption in America*. New York: New York University Press, 2013.

Chung, Hyun Kyung. *Struggle to Be the Sun Again: Introducing Asian Women's Theology*. Maryknoll, NY: Orbis Books, 1990.

Chung, Soojin. "The Missiology of Pearl Sydenstricker Buck," *International Bulletin of Mission Research* 41, no. 2 (2017): 134–41.

Chung, Soojin. "Transnational Adoption: A Noble Cause? Female Missionaries as Pioneers of Transnational Adoption, 1945–1965," *Evangelical Missions Quarterly* (2016).

Church, Louisa Randall. "Parents: Architects of Peace," *American Home*, November 1946.

Cole, David C., and Princeton N. Lyman. *Korean Development: The Interplay of Politics and Economics*. Cambridge, MA: Harvard University Press, 1971.

Conn, Peter. *Pearl S. Buck: A Cultural Biography*. New York: Cambridge University Press, 1996.

Crenson, Matthew A. *Building the Invisible Orphanage: The Prehistory of the American Welfare System*. Cambridge, MA: Harvard University Press, 1998.

del Mar, David Peterson. *The American Family: From Obligation to Freedom*. New York: Palgrave Macmillan, 2011.

Doran, Mary S., and Bertha C. Reynolds. *The Selection of Foster Homes for Children: Principles and Methods Followed by the Boston Children's Aid Society with Illustrative Cases*. New York: School of Social Work, 1919.

Dower, John *War without Mercy: Race and Power in the Pacific War*. New York: Pantheon Books, 1986.

Dubinsky, Karen. *Babies without Borders: Adoption and Migration across the Americas*. New York: New York University Press, 2010.

Eiduson, Bernice T., and Jean B. Livermore. "Complications in Therapy with Adopted Children," *American Journal of Orthopsychiatry* 23 (1953): 795–802.

Ehrenreich, John H. *The Altruistic Imagination: A History of Social Work and Social Policy in the United States*. Ithaca, NY: Cornell University Press, 1985.

Emerson, Michael O., and Christian Smith. *Divided by Faith: Evangelical Religion and the Problem of Race in America*. New York: Oxford University Press, 2001.

Fabella, Virginia, and Sun Ai Park Lee, eds. *We Dare to Dream: Doing Theology as Asian Women*. Maryknoll, NY: Orbis Books, 1990.

Fanon, Frantz. *The Wretched of the Earth*. New York: Grove Press, 1963.

Finstuen, Andrew, Grant Wacker, and Anne Blue Wills, eds. *Billy Graham: American Pilgrim*. Oxford: Oxford University Press, 2017.

Fogg-Davis, Hawley. *The Ethics of Transracial Adoption*. Ithaca, NY: Cornell University Press, 2002.

Foglesong, David S. "Roots of 'Liberation': American Images of the Future of Russia in the Early Cold War, 1948–1953," *International History Review* 21 (1999): 57–79.

Fradkin, Helen. *The Adoption Home Study*. Trenton: Bureau of Children's Services, 1963.

Frederick, Thomas V. "An Interpretation of Evangelical Gender Ideology: Implications for a Theology of Gender," *Theology & Sexuality* 16, no. 2 (2010): 183–192.

Friedan, Betty. *The Feminine Mystique*. New York: W. W. Norton and Co., 1963.

Fry, Annette Riley. "The Children's Migration," *American Heritage* (1974): 4–10, 79–81.

Gillespie, Natalie. *Successful Adoption: A Guide for Christian Families*. Nashville: Thomas Nelson, 2006.

Gish, Clay. "Rescuing the 'Waifs and Strays' of the City: The Western Emigration Program of the Children's Aid Society," *Journal of Social History* 33, no. 1 (1999): 121–141.

Goddard, Henry Herbert. *Psychology of the Normal and Subnormal*. New York: Dodd, Mead, and Company, 1919.

Gordon, Linda. *Pitied but Not Entitled: Single Mothers and the History of Welfare, 1890–1935*. New York: The Free Press, 1994.

Gordon, Linda. *The Great Arizona Orphan Abduction*. Cambridge, MA: Harvard University Press, 1999.

Graham, Franklin, and Jeanette W. Lockerbie. *Bob Pierce: This One Thing I Do*. Waco, TX: Word Books, 1983.

Graves, Kori A. *A War Born Family: African American Adoption in the Wake of the Korean War*. New York: New York University Press, 2020.

Grow, Lucille J., and Deborah Shapiro. *Black Children—White Parents: A Study of Transracial Adoption*. New York: Child Welfare League of America, 1974.

Hadden, Jeffrey K. "H. Paul Douglass: His Perspective and His Work," *Review of Religious Research* 22, no. 1 (1980): 66–88.

Haney, Charles J., Choe, Sang-Hun, and Mendoza, Martha. *The Bridge at No Gun Ri: A Hidden Nightmare from the Korean War*. New York: Henry Holt, 2001.

Hankins, Barry. *American Evangelicals: A Contemporary History of a Mainstream Religious Movement*. Lanham, MD: Rowman & Littlefield Publishers, 2008.

Harris, Theodore F. *Pearl S. Buck: A Biography*. New York: John Day, 1969.

Hart, D. G. "After the Breakup, Heartbreak: Conservative Presbyterians without a Common Foe," *Journal of Presbyterian History* 86, no. 2 (2008): 61–70.

Hart, James D. *The Popular Book: A History of America's Literary Taste*. Berkeley: University of California Press, 1950.

Haugaard, Jeffrey J. "Is Adoption a Risk Factor for the Development of Adjustment Problems?" *Clinical Psychology Review* 18, no. 1 (1998): 47–69.

Hefley, James C. *God Goes to High School: An In-Depth Look at an Incredible Phenomenon*. Waco, TX: Word, 1970.

Helgren, Jennifer. *American Girls and Global Responsibility: A New Relation to the World during the Early Cold War*. Newark, NJ: Rutgers University Press, 2017.

Henry, Carl F. H. *The Uneasy Conscience of Modern Fundamentalism*. With a foreword by Richard J. Mouw. Grand Rapids, MI: Wm. B. Eerdmans Publishing, 2003.

Herman, Ellen. "The Difference Difference Makes: Justine Wise Polier and Religious Matching in Twentieth-Century Child Adoption," *Religion and American Culture* 10 (2000): 57–98.

Herman, Ellen. *Kinship by Design: A History of Adoption in the Modern United States*. Chicago: University of Chicago Press, 2009.

Herman, Ellen. "The Paradoxical Rationalization of Modern Adoption," *Journal of Social History* 36 (2002): 339–385.

Hodgson, Dorothy L. *The Church of Women: Gendered Encounters between Massai and Missionaries*. Bloomington: Indiana University Press, 2005.

Hollinger, David A. *Protestants Abroad: How Missionaries Tried to Change the World but Changed America*. Princeton, NJ: Princeton University Press, 2017.

Hollinger, Joan Heifetz. "Beyond the Best Interests of the Tribe: The Indian Child Welfare Act and the Adoption of Indian Children," *University of Detroit Law Review* 66 (1989): 451–501.

Hollinger, Joan Heifetz. *A Guide to the Multiethnic Placement Act of 1994 as Amended by the Interethnic Adoption Provisions of 1996*. Washington, DC: ABA Center on Children and the Law, 1998.

Holman, Portia. "Some Factors in the Aetiology of Maladjusted Children," *Journal of Mental Science* 99 (1953): 654–688.

Holt, Marilyn Irvin. *Indian Orphanages*. Lawrence: University Press of Kansas, 2001.

Holt, Marilyn Irvin. *The Orphan Trains: Placing Out in America*. Lincoln: University of Nebraska Press, 1992.

Hong, Jane. *Opening the Gates of Asia: A Transpacific History of How America Repealed Asian Exclusion*. Chapel Hill: University of North Carolina Press, 2019.

Howe, Ruth-Arlene W. "Transracial Adoption (TRA): Old Prejudices and Discrimination Float Under a New Halo," *Boston University Public Interest Law Journal* 6 (1997): 409–472.

Hubinette, Tobias *Comforting an Orphaned Nation*. Seoul: Jimoondang, 2006.

Hutchinson, Mark, and John Wolffe. *A Short History of Global Evangelicalism*. New York: Cambridge University Press, 2012.

Hutchison, William R. *Errand to the World: American Protestant Thought and Foreign Missions*. Chicago: University of Chicago Press, 1993.

Johnson, Sylvester A. *The Myth of Ham in Nineteenth-Century American Christianity: Race, Heathens, and the People of God*. New York: Palgrave Macmillan, 2004.

Johnson, Todd M. et al., eds. *2010Boston: The Changing Contours of World Mission and Christianity*. Eugene, OR: Pickwick Publications, 2015.

Joshi, Khyati Y., and Jigna Desai, eds. *Asian Americans in Dixie: Race and Migration in the South*. Urbana: University of Illinois Press, 2013.

Joshi, Khyati Y. *White Christian Privilege: The Illusion of Religious Equality in America*. New York: New York University Press, 2020.

Joyce, Kathryn. *The Child Catchers: Rescue, Trafficking, and the New Gospel of Adoption*. New York: PublicAffairs, 2013.

Kadushin, Alfred. "A Study of Adoptive Parents of Hard-to-Place Children," *Social Casework* 43 (1962): 227–33.

Kane, Herbert J. *A Concise History of the Christian World Mission: A Panoramic View of Missions from Pentecost to the Present*. Grand Rapids, MI: Baker Academic, 1978.

Kennedy, Randall. *Interracial Intimacies: Sex, Marriage, Identity, and Adoption*. New York: Pantheon Books, 2003.

Ketchum, Betty K. "An Exploratory Study of the Disproportionate Number of Adopted Children Hospitalized at Columbus Children's Psychiatric Hospital." Masters thesis, Ohio State University, 1962.

Kevles, Daniel J. *In the Name of Eugenics: Genetics and the Uses of Human Heredity.* Cambridge, MA: Harvard University Press, 1995.

Kim, Eleana J. *Adopted Territory: Transnational Korean Adoptees and the Politics of Belonging.* Durham, NC: Duke University Press, 2010.

Kim, Hosu. *Birth Mothers and Transnational Adoption Practice in South Korea: Virtual Mothering.* Berlin: Springer, 2016.

Kim, Kirsteen, and Andrew Anderson. *Edinburgh 2010: Mission Today and Tomorrow.* Eugene, OR: Wipf and Stock Publishers, 2011.

Kim, Kirsteen. *Joining in with the Spirit: Connecting Local Church and World Mission.* London: SCM Press, 2012.

Kim, Sebastian C. H., and Kirsteen Kim. *A History of Korean Christianity.* New York: Cambridge University Press, 2014.

Kim, Sebastian C. H., ed. *Christian Theology in Asia.* Cambridge: Cambridge University Press, 2008.

King, David P. *God's Internationalists: World Vision and the Age of Evangelical Humanitarianism.* Philadelphia: University of Pennsylvania Press, 2019.

King, David P. "Seeking Global Vision: The Evolution of World Vision and American Evangelicalism." Ph.D. dissertation, Emory University, 2012.

Kirk, H. David. *Adoptive Kinship: A Modern Institution in Need of Reform.* Toronto: Butterworths, 1981.

Klein, Christina. *Cold War Orientalism: Asia in the Middlebrow Imagination, 1945–1961.* Berkeley: University of California Press, 2003.

Kline, Wendy. *Building a Better Race: Gender, Sexuality, and Eugenics from the Turn of the Century to the Baby Boom.* Berkeley: University of California Press, 2001.

Knight, Robert P. "Some Problems in Selecting and Rearing Adopted Children," *Bulletin of the Menninger Clinic* 5 (1941): 65–74.

Kohlsaat, Barbara, and Adelaide M. Johnson. "Some Suggestions for Practice in Infant Adoptions," *Social Casework* (1954): 91–99.

Künnemann, Vanessa. *Middlebrow Mission: Pearl S. Buck's American China.* Bielefeld, Germany: Transcript Verlag, 2015.

Kunzel, Regina G. *Fallen Women, Problem Girls: Unmarried Mothers and the Professionalization of Social Work, 1890–1945.* New Haven, CT: Yale University Press, 1993.

Kurashige, Lon. *Two Faces of Exclusion: The Untold History of Anti-Asian Racism in the United States.* Chapel Hill: University of North Carolina Press, 2016.

Kushner, James A. "Urban Neighborhood Regeneration and the Phases of Community Evolution after World War II in the United States," *Indiana Law Review* 41, no. 3 (2008): 575–604.

Ladner, Joyce A. *Mixed Families: Adopting Across Racial Boundaries.* Garden City: Anchor Press, Doubleday, 1977.

Larson, Edward J. *Sex, Race, and Science: Eugenics in the Deep South.* Baltimore: Johns Hopkins University Press, 1995.

Latourette, Kenneth S. *A History of the Expansion of Christianity, vol 4: The Great Century in Europe and the United States of America.* Grand Rapids, MI: Zondervan, 1970.

Lee, Barb, dir. *Adopted: The Movie*. Point Made Films, 2008.

Lee, Lorie Henry. "'Now That You Have Seen': A Historical Look at Compassion International 1952–2013." Ph.D. dissertation, Southeastern Baptist Theological Seminary, 2014.

Lian, Xi. *The Conversion of Missionaries: Liberalism in American Protestant Missions in China, 1907–1932*. University Park: Penn State University Press, 2013.

Lindman, Janet Moore. "The Manly Christian: Evangelical White Manhood." In *Bodies of Belief: Baptist Community in Early America*. Philadelphia: University of Pennsylvania Press, 2008.

Lockridge, Frances, and Sophie van S. Theis. *Adopting a Child*. New York: Greenberg, 1947.

Longfield, Bradley J. "For Church and Country: The Fundamentalist-Modernist Conflict in the Presbyterian Church," *Journal of Presbyterian History* 78, no. 1 (2000): 35–50.

Lotz, Denton. "The Evangelization of the World in This Generation: The Resurgence of a Missionary Idea Among the Conservative Evangelicals." Ph.D. dissertation, University of Hamburg, 1970.

Louise, Andrea. *How Chinese Are You? Adopted Chinese Youth and Their Families Negotiate Identity and Culture*. New York: New York University Press, 2015.

Lovelock, Kirsten. "Intercountry Adoption as a Migratory Practice: A Comparative Analysis of Intercountry Adoption and Immigration Policy and Practice in the United States, Canada, and New Zealand in the Post WWII Period," *International Migration Review* 34, no. 3 (2000): 907–49.

Luther, Martin. *Luther's Works: Lectures on Galatians, Chapters 1–4*. Saint Louis, MO: Concordia Publishing House, 1963.

Mandler, Peter, ed. *The Uses of Charity: The Poor on Relief in the Nineteenth-Century Metropolis*. Philadelphia: University of Pennsylvania Press, 1990.

Marglin, Stephen A., and Juliet B. Schor, eds. *The Golden Age of Capitalism: Reinterpreting the Postwar Experience*. Oxford: Clarendon Press, 1992.

Mason, Mary Ann. *From Father's Property to Children's Rights: The History of Child Custody in the United States*. New York: Columbia University Press, 1994.

May, Elaine Tyler. *Barren in the Promised Land: Childless Americans and the Pursuit of Happiness*. New York: Basic Books, 1995.

McKee, Kimberly D. "Monetary Flows and the Movements of Children: The Transnational Adoption Industrial Complex," *Journal of Korean Studies* 21, no. 1 (2016): 137–78.

McLeod, John, Bryan Cheyette, and Martin Paul Eve. *Life Lines: Writing Transcultural Adoption*. London: Bloomsbury Academic, 2017.

Melosh, Barbara. "Adoption Stories: Autobiographical Narrative and the Politics of Identity," in *Adoption in America: Historical Perspectives*, ed. E. Wayne Carp. Ann Arbor: University of Michigan Press, 2002. 218–245.

Melosh, Barbara. *Strangers and Kin: The American Way of Adoption*. Cambridge, MA: Harvard University Press, 2002.

Minow, Martha, ed. *Family Matters: Readings on Family Lives and the Law*. New York: The New Press, 1993.

Mintz, Steven, and Susan Kellogg. *Domestic Revolutions: A Social History of American Family Life*. New York: The Free Press, 1989.

Modell, Judith S. *Kinship with Strangers: Adoption and Interpretations of Kinship in American Culture*. Berkeley: University of California Press, 1994.

Modell, Judith, and Naomi Dambacher, "Making a 'Real' Family: Matching and Cultural Biologism in American Adoption," *Adoption Quarterly* 1, no. 2 (1997): 3–33.

Mondloh, Raymond. "Changing Practice in the Adoption Home Study," *Child Welfare* 48 (1969): 148–156.

Moon, Katherine. *Sex among Allies: Military Prostitution in U.S.-Korea Relations*. New York: Columbia University Press, 1996.

Moon, Young Mi. *Nobody Listened to Her Story: The Story of Pei Moon*. Seoul: Samteo Press, 1999.

Moore, Russell. *Adopted for Life: The Priority of Adoption for Christian Families and Churches*. Wheaton, IL: Crossway, 2015.

Muck, Terry C., Frances S. Adeney, and A. Moreau. *Christianity Encountering World Religions: The Practice of Mission in the Twenty-First Century*. Grand Rapids, MI: Baker Academic, 2009.

Mullins, Mark R., and Richard Fox Young, eds. *Perspectives on Christianity in Korea and Japan: The Gospel and Culture in East Asia*. Lewiston, NY: Edwin Mellen Press, 1995.

Nelson, Claudia. *Little Strangers: Portrayals of Adoption and Foster Care in America, 1850–1929*. Bloomington: Indiana University Press, 2003.

Neufeld, John. *Edgar Allan*. New York: S. G. Phillips, 1968.

Ninivaggi, Cynthia Carter. "The Traffic in Children: Adoption and Child Relinquishment in the United States." Ph.D. dissertation, Temple University, 1996.

Novy, Marianne, ed. *Imagining Adoption: Essays on Literature and Culture*. Ann Arbor: University of Michigan Press, 2001.

Nutt, Rick. *The Whole Gospel for the Whole World: Sherwood Eddy and the American Protestant Mission*. Macon, GA: Mercer University Press, 1997.

O'Connor, Stephen. *Orphan Trains: The Story of Charles Loring Brace and the Children He Saved and Failed*. Boston: Houghton Mifflin, 2001.

Oak, Sung-Deuk. *The Making of Korean Christianity: Protestant Encounters with Korean Religions, 1876–1915*. Waco, TX: Baylor University Press, 2013.

Oh, Arissa. *To Save the Children of Korea: The Cold War Origins of International Adoption*. Stanford, CA: Stanford University Press, 2015.

Oscar, Riddle. *Biographical Memoir of Charles Benedict Davenport 1866–1944* (PDF). National Academy of Sciences, 1947.

Pate, SooJin. *From Orphan to Adoptee: U.S. Empire and Genealogies of Korean Adoption*. Minneapolis: University of Minnesota Press, 2014.

Patterson, James A. "Robert E. Speer, J. Gresham Machen, and the Presbyterian Board of Foreign Missions," *Journal of Presbyterian Historical Society* 64, no. 1 (1986): 58–68.

Patton, Sandra. *BirthMarks: Transracial Adoption in Contemporary America*. New York: New York University Press, 2000.

Patton-Imani, Sandra. "Orphan Sunday: Narratives of Salvation in Transnational Adoption," *Dialog: A Journal of Theology* 51, no. 4 (Winter 2012): 294–304.

Pavao, Joyce Maguire. *The Family of Adoption*. Boston: Beacon Press, 1998.

Perry, Samuel L. *Growing God's Family: The Global Orphan Care Movement and the Limits of Evangelical Activism*. New York: New York University Press, 2017.

Peterson, Mark A. *Korean Adoption and Inheritance: Case Studies in the Creation of a Classic Confucian Society*. Ithaca, NY: Cornell University Press, 1998.

Pierce-Dunker, Marilee. *Man of Vision*. Waynesboro, GA: Authentic and World Vision, 2005.

Quiroz, Pamela Anne. *Adoption in a Color-Blind Society*. Lanham, MD: Rowman & Littlefield Publishers, 2007.

Quiroz, Pamela Anne. "From Race Matching to Transnational Adoption: Race and the Changing Discourse of US Adoption," *Critical Discourse Studies* 5, no. 3 (2008): 249–64.

Reeves, Richard. *President Nixon: Alone in the White House*. New York: Simon & Schuster, 2002.

Rigert, Joe. *All Together: An Unusual American Family*. New York: Harper & Row, 1973.

Rindfuss, Ronald R., and James A. Sweet. *Postwar Fertility Trends and Differentials in the United States*. New York: Academic Press, 1977.

Roark, Dallas M. "J. Gresham Machen: The Doctrinally True Presbyterian Church," *Journal of Presbyterian Historical Society* 43, no. 2 (1965): 174–81.

Robert, Dana L. *American Women in Mission: The Modern Mission Era 1792–1992*. Macon, GA: Mercer University Press, 1997.

Robert, Dana L. "The 'Christian Home' as a Cornerstone of Anglo-American Missionary Thought and Practice." In *Converting Colonialism: Visions and Realities in Mission History, 1706–1914, ed*. Dana L. Robert. Grand Rapids, MI: Curzon-Eerdmans, 2008. 134–165.

Robert, Dana L. *Christian Mission: How Christianity Became a World Religion*. Malden, MD: Wiley-Blackwell, 2009.

Robert, Dana L. *Faithful Friendships: Embracing Diversity in Christian Community*. Grand Rapids, MI: William B. Eerdmans, 2019.

Robert, Dana L. "The First Globalization: The Internationalization of the Protestant Missionary Movement between the World Wars," *International Bulletin of Missionary Research* 26, no. 2 (2002): 50–66.

Robert, Dana L. "'Rethinking Missionaries' from 1910 to Today," *Methodist Review* 4 (2012): 1–10.

Roberts, Dorothy. *Shattered Bonds: The Color of Child Welfare*. New York: Basic Books, 2002.

Robinson, Virginia P., ed. *Jessie Taft: Therapist and Social Work Educator, A Professional Biography*. Philadelphia: University of Pennsylvania Press, 1962.

Rogers, Carl R. *On Becoming a Person: A Therapist's View of Psychotherapy*. Boston: Houghton Mifflin, 1961.

Rohrer, Norman. *Open Arms*. Wheaton, IL: Tyndale House Pub, 1987.

Rosenberg, Emily S. *Spreading the American Dream: American Economic and Cultural Expansion, 1890–1945*. New York: Hill and Wang, 1982.

Rosenberg, Rosalind. *Beyond Separate Spheres: Intellectual Roots of Modern Feminism*. New Haven, CT: Yale University Press, 1982.

Rothman, Barbara Katz. *Weaving a Family: Untangling Race and Adoption*. Boston: Beacon Press, 2005.

Rothstein, Richard. *The Color of Law: A Forgotten History of How Our Government Segregated America*. New York: Liveright Publishing Corporation, 2017.

Said, Edward W. *Orientalism*. New York: Vintage, 1979.

Sanders, Nichole Sanders. "The Medicalization of Childhood in Mexico during the Early Cold War, 1945–1960." In *Gender, Sexuality, and the Cold War: A Global Perspective*, ed. Philip E. Muehlenbeck. Nashville, TN: Vanderbilt University Press, 2017.

Saunders, Kenneth. "The Passing of Paternalism in Missions," *Journal of Religion* 2, no. 5 (1922): 466–75.

Schafer, Axel R. *Countercultural Conservatives: American Evangelicalism from the Post-war Revival to the New Christian Right*. Madison: University of Wisconsin Press, 2011.

Schapiro, Michael. *A Study of Adoption Practice, Volume III: Adoption of Children with Special Needs*. New York: Child Welfare League of America, 1956.

Schechter, Marshall D. "Observations on Adopted Children," *Archives of General Psychiatry* 3 (1960): 21–32.

Scheper-Hughes, Nancy. "Theft of Life," *Society* 27, no. 6 (1990): 57–62.

Shaefer, Richard T. *Encyclopedia of Race, Ethnicity, and Society*. Thousand Oaks, CA: Sage Publications, 2008.

Shaffer, Robert. "Pearl S. Buck and the East and West Association: The Trajectory and Fate of 'Critical Internationalism,' 1940–1950," *Peace & Change* 28, no. 1 (2003): 1–36.

Showalter, Elaine. *Insights, Interviews & More*. New York: HarperCollins Publishers, 1997.

Shurtleff, William, and Akiko Aoyagi. *History of Meals for Millions, Soy, and Freedom from Hunger*. Lafayette, CA: SOYINFO Center, 2011.

Silver, Charles. "Pearl Buck, Evangelism, and Works of Love: Images of the Missionary in Fiction," *Journal of Presbyterian History* 51, no. 2 (1973): 216–34.

Simon, Rita James, and Howard Alstein. *Transracial Adoption*. New York: Wiley, 1977.

Skidelsky, Robert. *Keynes: The Return of the Master*. New York: PublicAffairs, 2010.

Smith, Eve P., and Lisa A. Merkel-Holguín, eds. *A History of Child Welfare*. New Brunswick, NJ: Transaction Publishers, 1996.

Smolin, David M. "Of Orphans and Adoption, Parents and the Poor, Exploitation and Rescue: A Scriptural Critique of the Evangelical Christian Adoption and Orphan Care Movement," *Regent Journal of International Law* 8, no. 2 (2012): 6–8.

Song, C. S. *Tell Us Our Names: Story Theology from an Asian Perspective*. Eugene: Wipf & Stock, 2005.

Sorosky, Arthur D., Annette Baran, and Reuben Pannor. *The Adoption Triangle: Sealed or Opened Records: How They Affect Adoptees, Birth Parents, and Adoptive Parents.* San Antonio, TX: Corona Publishing, 1978.

Stern, Alexandra Minna, and Howard Markel, eds. *Formative Years: Children's Health in the United States, 1880–2000.* Ann Arbor: University of Michigan Press, 2002.

Stoltzfus, Brenda, and Saundra Pollock Sturdevant. *Let the Good Times Roll: Prostitution and the U.S. Military in Asia.* New York: New Press, 1992.

Stone, Jon R. *On the Boundaries of American Evangelicalism: The Postwar Evangelical Coalition.* New York: St. Martin's Press, 1997.

Stoneman, Albert H. "Adoption of Illegitimate Children: The Peril of Ignorance," *Child Welfare League of America Bulletin* 5 (1926).

Stonesifer, Elsie. "The Behavior Difficulties of Adopted and Own Children," *Smith College Studies in Social Work* 13 (1942).

Strong-Boag, Veronica. *Finding Families, Finding Ourselves: English Canada Encounters Adoption from the Nineteenth Century to the 1990s.* Don Mills, Ontario: Oxford University Press, 2006.

Sutton, Matthew Avery. *American Apocalypse: A History of Modern Evangelicalism.* Cambridge, MA: The Belknap Press of Harvard University Press, 2014.

Sweeney, Douglas A. "The Essential Evangelicalism Dialectic: The Historiography of the Early Neo-Evangelical Movement and the Observer-Participant Dilemma." *Church History* 60, no. 1 (1991): 70–84.

Tansey, B. J., ed. *Exploring Adoptive Family Life: The Collected Adoption Papers of H. David Kirk.* Port Angeles, WA: Ben-Simon Publications, 1988.

Theis, Sophie van S. "Some Aspects of Good Adoptive Practices," *Child Welfare* 19 (1940): 1–3.

Theis, Sophie van S. "The Passing of the Orphanage," *New York Times Magazine,* January 18, 1953, 16.

Thompson, Michael G. *For God and Globe: Christian Internationalism in the United States between the Great War and the Cold War.* Ithaca, NY: Cornell University Press, 2015.

Towle, Charlotte. "The Evaluation of Homes in Preparation for Child Placement," *Mental Hygiene* 11 (1927): 460–81.

Trenka, Jane Jeong, Julia Chinyere Oparah, and SunYung Shin, eds. *Outsiders Within: Racial Crossings and Adoption Politics.* Cambridge, MA: South End Press, 2006.

Vanderpol, Gary. "The Least of These: American Evangelical Parachurch Missions to the Poor, 1947–2005." Ph.D. dissertation, Boston University, 2010.

Watson, B., and Clarke, M., eds. *Child Sponsorship: Exploring Pathways to a Brighter Future.* Basingstoke: Palgrave Macmillan, 2014.

Wellisch, E. "Children without Genealogy—A Problem of Adoption," *Mental Health* 13 (1952): 41–42.

Westbrook, Robert B. "'I Want a Girl, Just Like the Girl That Married Harry James': American Women and the Problem of Political Obligation in World War II," *American Quarterly* 42, no. 4 (1990): 587–614.

Woo, Susie. *Framed by War: Korean Children and Women at the Crossroads of US Empire*. New York: New York University Press, 2019.

Wu, Ellen D. *The Color of Success: Asian Americans and the Origins of the Model Minority*. Princeton, NJ: Princeton University Press, 2015.

Wu, Frank H. *Yellow: Race in America Beyond Black and White*. New York: Basic Books, 2002.

Yamazaki, Yuki. "American Catholic Mission to Japanese in the United States: Their Intersection of Religion, Cultures, Generations, Genders, and Politics, 1910 to 1970." Ph.D. dissertation, The Catholic University of America, 2011.

Yates, Timothy. *Christian Mission in the Twentieth Century*. Cambridge: Cambridge University Press, 1996.

Zeiger, Susan. *Entangling Alliances: Foreign War Brides and American Soldiers in the Twentieth Century*. New York: New York University Press, 2010.

Websites

"Orphan Process," United States Citizenship and Immigration Services. Accessed May 2020. www.uscis.gov/adoption/immigration-through-adoption/orphan-process.

"Orphans," United Nations International Children's Emergency Fund. Accessed May 2020. www.unicef.org/media/media_45279.html.

Compassion International. Accessed May 2020. www.compassion.com.

World Vision. Accessed May 2020. www.worldvision.org.

The Adoption History Project. Accessed May 2020. https://pages.uoregon.edu/adoption/.

Ekbladh, David. "How to Build a Nation," *Wilson Quarterly* Archives. Accessed May 2020. http://archive.wilsonquarterly.com/essays/how-build-nation.

Korean War Children's Memorial. Accessed May 2020. http://koreanchildren.org/.

INDEX

abortion, 49, 121

abuse, of adoptees, 77–79, 81

Acheson, Dean, 1

Adelson, Joseph, 7

Adopted (documentary), 153–54

The Adopted Break Silence (Paton), 126

adoptees, 76, 149, 153, 164n46; abuse of, 77–79, 81; culture of, 12, 43–44, 50–51, 76, 155; death of, 69, 78, 79; identity and, 12–13, 44, 84, 115, 125

adoption. *See specific topics*

adoption agencies, 18–19, 93, 99–100, 128, 155; domestic, 8, 12, 76–77, 120, 157; racism in, 122–24; transnational, 17, 87–89, 94–96. *See also specific agencies*

adoption evangelists, 3–4 116–117, 131–32, 141–43, 157. *See also* audience, for adoption evangelicals; missionaries, Christian; *specific evangelists*

adoptive parents, 52, 96, 125–29, 132, 155–56; financial instability of, 77–79, 128; religious matching criteria for, 17, 57–58, 71–76; white Americans as, 2, 43–44, 105–6, 115, 123, 153–54

African Americans, 5, 28, 100, 116, 148; children, 96, 104, 105–6, 135–37, 156

Albert, Beth, 31–32

Alex (adoptee), 129, 133

All the Children of the World (Doss, H.), 132

Amerasian children, 87–88, 90, 94, 103–4, 107–11, 114, 143, 157. *See also* G.I. babies; mixed-race children

American Joint Committee for Assisting Japanese-American Orphans (organization), 165n62

American Mercury (magazine), 65

Anagnost, Ann, 155

Angel Unaware (Evans), 42

Anti-Asian racism, 8–10, 50–51, 84

anti-communist rhetoric, 3, 97, 107, 141

anti-racist, 15–16, 52, 82, 100, 102, 148; Buck, P., as, 17–18, 88, 90, 96–98, 142; Doss, H., as, 126–27, 134, 142–43; ecumenical Christians as, 17–18, 98, 134–35; transnational adoption as, 120, 141, 142, 144–46

Asbury, William F., 70

Asian Americans, model minority myth for, 9, 10, 43, 51, 103, 146

Asian children, 1, 10, 22, 50–51, 81, 99

Asiatic Exclusion (U.S. policy), 8–9, 100

audience, for adoption evangelicals, 18, 29, 105, 116–17, 119, 128, 143; HAP addressing, 33, 53, 65, 85

Aylward, Gladys, 31, 34–35

baby boom, U.S., 4, 124

The Bad Seed (March), 121–22

Baltimore, Maryland, 136

Baptist General Convention, 38

Bethany Christian Services, 150

Bible, 15, 47–48, 61–62, 82, 101–2, 120, 151–52, 172n14

biological parents, 8, 13, 59, 124

Blake, Eugene Carson, 73

blood, bad, 120–22

ABOUT THE AUTHOR

SOOJIN CHUNG is Assistant Professor in the Department of Practical Theology at Azusa Pacific University. Her research interests include Christian internationalism, race and religion, and gender in world Christianity.